Privatization and
popular capitalism

Privatization and popular capitalism

Peter Saunders and
Colin Harris

Open University Press
Buckingham · Philadelphia

Open University Press
Celtic Court
22 Ballmoor
Buckingham
MK18 1XW

and
1900 Frost Road, Suite 101
Bristol, PA 19007, USA

First Published 1994

A catalogue record of this book is available from the British Library

ISBN 0 335 15708 4 (pbk)   0 335 15709 2 (hbk)

Library of Congress Cataloging-in-Publication Data

Saunders, Peter R.
    Privatization and popular capitalism/Peter Saunders and Colin Harris.
      p.   cm.
    Includes bibliographical references and index.
    ISBN 0–335–15709–2. – ISBN 0–335–15708–4 (pbk.)
      1. Privatization–Great Britain.   2. Government ownership–Great Britain.   3.
    Industry and state–Great Britain.   4. Capitalism–Great Britain.   5. Great
    Britain–Economic policy–1945–
    I. Harris, Colin (Colin Neil), 1956–   .   II. Title.
    HD4145.S28   1994
    338.941–dc20
                                                                              93–41298
                                                                                   CIP

Typeset by Type Study, Scarborough
Printed in Great Britain by St Edmundsbury Press, Bury St Edmunds, Suffolk

Contents

Note on authorship

The research on which this book is based was divided into two parts: a survey of employees and trade unions, and a survey of the general public and of non-work-based voluntary organizations.

Colin Harris was responsible for the survey of employees and their unions. He undertook the interviews and data analysis on this part of the research, and he produced the material for Chapter 4 and the third section of Chapter 5. This part of the research will be analysed and presented more fully in his forthcoming University of Sussex doctoral thesis, 'Privatisation and the Employee'.

Peter Saunders took responsibility for the survey of the public and he carried out the data analysis on this part of the project. He also conducted the interviews with business, environmental and leisure groups. He wrote Chapters 1, 2, 3, 6 and 7 and the sections of Chapter 5 dealing with land and capital.

Acknowledgements

The research on which this book is based has benefited from the help and input of many individuals and organizations.

First, we gratefully acknowledge the help and cooperation of all those people – the householders in the South and North-West of England, the employees at North West Water and Southern Water, and the various managers, trade union officials and officers of pressure groups – who agreed to give the interviews on which so much of this book is based.

The managements at Southern Water and North West Water were enormously helpful throughout the research, and we are very grateful for all the efforts they made in helping us organize the study of employees. We particularly wish to mention David Beattie at Southern Water who gave us a lot of help throughout the research. We also wish to thank Strathclyde Regional Council for the help and cooperation they gave us in organizing the control group survey.

The task of conducting the household interviews was delegated to Market and Opinion Research International Ltd. Helga Mittag carried out coding and other work at the data analysis stage of the project, and we wish to thank her as well as all those other friends and colleagues in the academic world who have commented on our ideas at various seminars and conferences in Britain and abroad.

The University of Sussex and the University of Brighton have both given technical and financial support to the project. Thanks are also due to Hartmut Haussermann at the Universität Bremen for arranging a three-month visiting fellowship in 1992 which enabled part of the book to be written.

Finally, we are most grateful to the Economic and Social Research Council which generously funded the research on which this book is based (research grant number R000231082).

Peter Saunders and Colin Harris
Brighton, August 1993

1 The emergence of popular capitalism

The place is the new Stock Exchange building in Manchester. It is December 1986. About a hundred people have crowded into the foyer to watch the start of dealing in the newly privatized shares of British Gas. As the crowd sees the price rising on early trading, they cheer. When the price falters, they boo. The management of the Stock Exchange has never seen scenes like this before. It is as if the stoats and the weasels have taken over Toad Hall. The general manager of the Stock Exchange northern unit tells reporters, 'It was just like a bookie's office' (*Sunday Times*, 21 December 1986).

More than a hundred years earlier, Karl Marx had sat in the Reading Room of the British Museum in London and developed a theory based on the simple proposition that modern societies are irreconcilably divided between a small class of capitalists who own all the productive assets, and a large class of workers who own nothing. The theory further predicted that ownership of capital would become increasingly concentrated in fewer and fewer hands while the size of the propertyless proletariat was destined to swell.

In the mid-nineteenth century, this theory seemed all too plausible, for it clearly was the case that a small number of individuals or families owned most of the land and the factories while the mass of the population owned nothing. But capitalism has changed dramatically over the intervening hundred years and the ownership of capital in Britain has become dispersed and fragmented rather than concentrated. It is simply not possible today to draw a clear distinction between a class of 'capitalists' who own all of the country's productive resources, and a class of 'workers' who own nothing, for most workers have a direct or indirect financial stake in capitalist enterprises, and most companies are owned directly or indirectly by millions of workers. The cheering crowd which gathered in the Manchester Stock Exchange on that cold December morning in 1986 is the visible proof of the bankruptcy of Marx's fatalistic predictions.

The extension of capital ownership in the twentieth century

Three crucial changes have occurred since Marx's time. The first was the spread of joint-stock companies. The second was the growth of institutional share ownership. And the third, very recent in origin, has been the extension of individual share ownership.

Joint-stock companies

The first of these changes occurred back in the nineteenth century when capitalism developed from a system of individual proprietorship into one based upon joint-stock ownership. As the scale of production grew and companies expanded, so the need for additional investment funds led the original owners to sell 'shares' in their enterprises to other individuals who were willing to risk their money in return for a slice of the profits. This produced two significant results. One was that ownership of capital became slowly dispersed, although the number of individuals who could afford to own and trade in shares was, of course, still very small. The other was that the Dickensian figure of the top-hatted owner gradually gave way to that of the grey-suited manager running the company on behalf of hundreds or even thousands of people, each of whom owned a small slice of the total equity.

Of course, some individuals and families still own the lion's share of some large companies (the Sainsbury family still owns 43% of the supermarket chain, for example), and in every generation new capitalist entrepreneurs have emerged to form their own companies and amass a personal fortune (people like Richard Branson, owner of Virgin; Anita Rodick, founder of The Body Shop; and Alan Sugar, founder of Amstrad). But most of the major companies in Britain are today owned principally by shareholders rather than by individual proprietors and their families. Ownership of capital has in this way been divorced from its day-to-day control, for the shareholders who own these companies do not run them. Rather, they elect a board of directors to oversee the management and to ensure that decisions are taken which will maximize profits and hence increase their dividends.

Institutional share ownership

The second important change since Marx's time has been the rise of the financial institutions. This change reflects the growing prosperity of millions of ordinary people in Britain, particularly in the years following the end of the Second World War, for increasing real incomes have enabled many of us to join private pension schemes, to take out life assurance policies, to invest small sums of money in investment trusts, and to purchase homes with the aid of endowment mortgages. As a result, every month, millions of pounds' worth of pension contributions, savings and endowment instalments are paid by millions of British workers and their families into pension funds, unit trusts and insurance companies. The managers of these funds then invest these huge sums by buying assets such as land, government securities and stocks and shares. The profits which the fund managers are able to secure from these investments are then used to pay people their pensions and to redeem their life policies when they fall due.

The emergence of these institutions is an indication of how widely share ownership has been dispersed since the war. Over half of the employed population, for example, now belongs to a private pension scheme, and in 1986 the investments in stocks and shares made on their behalf averaged some £12,000 per head (Moore 1986a). Some 2½ million people subscribe to unit trusts (*Sunday Times*, 30 April 1989). Over two-thirds of the population are now homeowners, and many of them are purchasing through endowment mortgages. Many millions of people subscribe to equity-linked life assurance schemes. Most of us, therefore, have a small stake of one kind or another in the nation's productive assets, and we benefit accordingly from the profits which capitalist firms are able to make.

This dispersed pattern of capital ownership is, however, also a very indirect form of ownership. It is true that the worker who pays into a superannuation scheme and the householder who takes out an endowment mortgage both establish a significant property right in the sense of a claim or title to a flow of revenue from the investments made on their behalf. But this is ownership of capital twice removed, for not only is ownership of companies divorced from their everyday management, but so, too, is ownership of the shares themselves separated from the way they are managed and controlled. Most people who belong to private pension schemes or who take out 'with profits' life assurance policies do not have a clue how their monthly premiums are being invested. They may be 'little capitalists', in the sense that they own a slice of the nation's capital assets and they benefit from their exploitation, but in most cases they appear to be oblivious of the fact. As Peter Walker, a former Conservative MP and the founder of Britain's first unit trust, recognized in a radio interview, people with unit trusts, pensions and life policies 'don't in reality take much note or interest of the considerable underlying investments in which they have a vested interest' (BBC 1989, p. 10).

Furthermore, not only do these indirect owners fail to understand the nature of their investments, but the growth of the financial institutions has steadily been squeezing out the small number of individuals who buy shares directly rather than through institutional intermediaries. The extension of indirect ownership of shares since the war has gone hand in hand with a relative and absolute contraction in direct ownership.

The proportion of total capital owned directly by individuals has been falling steadily for the last forty years. In 1957, two-thirds of company shares registered in Britain were owned by individuals (Chapman 1990, p. 8). Ten years later it was down to 50%. By 1990, the proportion had fallen to just 20%. According to Gavin Oldham, founder of the Share Centre, just ninety financial institutions now control three quarters of all the equity investment in the United Kingdom, and the biggest ten of these alone control 20% of all

Table 1.1 Ownership of UK listed equities by individuals and institutions, 1963–89 (%)

	1963	1975	1981	1989
Individuals	53.8	37.5	28.2	20.0
Pension funds	6.5	16.9	26.7	32.0
Insurance companies	10.1	15.9	20.5	20.0
Unit and investment trusts	12.6	14.6	10.3	8.0
Government, overseas, etc.	17.0	15.1	14.3	20.0

Source   CBI (1990), p. 15

the money invested (Oldham 1990, p. 14). Thus, while millions of us have an indirect stake in all this equity, only a few hundred people actually control it.

Shares in privatized companies

It is at this point, however, that the third important change since Marx's day has to be taken into account, for since the early 1980s there has occurred a dramatic reversal in the absolute decline of individual share ownership. As the figures in Table 1.1 demonstrate, the relative size of institutional holdings is still growing, and the relative size of individual holdings is still shrinking, but in absolute terms, the number of individuals owning shares has suddenly and dramatically expanded to an unprecedented degree.

When the Conservative Party was elected to government in Britain in 1979, individual share ownership had been in decline for years. Grout (1987a) estimates that in 1958, 7% of the adult population owned shares. By 1979, the proportion had fallen to just 4½%, representing approximately 2½ million people. These owners were mostly male, middle-class and late middle-aged. They represented a small and socially unrepresentative elite. They were certainly not the sort of people to gather together in public to cheer and boo as their share prices changed.

By the time the Conservatives won their fourth consecutive general election victory in 1992, there were at least 11 million individual shareowners in Britain, representing a quarter of the total adult population (Treasury estimates, quoted in *The Independent*, 20 March 1991). While still not representative of the population as a whole, these owners were drawn from all parts of the country, all age groups, both genders and all social classes. Over half of the professional and managerial classes owned shares by the late 1980s, but so, too, did nearly one-third of other white-collar workers and a quarter of skilled manual workers (see Table 1.2). Even among unskilled manual workers, one in ten owned shares. The stock market – 'one of the great, closed distant institutions of the upper classes' (Leadbeater 1987, p. 19) – was in the 1980s simply blown open to the working and lower-middle classes. In the space of just a dozen years, share ownership had been transformed into a mass

Table 1.2 Share ownership by socio-economic group (%)

Professional	55
Employers and managers	51
Intermediate and junior non-manual	31
Skilled manual and own account	24
Semi-skilled manual and personal service	15
Unskilled manual	9

Source Central Statistical Office (1990)

phenomenon and, as the events in Manchester in 1986 indicated, the movement of share prices had likewise become a mass spectacle.

Various factors contributed to this extraordinary growth in the number of shareowners over such a short period. One is that the government introduced a number of tax-exempt savings and investment schemes during the 1980s, and these attracted people into building up small portfolios of holdings at a time when share prices were booming. In 1987, for example, 'Personal Equity Plans' (PEPs) were launched to allow savers to invest in long-term holdings on a regular basis free of capital gains tax when eventually they come to sell. By 1989, 300,000 PEPs were being opened annually.

A second factor, again prompted by the government, was that during the 1980s an increasing number of employers established profit-sharing or share-option schemes through which their employees could build up equity stakes in their company. By 1990 around 900 profit-sharing share schemes and 1,000 savings-related share-option schemes were in operation covering 20% of listed British companies and nearly 2 million workers (CBI 1990).

Third, important changes affecting financial institutions themselves helped stimulate the growth of shareowning during the 1980s. One such change was the so-called 'Big Bang' of 1986 when (among other changes) share trading at the London Stock Exchange was computerized. This obviously facilitated the handling of larger numbers of small transactions, and banks, building societies and specialist share shops soon took advantage of this to offer new purchase and selling services to small investors. Another even more significant change occurred in 1989 when the Abbey National Building Society (one of the largest in Britain) took advantage of changes in the law governing financial institutions to convert itself into a bank. Overnight this move created a huge number of new shareowners in Britain, for free shares were allocated to the 5.6 million borrowers and savers who had 'owned' the former mutually organized society. It was estimated by the Abbey National that 4 million of these people had never owned shares before (*The Independent*, 31 March 1989).

By far the biggest single cause of the dramatic expansion in the number of individual shareowners in Britain was, however, the government's privatization programme. Between 1979 and 1992, the government disposed of a staggering £41.5 billion worth of state assets (written reply, Hansard, 24 January 1992, vol. 202, col. 388–9w), and most of this was sold off through Stock Market flotation.

They sold the telephone system and the gas industry, electricity generating and electricity distribution. They sold Jaguar cars and Rover cars, Rolls Royce aeroengines and British Aerospace. They sold a bank – the TSB – which neither they nor anybody else actually owned. They turned British Steel from a loss-making albatross into a slimmed-down profitable concern and they sold that. They sold tiny companies which nobody even knew they owned, and they sold their stake in BP, the biggest company in Britain and the third largest oil company in the world. They sold the national airline, and they sold seven national airports including London Heathrow and London Gatwick, the world's busiest airports. They sold the ports and they sold the cross-Channel ferries, the coach companies, the road haulage industry and the railway catering service. They even managed to sell the water supply and sewage treatment and disposal industries. By 1992, all that was left of any note in the hands of the central government, apart from the BBC, was the coal industry, the railways and the Post Office, and there are plans to privatize even these three remaining industries before the turn of the century.

State assets have been sold off before by various governments, but the scale of sales since 1979 has been without precedent. According to one commentator, the transfer of property which took place through the 1980s as £41.5 billion of assets were shifted from state to individual ownership represents 'the largest transfer of power and property since the dissolution of the monasteries under Henry VIII' (Pirie 1988, p. 4). The privatization programme was, in its scale, a revolution.

Nor is there any international precedent for what happened in Britain after 1979. Britain was the first country in the world to embark on such a major programme of sales, and nowhere outside of the former socialist countries of eastern Europe has privatization proceeded with such vigour and to such an extent as in Britain. Indeed, when other countries did begin to sell state assets later in the 1980s, it was often in response to the British example (see Sunday Times, 17 May 1987; Swann 1988, p. 12). As Heald and Thomas (1986, p. 62) remark, there is no other example in the twentieth century of a British policy initiative achieving such a degree of influence in the international arena.

When a Gaullist–Giscardian coalition government was narrowly elected in France in 1986, it did seem for a time that the British record may be emulated or even surpassed across the Channel, for the National Assembly passed a general law enabling the sale of sixty-five state-owned companies representing an estimated total value equivalent to one-quarter of the total capitalization of the French Stock Exchange at the time. The sales began briskly, for half of these companies were privatized in the first twelve months of the programme, and the number of shareholders in France tripled between 1986 and 1987, but the world Stock Market crash of October 1987 soon stalled the programme and the subsequent return to power of the Rocard socialist government led to its abandonment (see Chapman 1990; Henig et al. 1988; Letwin 1988). Although the conservatives have recently been returned to power in France and seem committed to restarting the privatization programme, it is still very unlikely that it will come anywhere near matching what has been done in Britain.

As for other west European countries, privatization has been generally a small-scale affair. In the Netherlands, the government has raised $367 million principally through the sale of 23% of the national airline, KLM. The Italian government has likewise sold some of its holdings in Alitalia. The former West Germany raised only DM5 billion from sales between 1984 and 1987, although since reunification in 1990 privatization has taken on a new significance, with the Treuhand trying to find buyers for the run-down firms in the former GDR. The only other established capitalist country besides Britain to have embarked upon a substantial sales programme is Japan, whose giant Nippon Telephone and Telegraph has gradually come to market piece by piece, while shares have also been offered in the railways and national airline (for further discussion of privatization in other countries, see Chapman 1990; Fraser and Wilson 1988; Letwin 1988; Swann 1988; and Vickers and Wright 1988).

In eastern Europe, of course, many of the former socialist states are engaged on crash programmes of privatization aimed at creating rather than extending a private sector of the economy. In Hungary the State Property Agency hopes to raise around £1 billion through sales of up to 150 companies (*The Independent*, 6 July 1990), and in Russia where every citizen was given a voucher worth 10,000 roubles which could be traded or exchanged for shares in one or more of 5,000 state-owned companies, half of the economy was privately owned by the end of 1993.

The British experience since 1979 nevertheless remains unique among capitalist nations. Never before, and nowhere else outside of the former socialist bloc, has such an extensive transfer of property assets from the state to the people taken place. In just thirteen years of Conservative government, the size of the public sector was halved while the number of people owning shares was more than quadrupled. The government's critics see this programme of privatization as 'the dominant political development' of recent years (Heald and Thomas 1986, p. 64). The government's supporters see it as the Conservatives' most 'enduring success' (Clarke 1987, p. 69). Yet what appears, with the wisdom of hindsight, to have been a major radical policy innovation with dramatic implications for the British economy and society actually began as something much more timid. The history of privatization in Britain is the story of a trickle which later turned into a flood.

The problem of the nationalized industries

When the Conservatives came to power in 1979, nationalized industries and public corporations accounted for over 11% of the gross domestic product. They employed some 2 million workers – over 8% of the total workforce – and represented over 13% of total investment in the economy.

In some cases – the BBC, the National Grid and the Post Office, for example – these enterprises were initially established by government. More commonly, however, state-owned enterprises have begun life in private ownership and have only later been taken over by the government. Most of these – including the core basic industries like gas, coal, electricity, iron and steel, and the railways – were nationalized by the postwar Labour government, though some – like Rolls Royce, the shipbuilding industry, and various aircraft manufacturers – were only taken into state ownership in the 1970s.

There are various reasons why these different enterprises were nationalized (see Swann 1988). Sometimes – as in the case of the coal industry in the 1940s and shipbuilding in the 1970s – they were teetering on the brink of collapse, and public ownership was seen as the solution to long-standing problems of poor profitability and lack of investment. Sometimes the decision to nationalize was driven by the belief that a nationally coordinated strategy would prove more efficient than a fragmented and unplanned pattern of service delivery (such was the thinking behind the nationalization of the railways and the utilities after the war and the establishment of the National Bus Company in 1968). Sometimes, as in the decision back in 1914 to take a controlling interest in BP, nationalization has occurred on grounds of national security. And sometimes it has been seen as the only solution to the problems of so-called 'market failure' in industries enjoying what is known as a 'natural monopoly'.

More often than not, however, nationalization in Britain has been pursued as a matter of political principle. Ever since the 1920s, the British Labour Party has equated socialism with some form of public ownership of the means of production. The desire to secure ownership and control of a least the 'commanding heights' of the economy reflects two deeply held socialist convictions. One is that it is in some way immoral or ethically unjustifiable for private owners to make profit by selling resources like gas or water which exist in nature and upon which everybody else depends. The other is that capitalism is an essentially chaotic and anarchic way of organizing production in a society and that things could be produced and distributed far more rationally if all key resources were under the control of a state planning agency. It was mainly for these kinds of reason that the postwar Labour government pursued its radical nationalization programme, and, as we shall see, it is the same kinds of reason which explain why the Labour Party has remained so implacably hostile to the privatizations of the 1980s and 1990s.

Most of the enterprises which have been taken into state ownership have been run as public corporations on a model first developed by the prewar Labour leader of London County Council, Herbert Morrison. Morrison advocated the establishment of independent boards to run each of these industries. Ministers would appoint board members and could control their capital spending, but government and Parliament should retain an 'arm's-length' relationship with them, and it would be for the boards themselves to decide on policy. Furthermore, because the profit motive had been removed, Morrison thought (naively as it turned out) that board members could be trusted to act 'in the public interest'. Even though these industries were often monopoly suppliers of services (and where private sector competition was possible it was normally outlawed), Morrison saw no need for special safeguards for consumers.

The results were disappointing. Politicians leaned on nationalized industry chairmen to pursue policies which were politically expedient, trade unions used their monopoly power to secure higher wages and to resist modernization strategies, and management generally opted for a quiet life and took the path of least resistance (Kay 1987; Vickers and Yarrow 1989; Wiseman 1991). Removal of the need to make profits and of the threat of possible bankruptcy in the event of failure resulted in an absence of effective incentives for those who ran these industries, and the principle of 'arm's-length regulation' meant in practice that ministers were vague about setting and enforcing targets. In industries like coal and electricity supply, huge sums of money were squandered on investments which were probably unnecessary and which showed pitiful rates of return (Shackleton 1984, p. 63). Pricing policies became chaotic, often with seriously deleterious effects for consumers – see, for example, the problems created for domestic consumers by gas pricing policy in the 1970s (Moore 1983). Nationalized industry boards proved in practice to be largely unaccountable either to Parliament or to their customers, with the result that the industries were generally run inefficiently and with mounting and staggering levels of losses.

Vickers and Yarrow (1989) show that between 1968 and 1978, productivity in UK manufacturing rose by an average of 1.7% per year. In the state-owned electricity industry, however, it rose by just 0.7%. In the nationalized steel industry it fell by 2.5% per year. In the nationalized coal industry it fell by 4.4% per year. To a large extent, these figures reflect what was happening to relative employment costs in these industries. During the 1970s, employment costs per employee rose 18% faster than the national average in the electricity industry and 21% faster than average in the coal industry. In the gas industry these costs escalated 38% faster than average (Moore 1983). With productivity records this bad, rates of return to public sector industries were very low, if not negative. In 1979 the nationalized industries recorded a gross trading surplus before depreciation of just over £5½ billion – a 5% rate of return on assets valued at replacement cost. In the same year, however, they received subsidies of over £1½ billion and they consumed nearly £5 billion worth of capital. Net of subsidies and depreciation, therefore, they achieved a rate of return on capital of −0.86%.

Defenders of nationalization often argue that these industries should not be judged purely on financial performance criteria since they are expected to perform social obligations not expected of private sector companies, yet consumers were often the ones who suffered most as a result of their inefficiencies, and in 1981 a National Consumer Council survey of the nationalized industries found 'pervasive discontent with declining standards' (Moore 1986a, p. 6). It is difficult to avoid the conclusion that these industries were being run neither 'in the public interest' nor for the benefit of consumers, but in the interests of those who worked in them (Veljanovski 1987, p. 63). Given the political weaknesses of consumers and of taxpayers, neither of whom are normally in a position to organize to push their diffused interests, it was the producer interests within these industries who were best placed to extract benefits, and by and large that is exactly what they did.

In 1980, 90% of white-collar and manual workers in the nationalized industries were in trade unions, as compared with 75% and 39%, respectively, of private sector employees. Seventy-two per cent of manual workers in the nationalized industries worked in 'closed shops' (that is, there were agreements with management that nobody would be employed who did not belong to the union). The equivalent figure in the private sector was less than half (Thomas 1986, p. 300). During the 1960s and 1970s in particular, this industrial muscle was effectively used to resist restructuring of work practices and to push for higher wages. Between 1970 and 1983, for example, electricity supply workers increased their hourly earnings by around 17% relative to other manufacturing employees. Given the low level of productivity in the industry, this rise in pay was met by increases in electricity prices of 31% in real terms during the same period (Henney 1986, p. 15).

Attempts to raise efficiency in the nationalized industries were made in 1961, when they were told to break even over a five-year period, and again in 1967, when they were told to reduce labour costs, cut out cross-subsidization, and achieve an 8% real rate of return on new investments. Neither initiative had much impact, however, (for reviews, see Swann 1988; and Vickers and Yarrow 1985). Following the 1973 oil crisis, the Morrisonian principle of 'arm's-length' political control was finally dumped as the Conservative government took more direct control of the nationalized industries as part of its new industrial strategy, and in 1975, with public sector spending spiralling out of control and an ignominious plea for help to the IMF just around the corner, the Labour government imposed new 'External Financing Limits' (widely referred to as 'cash limits') which set a strict ceiling on the amount of money each nationalized industry was allowed to borrow from the central exchequer.

By 1976, a report by the National Economic Development Office found that there was no longer any proper framework for nationalized industries to make long-term decisions and there was no effective system for monitoring their performance. The response to this was yet another White Paper. This one, in 1978, sought to reinforce financial discipline by setting each industry a new 'financial target' of a 5% real rate of return on all its investments. It would then be for each board to determine its own future investment programme and its own pricing strategy within the constraints of its financial target and its cash limits. Yet within a month of publishing this White Paper, the government imposed a new freeze on electricity prices! A year later, the new Conservative government intervened to hold down gas prices. A Coal Board decision to close uneconomic pits was overridden following a strike threat by the miners' union, and the British Steel Board was overruled when it tried to close loss-making steel mills in Scotland. The nationalized industries were simply too big and too significant for ministers to allow them to pursue their own commercial rationality.

Political intervention often forced nationalized industries into commercially disastrous decisions (Swann 1988). The state airline (formerly BEA and later BA) was required to buy British-made planes even when foreign alternatives were better or more appropriate for its planning strategy. The Central Electricity Generating Board was obliged to burn British-produced coal even though cheaper supplies were available on world markets. The railways were told to keep unprofitable lines open whenever proposed closures threatened politically sensitive constituencies. And prices and investment plans were constantly subject to change depending upon shifts of political whim and electoral fortune. As Samuel Brittan (1984, p. 120) wrily observes: 'To say that politicians should not indulge in these practices is to say they should not be politicians'.

Gradually, the implications of this sorry history began to surface in political debate and argument. If the aim of all these reports and White Papers was to subject the nationalized industries to surrogate market forces, why not expose them to real ones? If government really did want to force these industries to operate on a commercial basis as if they were private sector firms, then why not adopt the logical solution and turn them into actual private sector firms? Licking their wounds in opposition between 1974 and 1979, some free-market radicals on the fringes of the Conservative Party began to think the unthinkable. Perhaps the answer to the problem of the nationalized industries was not to attempt to control them but rather to try to get rid of them.

The mainstream of the Party was not yet ready for such bold remedies, however. In 1978, the Party's policy group on the nationalized industries recommended simply that rates of return should be tightened up, and that where possible the industries should be opened up to competition from the private sector by ending their statutory monopoly rights. When the Party was returned to power the following year, it was initially this strategy that it pursued, for cash limits and financial targets were rigorously imposed while the monopoly in telecommunications was broadened to a duopoly in 1982 when a new private enterprise competitor, Mercury, was licensed to offer telephone services in competition with BT. In May 1979 the Conservative leadership apparently had little thought of privatizing state assets beyond offering local authority tenants the right to buy their council houses. In its election manifesto of that year, the only nationalized enterprises targeted for sale into the private sector were British Aerospace and British Shipbuilders (both nationalized by the preceding Labour administration) plus that part of the road haulage industry which had not been denationalized in the 1950s, the National Freight Corporation. Rather than promising to privatize the nationalized industries, the manifesto emphasized the need to make them more efficient by 'protecting the management of nationalised industries from constant Whitehall interference' (quoted by Wiltshire 1987, p. 5). As Wolfe (1989, p. 18) observes: 'At the time of the 1979 election, there was no hint of the political potential of privatisation or its future role in the Conservative government's program'.

How Margaret Thatcher and her ministers discovered Sid

Privatization began slowly and cautiously (for details, see Hyman 1989; and Price Waterhouse 1989). In 1979, 5% of the shares in BP were sold (scarcely a radical move given that the Labour government had sold 17% of BP two years earlier!) and the National Enterprise Board's holdings in the computer company ICL were transferred to private ownership by means of a trade sale. In 1980, more of the NEB's holdings were released through trade sales, the two largest being Fairey and Ferranti, but no public offers took place. Early in 1981, the manifesto promise to denationalize British Aerospace was redeemed when 51% of the government's holdings were sold on the Stock Exchange (the remaining shares stayed in government ownership until 1985). The National Freight Corporation, which had also been named in the manifesto, was privatized through a management buyout in 1982 (see Chapter 4 for further details). The other denationalization promised in the manifesto – that of British Shipbuilders – was, however, postponed and was eventually only achieved through a series of trade sales and management buyouts through 1985 and 1986.

Nineteen nationalized ports were sold, with over half of Associated British Ports going to market in 1983 and the remainder in 1984. Most ports, however, remained in state ownership, and only since the abolition of the National Docks Labour Scheme in 1989 has it seemed possible that they, too, may someday find a buyer (Chapman 1990). Britoil, the government's North Sea oil and gas exploration and production company, was sold in November 1982, though offers were received for only 27% of the shares and the rest had to be taken up by the underwriters. The only other share sales before the 1983 election were the public offerings in the drugs company Amersham International (sold in February 1982), and in the telecommunications group and part-owners of Mercury, Cable and Wireless (49% sold in 1981, with the rest disposed of in two further tranches in 1983 and 1985). There were also trade sales of the hotels owned by British Rail and of the British Airways subsidiary International Aeradio.

Total revenue from sales during the government's first term in office amounted to just £1.306 billion in offers to the public and a further £207 million in trade sales and buyouts. To put this in perspective, between 1979 and 1983 the government raised less than 4% of the amount it collected during its next two periods in power between 1983 and 1992 (see Figure 1.1). None of these sales excited much interest outside of the financial institutions and a few individual shareholders, although the Amersham, British Aerospace and Cable and Wireless sales all provoked criticism in some quarters when the shares began trading at a price well above the offer price. Few new shareholders were created by these sales, and in reality they broke no new ground, for in most cases they simply returned small and medium-sized firms to the competitive private sector whence they had come. As Kay (1987, p. 12) suggests, these industries were 'essentially peripheral to the public sector'.

More small enterprises – Enterprise Oil, the Wytch Farm oil well owned by British Gas, the Jaguar division of Leyland cars, and the Sealink ferries owned by British Rail – were sold off in the twelve months or so following the 1983 general election. None of this excited more than a flicker of interest among most members of the British public.

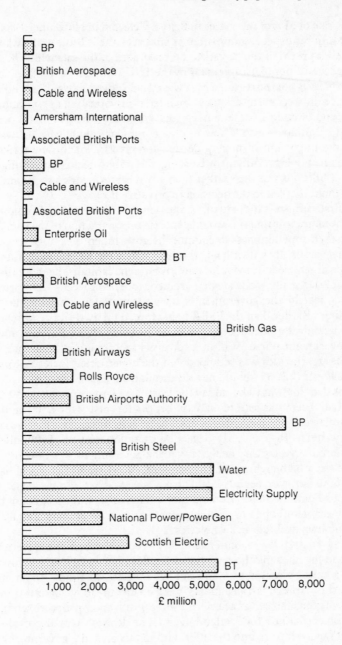

Figure 1.1   Gross proceeds from privatization flotations, 1979–92

The sale of 51% of the shares in British Telecom in November 1984 changed all that. In retrospect, commentators have seen the BT sale as the watershed in the development of the privatization programme, the sale which 'marked the emergence of popular capitalism in the UK' (Grimstone 1988, p. 33). This, however, was not the reason why it was done. Indeed, it was not until quite late on that ministers even seriously considered privatization as an option for this large and strategic state enterprise. In 1982, the problem dominating ministers' minds was not how to create popular capitalism, but was how to raise the huge sum of money needed for investment in new telecommunications technology without increasing the public sector borrowing requirement (PSBR). It was this, rather than any desire to spark a social and political revolution, that led to the decision to privatize BT.

At first, ministers thought of issuing bonds in order to raise the money, but it soon became clear that this would generate only a fraction of the sum required. Given their unwillingness to commit the government to a huge new debt, the Cabinet was finally left with no other alternative but a share issue as the answer to BT's urgent requirement for new investment capital. The more they looked at the idea, the more attractive it seemed, for the proceeds from privatization sales count, in the government's own accountancy language, as 'negative spending'. Rather than the PSBR being forced up by BT borrowing money, it could technically be reduced by a share issue which would bring money into the government purse. Within a few weeks of its initial announcement of a bond issue, the idea was scrapped and the government instead proposed in a White Paper that BT should be sold through a massive share issue.

This decision was risky, to say the least. The largest privatization up to that time had been the sale of half of Britoil for just over £500 million, and three-quarters of those shares had been left unsold in the hands of the underwriters. In the early 1980s, a flotation raising £500 million was considered large by City analysts, yet the government was now proposing to sell shares worth eight times this amount! Nowhere in the world had such a huge flotation ever been tried. The BT sale was *seven times larger* than any previous flotation on the London Stock Exchange, and the amount of money the government hoped to raise represented twice the amount usually raised in London by new issues in a whole year.

Many analysts were understandably sceptical when the government announced the sale, and there was talk of it 'flopping' or of its size 'crowding out' other stocks by soaking up all available investment funds. In an attempt to avoid this, special arrangements were made to allow investors to spread payments for shares over a period of three years, and a proportion of the shares was also earmarked for foreign buyers. The decision was also made to try to attract novice buyers into the offer, and to this end, the government financed various special offers including bonus shares and £20 million worth of telephone bill vouchers to stimulate wider public interest while also setting aside 10% of the shares for BT employees and pensioners (see Chapter 4 for details of employee schemes in this and other sales). In addition to all this, a £7½ million advertising campaign was launched in the newspapers and on television which set out to encourage ordinary men and women who might have a few hundred pounds saved up in the building society to take a risk and invest a minimum of £260 in BT instead. This was the first time a share issue had been advertised on British television.

Right up until the end, ministers apparently remained nervous: 'The government is reported to have sweated through a fortnight of waiting to see whether the shares would all sell on the domestic market' (Wiltshire 1987, p. 65). They need not have worried. The BT sale raised an extraordinary £3.9 billion – twice the amount raised over the previous five years by all the other government asset sales taken together. It attracted an unprecedented 2.3 million applications, far exceeding the government's expectations (according to the *Sunday Times*, ministers had hoped simply to exceed the 350,000 shareholders in ICI). Although the offer of shares was 9.7 times oversubscribed, every applicant got some, with the result that the big institutions went short. On the first day of trading, as the institutions clamoured to increase their holdings, the part-paid 50p shares closed at 93p – a profit of 86% on the part-paid price, or 33% on the fully-paid price of 130p. Everybody, not least the government, was taken aback by the enormous popularity and enthusiasm which the sale had provoked. As a result of this one privatization, the number of shareholders in Britain had been swollen to over 3 million. Inevitably, it was not long before ministers got around to increasing it still further.

In 1986 there were two new major sales. In September, the Trustee Savings Bank (TSB) was floated, although strictly speaking this was not a 'privatization' since the bank was not owned by the government, and, following a House of Lords ruling, the £1.3 billion proceeds from the sale went to the bank itself rather than to the central exchequer. As in the case of BT, the sale proved enormously popular. The 50p part-paid shares were eight times oversubscribed and they shot to a first day closing price of 86p, representing a 72% gain on the part-paid price or 36% on the full price.

The second sale that year was British Gas, the largest integrated gas supply business in the western world and a monopoly supplier at that. Just as the BT management had successfully resisted proposals that the company should be broken up and sold off in pieces in order to create a competitive market environment, so, too, the chairman of British Gas succeeded in keeping his empire in one piece. This added to the attractiveness of the shares, although it also meant that this became the biggest flotation yet and it obliged the government to cast its net even wider in search of new buyers. The shares were sold off in December 1986 in one huge tranche, and the government announced that it was hoping to attract 4 million applications. This was to be a people's share issue and everything possible was done to enable and encourage small investors to buy into it. As in the case of BT, payments were staggered over three financial years and bonus and voucher schemes were devised. British Gas employees were offered the same kind of free and matching shares package that had been devised for BT, and the minimum initial investment for members of the public was fixed at just £50. Finally, a massive advertising campaign was launched costing over £28 million pounds in which the public was insistently reminded to 'tell Sid' about the impending share issue. The elusive Sid never actually appeared in these advertisements, but the message was clear enough. As his name alone implied, Sid was one of the millions of ordinary middle-aged or elderly working-class people at whom this share issue was explicitly being targeted.

Sid responded magnificently. An unprecedented 4.6 million applications were lodged for British Gas shares, nearly twice the number received for the BT sale. The huge issue was four times oversubscribed and at the close of the first day's trading, the 50p shares stood at 61½p – a modest first day premium of 23% on the part-paid price or just 8.5% on the full price, but enough to send the boisterous crowd at the Manchester Stock Exchange home happy. It is estimated that by the end of 1986, the number of shareholders in Britain had increased to as many as 9 million (*Sunday Times*, 23 August 1987).

The success of the British Gas sale prompted a steady stream of privatizations. British Airways, Rolls Royce and BAA (owner of seven national airports) were all sold off in 1987, and in each case the issue was oversubscribed by at least nine times, leading to first day profits in the part-paid shares of between 37% and 68%. For the government and the punters alike, privatizations were becoming almost too easy. As *The Independent* (16 September 1987) observed: 'Weaned on British Gas and British Telecom, less sophisticated investors are understandably starting to view privatisation issues as a form of state handout to anyone who can be bothered to fill up the appropriate forms'. Such investors were, however, in for a nasty shock.

In October 1987, the government tried for its fourth big privatization of the year when it offered for sale the final 31.5% of its BP shares plus a simultaneous new issue. Valued altogether at over £7 billion, this was the biggest privatization yet and it was the world's biggest ever share issue. It was also the first big privatization to hit problems. Between fixing the sale price on 18 October and the start of trading twelve days later, the world's stock markets plummeted. In London, share prices lost 28% of their value in just two weeks – the biggest fall since the Wall Street crash of 1929. The BP share issue flopped, with its offer price now suddenly grossly overvalued, and only 270,000 applications (most of them made early before the crash occurred) were received. Most of the shares were left in the hands of unhappy underwriters.

It might have been expected that a disaster like this would have brought the privatization programme to an abrupt halt. As we saw earlier, the 1987 crash effectively ended privatization in France, but in Britain it had little long-term impact on either politicians or the share-buying public. There was a pause while the market recovered, but in just over a year, the sales started again with the cautious privatization of British Steel. This issue was not heavily advertised and there were only 650,000 applications for shares, but the offer was still oversubscribed three times. Most importantly, another flop had been avoided and the bandwagon soon began to roll once again.

The year 1989 marks the beginning of a new, third phase of privatization in Britain (Dunn and Smith 1990). In the first phase, between 1979 and 1984, proceeds were relatively small, the enterprises that were privatized were operating in competitive markets, few new shareholders were enlisted and the sales were motivated mainly by the desire to raise revenue, reduce demands on public sector borrowing, and raise efficiency by increasing competition. In the second phase the government began to sell off large and often monopolistic enterprises and the number of new shareholders grew rapidly. In this period, the desire to expand the number of shareholders and to create a new culture of 'popular capitalism' began to surface as a clear objective of the government, and the concern to foster increased competition was quietly forgotten. From 1989 onwards, privatization reached its climax as the government moved to sell off virtually every public sector industry, no matter how big, how monopolistic or how unprofitable. From 1989, privatization became almost an end in itself, a self-evident good that was pursued even against widespread public opposition and which was applied even to the most basic and traditional of state services. In this third phase, industries which ten years earlier nobody would have thought of privatizing were sold, and the momentum which had been built up proved unstoppable.

In July 1989, the Abbey National Building Society turned itself into a bank and gave all its depositors and borrowers free shares. As we saw earlier, this increased the number of shareholders in Britain by perhaps as many as 4 million. The sale which really marks the beginning of this third phase did not, however, occur until December 1989 when the ten Regional Water Authorities were privatized. This was in many ways the most difficult and astounding sale of all, for as we shall see in Chapter 2, it was deeply unpopular and encountered a series of daunting problems along the way. But despite the fact that there was a widespread feeling that it was unwise or even ethically wrong to sell such a basic and crucial industry into private ownership, the privatization itself was successfully carried through. Over 2½ million people applied for shares and the companies were oversubscribed on average 5.7 times. All this guaranteed healthy first day profits ranging between 36% and 57% on each company's part-paid 100p shares. The water privatization, which provides us with the particular case study examined in this book, attracted more buyers than any previous privatization other than British Gas.

Even the British Gas record of 4½ million applications was surpassed by the next huge flotation. The government decided that the electricity industry was too large to be sold off as a single entity, and, following protracted discussions, dogged opposition by top management in the CEGB, and a few false starts, the industry was eventually divided up into twelve English and Welsh regional supply companies, three power generating companies, a national grid company and two Scottish generation and supply companies.

The first of these to come to market, just one year after the water companies had been sold, were the twelve English electricity suppliers which between them also owned the new national grid company, Gridco. Following a massive and crass advertising campaign featuring a character called Frank N. Stein, an incredible 5.7 million people – one in ten of all the adults and children in Great Britain – made a total of over 12 million applications for shares in one, some or all of the companies. All twelve companies, with a combined value of over

£5 billion, were massively oversubscribed (some as many as fourteen times). Judged simply by the sheer numbers of people applying, this was, and remains, 'the most popular privatisation ever' (*The Times*, 10 December 1990). Predictably, prices of 100p part-paid shares showed huge first day premiums as they closed at between 142p and 166p.

In the run-up to the 1992 general election, the government then successfully sold off 60% of its shares in two of the three new generating companies, National Power and PowerGen (the third, Nuclear Electric, was retained in state ownership at least until 1994 following uncertainty about insurance risks and future decommissioning costs of nuclear power plants) as well as all of its shares in the two Scottish electricity companies, Scottish Power and Scottish Hydro. Again, all these issues were oversubscribed at least three times and showed healthy first day premiums of between 15% and 37%. A second tranche of BT shares was also sold in December 1991 and this attracted applications from 2.8 million people – more even than had applied for shares in the first BT offer which had set the mass privatization programme on its way back in 1984. The government raised over £5 billion from the sale and individual investors saw their 110p part-paid shares go to 125p on the first day's trading.

By the time the Conservatives were unexpectedly returned to power in the April 1992 general election, the privatization programme had almost been completed and the nationalized industries had virtually all been transferred into private ownership. There was still a mopping-up operation to do – remaining government holdings in BT, PowerGen and National Power would still have to be sold in the historic fourth term of office – but the rolling programme of massive public flotations had effectively come to an end. London's buses had still to be privatized, and plans were laid for the sale of British Coal (a deeply symbolic privatization given the clashes between Conservative governments and the National Union of Mineworkers in 1974 and 1984–5), postal services, and various British Rail operations, but none of these privatizations was likely to be accomplished by flotation on the Stock Market. The programme of huge public flotations had therefore virtually ended by 1992. In just thirteen hectic years of sales, the Conservatives had succeeded in selling off almost the entire public sector and in creating some 10 million new shareholders. The obvious question is: why did they do it?

Why privatize?

There has never been an official government statement about the objectives behind privatization. Over time, of course, various ministers have delivered speeches or written articles defending and justifying the policy, but the reasons they have given have seemed to change as the years have gone by and they have sometimes contradicted each other. What is clear is that the large-scale programme of sales began mainly for economic reasons, and only later did more political and sociological motives come to the fore. Indeed, it seems that, in the course of pursuing its mundane economic aims, the government unintentionally created a social and political phenomenon which it then sought to encourage and support, even at the cost of some of its earlier economic commitments.

Of course, ideology and dogma were present right from the start. Just as the Labour Party's decision to nationalize a great swathe of industries after 1945 was entirely consistent with its underlying belief in state ownership of the means of production, so the sequence of privatizations from 1979 onwards fitted well with the renewed Conservative commitment to the principles of private ownership and free enterprise. Privatization was in this sense the Conservative Party's Clause IV. But privatization was not the product of this ideology. The sales went with the grain of Thatcherism, but they cannot simply be explained as the result of Thatcherite ideology.

It is possible to detect five principal objectives behind the programme. The first was the concern to reduce public sector borrowing and to increase government revenue. The second was to increase efficiency. The third was to weaken the power of the public sector trade unions. The fourth was to enhance managerial autonomy and initiative while eliminating political interference in the internal affairs of these enterprises. And the fifth, which arose very late on but which eventually became the dominant rationale for continued sales, was the attempt to create what became known as 'popular capitalism'.

Improving government finances

From the very beginning of its first term in office, the government's primary objective was to reduce inflation. As part of this strategy, it felt that it was necessary to reduce government borrowing. Privatization offered two ways of achieving this. First, as we have seen, it has meant that borrowing by these major enterprises no longer counts against the PSBR. It also means that the deficits of loss-making companies no longer have to be covered by government borrowing. Second, the government has received revenue from the sale of assets which counts in its own accounting system as negative spending and thus helps to achieve the PSBR target.

A number of early sales can be explained in these terms (see Vickers and Yarrow 1989). The sale of shares in companies like Britoil, Enterprise Oil and BP seems to have been motivated at least in part by the desire to keep public sector borrowing in check, and, as we saw earlier, it was this same concern which led in 1984 to the decision to privatize BT. By 1986–7, the PSBR had more than halved as a result of privatization revenues (Hyman 1989). Net total government spending also fell by 2.6% as a result of these revenues, thereby helping finance tax cuts. It was this that led to the famous comment by Lord Stockton, the former Conservative Prime Minister, Harold Macmillan, that the government was 'selling the family silver': 'First of all the Georgian silver goes, and then all that nice furniture that used to be in the saloon. Then the Canalettos go' (*The Times*, 9 November 1985). In Stockton's view, privatization involved selling assets to cover current spending. Ministers themselves denied, however, that the desire for revenue was ever more than an 'incidental objective' of their privatization policy (see Kay 1987), and it does seem that the sums raised have not been large enough by themselves to finance any major expenditure or tax cuts. It was the impact on the PSBR rather than the prospect of a few billion pounds to spend which seems to have been the main attraction for ministers in the early to mid-1980s.

Increasing efficiency and fostering competition

We saw earlier that successive governments have wrestled unsuccessfully with the problem of inefficiency in the nationalized industries, and that in 1978, while still in opposition, a Conservative Party policy group had resolved to tackle the problem through a dual strategy of tightening financial controls while encouraging competition wherever possible. The subsequent imposition of stricter cash limits from 1979 did in fact improve efficiency in many of these industries. Indeed, it is one of the ironies of privatization through the 1980s that many enterprises targeted for future sale radically improved their productivity and profitability while still in the public sector (see Vickers and Yarrow 1989).

The second part of the strategy – liberalization of competition – was also pursued early on with a degree of success. In local government and the National Health Service, direct labour departments were forced to compete with outside contractors to supply a range of services from street cleaning to catering, and the result in most cases was a marked fall in labour costs. One study, for example, found that private contractors were 22% cheaper than direct labour, that direct labour departments themselves were 17% cheaper after liberalization than they had been before, and that there had apparently been no deterioration in the quality of service rendered (see Rentoul 1987). Long-distance coach services and, later, local bus routes were also liberalized by breaking up and selling the National Bus Company while also allowing existing private operators to compete for business and to tender for routes which had previously been protected. Again, the result was efficiency gains, with overall operating costs down as much as 30% and a 19% improvement in labour productivity (Wright *et al*. 1990). And within the core nationalized industries, statutory monopoly rights were gradually weakened to allow competition from the private sector to emerge. In telecommunications, for example, Mercury was licensed in 1982 to compete with BT and was given ten years to establish itself before other competitors (notably fibre-optic cable companies) were also allowed to offer telephone services.

In the early days of the privatization programme, there was no conflict between the desire to liberalize, by opening up competition, and the desire to privatize. Indeed, the minister who first assumed responsibility for privatiz-ation policy in 1983, John Moore (1983, p. 13), made it clear in an early speech that the key reason for privatizing state industries was to force them to compete in the private market, thereby raising their efficiency: 'The long-term success of the privatisation programme will stand or fall by the extent to which it maximises competition. If competition cannot be achieved, an historic opportunity will have been lost'.

Somewhere between 1984, before the sale of BT, and 1986, with the sale of

British Gas, this 'historic opportunity' was, however, lost, for the emphasis in government policy changed. Any serious attempt to encourage competition would have entailed breaking up huge state monopolies before they were sold, yet this was not tried. Not until the privatization of the electricity generating industry in 1991 did the government split a nationalized company into competing parts before selling it, and even then it created only two huge enterprises, although it also tried to encourage competitors to set up their own generation plants as well. Instead of encouraging competition, the government chose to privatize huge monopolies intact and to set up new regulatory agencies to monitor pricing policies in order to ensure that they did not abuse their position.

There are various reasons why this happened. In the case of BT, the government apparently felt that it was necessary to retain a single company of substantial size if it were to compete in producing new technology products on intensely competitive world markets (see Barclay 1986). In the very different case of British Gas, the major factor which prevented liberalization was the bullish obstinacy of the company's chairman, who insisted that it be kept together as an integral concern and who let it be known that he would create major political problems for the government if any attempt were made to do otherwise. But there are some cases where it is difficult to explain the failure to liberalize other than as a result of political pragmatism or greed. In a case like BAA, the government's failure to break up the company prior to sale is probably best explained by a concern to maintain the momentum of sales while also raising more revenue. A company which is assured of a monopoly market position is clearly worth more than several separate companies which to some extent have to compete with each other for business.

For whatever reasons, the government had by 1986 changed its mind about the importance of competition. In that year, the Treasury issued a statement (cited in Wiltshire 1987, p. 20) in which it claimed that privatization could improve efficiency even where it did not result in any increase in competition, and this was echoed in a ministerial speech which asserted that 'Privatisation increases productive efficiency whether or not a monopoly is involved' (Moore 1986b, p. 95).

The argument that a change of ownership from public to private can of itself improve a company's performance rests on both theoretical and empirical grounds. Theoretically, privatization changes the incentive structures for managers (see, for example, Rouse 1990; Veljanovski 1989; Yarrow 1989; Zeckhauser and Horn 1989). The lack of a share price in the state sector means that there is no clear indicator of performance, and this makes it easier for poor performance to go undetected. In the private sector, by contrast, even monopolistic firms must compete with other firms to attract investment money, and this means that companies must perform well in order to induce individuals and institutions to buy their shares and bankers to lend them funds. As Letwin (1988, p. 45) explains:

Every private sector company . . . is bound to compete in at least one respect, since it must attract private equity and private debt in competition with other potential investments and borrowers . . . Privatised companies are pushed towards efficiency by competition imposed in the financial market place.

Empirically, the argument that private firms are more efficient than state-owned ones receives some support from studies which have tried to compare the performance of firms operating in the private and the public sector. In Australia, for example, the private internal airline carries 103% more freight and 17% more passengers per employee than its state-owned rival, while in the United States, private water utilities operate 25% more efficiently than public ones due to better labour productivity and greater utilization of capital equipment (Hanke and Walters 1987). Other American studies have found superior private sector operations in waste collection services, electric power, fire protection, public transport and postal services (see Savas 1982), and a comparison of private and state-owned banks in Australia showed that managers in the public sector tended to opt for low-risk, low-return strategies since they lacked any incentive to entrepreneurship (Zeckhauser and Horn 1989).

In Britain, Pryke (1986) compared the privately owned British Caledonian with the then nationalized British Airways, the privately owned European Ferries with the then nationalized Sealink, and two private retailers (Comet and Currys) with the then nationalized Gas and Electricity showrooms. In each case, he concluded that the state-owned enterprise compared badly with its private sector counterpart, although his conclusions have been challenged by critics and other studies claimed to have found no difference in public and private sector efficiency (for review, see Bishop and Kay 1988; Swann 1988; and Veljanovski 1987).

On balance, the arguments and the evidence seem to indicate that it is competition rather than ownership which has the biggest impact on efficiency. Looking at the performance of the companies in Britain which have been privatized, for example, many seem to have raised their profitability since they were sold, but the most impressive results are among those firms operating in a competitive market (see Hyman 1989). Evidence that monopolistic firms have performed more efficiently since they have been privatized is much less clear-cut, and, as Kay (1987) concludes, liberalization has proved far more significant than privatization as a factor likely to enhance a firm's efficiency.

Seen in this light, the government's concern to raise efficiency by selling the nationalized industries only really made sense in the early years when companies were sold into competitive market environments. By the time of the British Gas sale in 1986, the concern with creating competition seems to have been forgotten, and the desire to increase efficiency thus became less and less significant as a reason for the privatization programme. By then, however, sociological and political objectives were beginning to displace economic ones in the government's thinking about privatization.

Reducing the power of the unions

We saw earlier that the nationalized industries provided fertile ground for the development of strong trade unionism in the 1960s and 1970s. More workers were unionized than in the private sector, there were more closed shop agreements with employers, wage settlements were generally higher than those elsewhere, and attempts at rationalization and modernization were often thwarted by threatened or actual union resistance.

In its unpublished 1978 report on the nationalized industries, the Conservative Party emphasized the need to do something to reduce the power of the unions. According to Swann (1988, p. 235), 'The main concern, indeed obsession, was how best to cope with public sector union pressure'. Bitter memories of 1974 doubtless played a part in this, for in that year a strike by coal miners had reduced Britain to a three-day working week and had resulted in the fall of the Heath Conservative government. As the 1978 Conservative Party report somewhat bitterly observed, the public sector unions 'have the nation by the jugular vein' (quoted in Heald and Steel 1986, p. 70).

The problem was twofold. First, the nationalized industries provided essential goods and services – energy, transport, communications – on which many other activities depended. Governments therefore often had to give in to union demands or (as in 1974 and again in the 'winter of discontent' in 1978–9) face chaos and disruption. Second, these industries were statutory monopolies. When the unions took action, governments had no other source of supply to turn to.

Privatization provided the Conservative governments of the 1980s with at least a partial solution to both of these problems. By breaking the umbilical cord linking the nationalized industries to the Treasury, it was hoped that privatization would prevent the managers of these enterprises from simply giving in to union pressure since they could no longer turn to the Exchequer to foot the bill. Furthermore, removal of the statutory monopolies enjoyed by the nationalized industries would enable new private sector competitors to emerge, and this too could weaken the power of the unions by providing alternative sources of supply which could be stepped up in the event of industrial action (Dick 1987).

Taken together with the government's legislation outlawing closed-shop agreements, enforcing secret strike ballots and prohibiting secondary picketing, privatization was therefore part of the assault on the power of organized labour in the 1980s. It should, however, be noted that in 1978 the Conservatives had little thought of privatizing the heartlands of the public sector. Liberalization (that is, the introduction of competition), not privatization, was originally the strategy designed to tackle the union problem. Furthermore, the industries where union power had posed the biggest problems – electricity and coal – have been among the last to be privatized, and by the time these sales reached the agenda, public sector union militancy was virtually a thing of the past. It is probably true to say, therefore, that privatization appealed to ministers because of its potential to tame the unions, but that this was not a major reason why it was undertaken in the first place.

Freeing the managers

In the public sector, as we saw earlier, nationalized industry managements had constantly to mould their decisions and policies according to the shifting whims of their political masters. When the pressure was on politicians to reduce unemployment, the nationalized industries would be told to step up recruitment or to avoid creating redundancies. When the pressure was on politicians to find more revenue to finance tax cuts or new spending programmes, the industry chairmen would be told to begin to pay off their debts to the government by pushing up their prices. When rising prices put pressure on the politicians to tackle the inflation problem, these same chairmen would be called in again by the relevant ministers and would be told this time to hold down their prices, even if it meant wrecking a planned programme of new investment. Pressure from management or unions in some other industry threatened by cheaper and more efficient overseas competition would result in ministers overturning nationalized industry purchasing decisions, and ordering chairmen to buy British equipment rather than cheaper or more appropriate equipment from overseas. Pressure from one or other region of Britain similarly led to interference in their investment strategies, for ministers would suddenly decide that a new plant should be built in a different place, or that an old plant in a politically sensitive area should be kept open even though it had been scheduled for closure.

Battered from all sides by competing demands, ministers used the nationalized industries to achieve their own short-term political objectives. Governments never gave their managers clear signals about what they wanted and were never able to leave them alone to get on with the job. Rather than operating at arm's length, they found themselves operating from within the minister's pocket, and, increasingly, they did not like it.

A key reason for privatizing the nationalized industries was, therefore, that it would depoliticize them and free their managements to manage. Indeed, according to a former adviser to the Prime Minister, this was the 'first and foremost' of the government's motives for the privatization programme (Walters 1989, p. 250). Once in the private sector, ministers would be unable to pressure companies into policies which were not in their commercial interests, and this in turn would reduce the intensity of interest-group demands upon politicians since it would no longer be in the power of government to accede to them.

The managements themselves were, understandably, generally sympathetic to this kind of argument, for they were keen to extend their autonomy, and the imposition of ever-tighter cash limits during the 1980s made escape into the private sector seem increasingly attractive. In the private sector they would be left alone to make medium- and long-term policy, and there would be other advantages as well. They could diversify in a way that was prohibited to them under state ownership. They could seek new sources of finance without having constantly to beg at the Treasury and to take their chance against the competing demands of the health service or the defence budget. And, as we shall see in Chapter 4, they could pay themselves much bigger salaries.

Faced with a proposal to privatize, the principal objective of most nationalized industry managements was to ensure that they passed into the private sector with as many of their existing advantages still intact as could possibly be secured. In particular, those at the head of these industries were influential in ensuring that they were not broken up on privatization. When, late on in the programme, the government did begin to insist on a limited degree of restructuring, it faced major opposition from industry chiefs. In the electricity industry, the CEGB chairman fought bitterly and publicly against the division into three generating companies and the detachment of the national grid, and when the plans were decided he was described in the press as 'outraged' (*Sunday Times*, 7 February 1988). In the water industry, the government's eventual decision to separate water and sewage services from river management led to a major public confrontation with most of the ten water authority chairmen and resulted in the most prominent of them switching from being the principal advocate of privatization to being its most vociferous opponent (the story of the water privatization is discussed in Chapter 2). In other privatizations such as BT, British Gas and BAA, however, the chairmen got almost exactly what they wanted as their public sector monopolies were turned intact into private sector monopolies, thereby giving them the best of both worlds.

Creating 'popular capitalism'

All four of the preceding factors were important at one time or another in helping shape or underpin the government's privatization programme. But as time went on, so the broadly economic arguments became rather less important as a new set of essentially sociological aims began to dominate the government's thinking. Fuelled by the unexpected public enthusiasm shown for the BT share issue, and buoyed by the avalanche of applications for British Gas shares two years later, the government had by 1986 developed a completely new agenda for its privatization programme. As the *Financial Times* (5 November 1988) recognized:

> The programme began as a halting, ill-defined attempt to realise easily saleable assets, the receipts from which could be written off against public spending and cut the public sector borrowing requirement. It grew into . . . what the government hopes will be one of its most enduring contributions to British society, that is the rebirth, or some would say birth, of popular capitalism in the UK.

As people scrambled to buy shares in the various privatization issues that followed the first BT sale, so ministers began to realize the ideological and political potential of what they were doing. Gradually, a heroic vision was adopted in which the mass of the population would own shares and the culture of Britain would be transformed as a result. This vision was finally spelled out in the Conservative Party's 1987 election manifesto which promised to privatize more industries in order to bring about a 'historic transformation' in British society in which share ownership 'would become the expectation of the many', as widespread and taken for granted as ownership of cars, televisions, washing machines and foreign holidays.

This vision, like all revolutionary dreams, was rather vague when it came to more detailed objectives, but it rested on the assumption that people would only begin to understand capitalism, and thus appreciate its benefits, if they felt part of it. Privatization could therefore help change people's values and behaviour by enabling them to buy small stakes in the large enterprises which supplied them with basic everyday goods and services. It was this change in values and behaviour, linked to a spread of share ownership, which became known as 'popular capitalism'.

The idea of privatization as the means to realize a new popular capitalism was perhaps best expressed by the Conservative minister, John Moore. In a speech quoted by Aharoni (1988, p. 41), he said:

> Our aim is to build upon our property-owning democracy and to establish a people's capital market, to bring capitalism to the place of work, to the high street, and even to the home. As we dispose of state-owned assets, so more and more people have the opportunity to become owners . . . [T]hese policies also increase personal independence and freedom, and by establishing a new breed of owner, have an important effect on attitudes.

But it was an idea shared by many others who were caught up in the privatization programme. The chairman of the Confederation of British Industry, for example, thought that mass share ownership would help people understand capitalism better:

> The vision we share is of a country where the majority of its citizens are part owners of the large and small companies that create the wealth that we all enjoy . . . They will thus become more aware of and feel part of the system by which wealth is created.
>
> (CBI 1990, p. 7)

And a leading figure in the 'new right' Adam Smith Institute suggested that wider share ownership would dilute the appeal of ideologies which are hostile to capitalism:

> Perhaps most importantly of all, the wide ownership extends the stake in capitalism itself as well as in privatisation as a policy. Wide ownership involves more people understanding the role of investments and profits and less likely to be deluded by false attacks on business.
>
> (Pirie 1988, pp. 71–2)

What is immediately striking about comments like these is that they rest entirely upon assertion and faith. Although the political and sociological concern to create a popular capitalism has effectively displaced earlier economic objectives in the privatization programme, no evidence has been put forward to support the claims which are now being made. The earlier objectives – and notably the concern to increase efficiency – were the subject of an enormous amount of research and argument by economists concerned to discover whether privatization really did achieve what the government said it wanted to achieve. The new objective – the creation of popular capitalism – has, by contrast, been the subject only of polemic and assertion, for virtually no sociological research has been carried out to assess and evaluate it. The crucial link between ownership of shares and changed values and behaviour is simply assumed, yet it rests on an extremely crude materialist premise which few sociologists would uncritically endorse, and it completely ignores the question of what share ownership means to the people involved. It is not even clear from most of what has been said what exactly 'popular capitalism' might look like.

The elements of popular capitalism

The culture of popular capitalism which the government hopes to create through the privatization programme has four principal elements. First, unlike the nationalized industries which are thought to have been 'captured' by powerful producer interests such as trade unions and corporate management, privatized companies are said to be consumer-orientated. In popular capitalism, the consumer is sovereign. Second, privatization is intended to break down the traditional class-based divisions in industry between 'bosses' and 'workers', 'them' and 'us'. In popular capitalism, employees identify with the aims and objectives of the companies that employ them. Third, it is hoped that the spread of share ownership will increase electoral support for the Conservative Party and will undermine the appeal of collectivist ideologies. In popular capitalism, socialism is shunned by the masses. Finally, the new shareowners will, it is argued, develop a clearer understanding of the private enterprise system and the profit motive. The traditional ambivalence or even antipathy towards capitalism in British culture will in this way be overcome and the moral foundations of a market-based economy will be reinforced. In popular capitalism, everybody is a petty bourgeois.

Empowerment of consumers

The language of popular capitalism is the language of consumerism. 'Meeting the demands of the "sovereign" consumer becomes the new and overriding institutional imperative' (Keat 1991, p. 3). In the public sector, it is argued, industries are run for the benefit of those employed in them and the interests of consumers are often neglected. In a speech given in 1981, the then Chancellor, Sir Geoffrey Howe, made the point clearly: 'The consumer is sovereign in the private sector. In the public sector he is dethroned by subsidy or monopoly' (quoted in Heald and Steel 1986, p. 64). It follows from this, as John Moore

(1983, p. 13) argued, that the 'main prize' from privatization 'is for the consumer'.

Privatization, it is claimed, benefits consumers by reducing prices, raising quality and enhancing the accountability of those who provide the goods or services (see Redwood 1990). In the public sector, consumer interests are safeguarded by the principle of democratic accountability. The chain of accountability is, however, a long and indirect one. Nationalized industry managers are accountable to the relevant minister, who is in turn accountable to Parliament, which is in turn accountable to the electorate. A customer with an unresolved grievance with a nationalized industry has therefore to depend upon an agent – a Member of Parliament or a consumer body – to take up the case on his or her behalf. As Atkinson (1989, p. 17) puts it:' 'Letter writing is the consumer's pathetic response to monopoly exploitation by nationalised industries'.

In the private sector, by contrast, there is no need to contact MPs or write letters to consumer watchdogs. The aggrieved customer simply goes elsewhere. The difference between state provision and private provision is that only in the latter can the consumer 'exit' from an unsatisfactory relationship, and it is this power to shift to a competitor which drives private firms to do all they can to meet consumer preferences. To quote Atkinson (1989, p. 17) again: 'It requires no government legislation, consumers committees or thousands of letters to GEC or Marks and Spencer for an improvement in customer service. The consumer cracks the whip and the commercially constrained come running'.

But will private companies still come running when they have no effective competitors? As we have seen, it is not generally possible for domestic consumers to choose between competing utilities for the supply of services like electricity and water to their homes. In these cases of 'natural monopoly', the government has established regulators to monitor the quality of service and to limit prices to a point at which they would stabilize were a competitive market operating. Whether these regulators do in fact perform the role of a surrogate market in safeguarding the interests of consumers is a question addressed in Chapter 3.

Involvement of employees

Although privatization is explicitly intended to shift power from producers to consumers, its advocates still nevertheless maintain that it can bring advantages for employees as well as for customers. For high-level employees, of course, the advantages are obvious, for we have seen how privatization increases managerial autonomy as well as managerial remuneration. But lower down the hierarchy, too, workers are said to benefit. In his 1983 speech, John Moore (1983, p. 2) promised 'better pay, conditions and employment opportunities for the employees'. Furthermore, the industrial relations climate is intended to improve as workers begin to accumulate shares in their companies, for worker share ownership is an integral element of the new popular capitalism.

Every major privatization has deliberately encouraged workers to buy shares in their company, and most have set aside a small number of free shares for all employees who wanted them, with the result that over 90% of employees in most of these companies own shares in them. The assumption is that, owning a small stake in the company, workers will come to identify their interests with those of the company management and will recognize that their prosperity rises as the profitability of their company rises. Horizontal class-based identification ('labour' versus 'capital') should in time give way to vertical identification, and workers' interests as shareholders will eventually come to complement their interests as wage-earners, thereby reducing the appeal of militant trade unionism: 'Employees who are also owners see immediately the absolute identity of interest between themselves and the success of the companies for which they work, and they take steps to ensure that success' (Moore 1986a, p. 5).

Late in 1987, during the week of the annual TUC conference, the Chancellor of the Exchequer, Nigel Lawson, drew attention to the fact that the number of shareholders in Britain had for the first time exceeded the number of members of trade unions affiliated to the Trades Union Congress. The message was clear: organized labour was in decline, popular capitalism was in the ascendant. Whether this statistic is in fact as sociologically significant as it sounds is an issue taken up in Chapter 4, where we consider how privatization has affected those who are employed in the former nationalized industries.

Undermining socialism

The political objectives of the privatization programme appear to be twofold. First, there is the simple aim of winning votes. Second, there is the hope, often expressed by the former Prime Minister, Margaret Thatcher, that the popular appeal of socialism could be defeated and that socialist ideas would disappear from the political agenda.

The first of these objectives is rarely formally acknowledged, but few commentators seem to doubt that the Conservatives have made electoral gains as a result of the spread of share ownership. As Rentoul (1987, pp. 2–3) suggests: 'Privatisation is designed to create support for the Conservative Party. Wider share ownership creates a larger class of people who have a self-interest in maintaining a Conservative government'. Because the Labour Party has through most of this period promised to stop the privatizations and even in one way or another to take back into state ownership some of the assets which have already been sold, this is assumed to have alienated the new army of small investors. And because most privatization issues have been oversubscribed and have produced large first day percentage profits for those who 'stag' them, it is further assumed that those who hope to profit in the future will tend to vote Conservative in order to secure further windfall gains in the future.

Whether or not this beguilingly simple theory is actually true, many politicians (Labour as well as Conservative) seem to think it is true. This leads some commentators to suggest that the privatization programme has rather cynically been manipulated by Conservative election strategists to ensure attractive premiums on early trading of privatization stock. Put bluntly, the accusation is that the Tories have effectively been buying votes (Vickers and Yarrow 1988).

The second political objective, more explicitly addressed by Conservative politicians, was to banish socialism from the political agenda by shifting the political centre of gravity. Many on the political right believe that socialism appeals to the material self-interest of those who own very little. It thrives on envy. It follows that socialism can be defeated by ensuring that most people own something. This means they will be less susceptible to promises to redistribute wealth since they themselves will stand to lose as much as they gain, and they will feel less envious of others more prosperous than themselves. The spread of share ownership can therefore undermine the very foundations of socialism's popular appeal by 'weaning away British culture from its acceptance of state provision and intervention' (Henig *et al.* 1988, p. 463).

The question of whether privatization has in fact brought the Conservatives any electoral advantage or has reduced the popular appeal of socialism is one addressed in Chapter 6.

A *spirit of enterprise*

The British economy has been in a long-term decline relative to its major industrial competitors through most of the twentieth century. There are many competing explanations for why this has happened, but one which found favour with the Conservatives from the 1970s onwards held that there was a fundamental *cultural* problem in Britain. British culture, it is thought, is fundamentally anti-industrial and anti-entrepreneurial. Many people see industrial work as demeaning, evaluate a genteel non-vocational arts education over a more practical scientific and technological training, and see profit as something rather shameful.

During the 1980s, many leading Conservatives seem to have been convinced by this kind of argument, and they added to it their belief that the postwar welfare state and mixed economy had simply exacerbated the problem by turning people's attention from the creation of wealth to the question of how it should be distributed. The then Prime Minister, for example, spoke in 1988 of her fear 'that the British sense of enterprise and initiative would have been killed by socialism' (quoted by Keat 1991, p. 1). The Chancellor, Nigel Lawson, similarly delivered a speech in 1984 in which he identified as 'our goal' the transformation of 'the culture and psychology of two generations' (quoted by Morris 1991, p. 29). And Lord Young, formerly Employment Secretary and then Secretary of State for Trade and Industry, was in no doubt in 1985 that cultural antipathy to the core values of entrepreneurial capitalism was the fundamental explanation for Britain's poor economic performance. 'I believe very strongly,' he said, 'it is because of our culture, because of the sort of circumstances in the fifties and particularly the sixties and seventies when profit-making, making money, was somehow not quite nice' (quoted by Turner 1990, p. 121).

The new popular capitalism was intended to change all that. At its most ambitious, privatization was about turning a culture upside down, challenging the anti-enterprise ethic and instilling in the British people a new understanding and respect for entrepreneurial talent and successful profit-makers. As Grout (1987b, p. 13) suggests, the privatization policy was 'aimed at creating an enterprise culture, nothing less than a fundamental change in attitudes to wealth creation in the economy'. And the tool expected to bring about this remarkable transformation was wider share ownership. As Dick (1987, p. 18) observes: 'Wider direct ownership of shares is . . . designed to promote an enterprise culture.'

At its boldest, therefore, privatization is part of a strategy of cultural reconstruction. It is intended to propogandize capitalism by example. The creation of millions of new shareholders has become integral to a cultural re-education programme which will spread knowledge and understanding of how capitalism works and how the profits made by capitalist firms are used to generate wealth from which everybody benefits. As Veljanovski (1987, p. 106) suggests:

> The government believes that privatisation will create a property-owning democracy and that this will significantly alter attitudes. By enabling people to share in the success and failures of the economy more directly it will foster a nation of entrepreneurs and wealth creators.

Veljanovski immediately adds: 'It is impossible to evaluate the truth of these assertions', but Chapter 7 attempts to do just that.

Conclusion

When the Conservatives came to power in 1979, state-owned industries played a pervasive role in virtually all aspects of everyday life. When I awoke each morning I would switch on the bedside lamp powered by electricity supplied by a state-owned utility. I would then turn on the radio and tune in to the BBC, a state-owned broadcasting corporation. Stumbling into the bathroom, I would shave and shower with water piped to my house by a state-owned authority and taken away again by that same body. After that I would go downstairs and pick up the mail delivered by the state monopoly postal service. I cooked my breakfast using gas provided by the state monopoly gas corporation. The telephone might ring. It was rented from the state telecommunications body, for no one else was permitted to supply telephones, and it was plugged into a network owned and run by that same body. When I eventually left for work, I would either use the state-owned bus and train service, or would drive my car (manufactured by the state-owned Rover group) on a road network built and maintained by the state. Everyday life at that time was permeated by state provisioning in ways that most of us did not even think about.

Today all this has changed. The electricity company which lights my bedside lamp has been privatized and the BBC now faces tough new competition from private franchises and from cable and satellite companies. The water and sewage undertakings are likewise now in the private sector, as is the gas company. Telecommunications have been privatized. I can now buy a phone from any supplier I choose, and rather than use BT I can if I wish select a service from Mercury, or from a cable company, or even use the privately-owned cellular network. The buses have been deregulated and many train services may soon be privatized. The Rover car group has been sold into the private sector and there are even plans to enlist private companies in building and running new toll roads. Only the postman and postwoman still look the same, but if the problems can be sorted out, then the Post Office, too, could be privatized sometime after 1994.

The privatization programme has represented a remarkable shift from state to private ownership and provisioning of a range of basic goods and services in Britain. It has in this sense touched every one of us. But has it really affected us? Does it matter to the householder who turns on the tap that the water is now supplied by a private firm? Does it matter to the person who comes to read our gas meter that his or her employer is now a private sector company? Does it matter to the millions of people who now own a few hundred pounds' worth of privatized equity that they possess a tiny slice of one or two companies which before they owned only indirectly as citizens? Has privatization brought about any significant and lasting changes in the way we live? Is it an important sociological phenomenon?

It is in an attempt to answer this question that this book has been written.

2 Water floats

Of all the privatizations carried out by the British government after 1979, the sale of the ten regional water and sewage businesses of England and Wales was undoubtedly the most difficult and the most contentious. The government encountered problems which it had never encountered before, and at different times the sale provoked resistance from groups as diverse as the European Commission, local authorities, farmers, the Confederation of British Industry, the water industry chiefs, the water industry unions and the environmental lobby. The sale was also extremely unpopular with the British public, over three-quarters of whom opposed it. At one point the whole privatization plan had to be withdrawn and rethought, and there were several occasions when it seemed that it would never happen at all.

Even before the sale, many of those who knew the industry recognized that there were a number of unique problems which would have to be overcome. The managing director of Thames Water, by far the largest of what were then the ten Regional Water Authorities (RWAs), warned: 'Privatisation of the water industry presents a combination of some of the most difficult questions and issues to have arisen to date in the government's programme of privatisation of public sector industries' (Harper 1988, p. 215). Similarly, a business analyst with Price Waterhouse, who have themselves acted for the government in a number of privatizations, was in no doubt that 'This is the most complex privatisation there will ever be' (Dockray 1987, p. 398). Water privatization was, therefore, an extreme case, for all the issues, problems and concerns which arose in other sales seemed to arise in the case of water in clearer and sharper focus. It is, in this sense, the ideal case study.

The water industry before privatization

At the time when it was privatized, the water industry in England and Wales employed over 50,000 people and controlled assets valued (on a current replacement cost basis) at over £28 billion. After electricity, this makes water

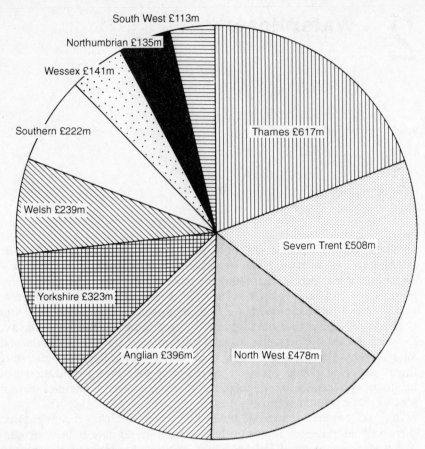

Figure 2.1   Turnover of the ten Regional Water Authorities before privatization
Source   The Independent (7 July 1989)

the biggest industry in Britain – BT, for example, had assets worth £16 billion when it was floated, and British Gas had assets of just £11 billion (see Jones 1987; Rees and Synnott 1988). In the financial year 1988–9 (the last before privatization), it had a turnover of over £3 billion, an operating profit of over £1 billion, and its capital expenditure also exceeded £1 billion. It was, by any criteria, a huge industry.

The industry before 1974

The water industry performs three main functions. First, and most obviously, it abstracts water from rivers, reservoirs and underground sources, purifies it, and pumps it to millions of domestic, industrial and agricultural users. Every day the industry supplies around 18,000 megalitres of clean piped water to its customers. Second, it takes away virtually the same volume of dirty water, treats it to remove the impurities, and returns it to the rivers or the sea. Third, it maintains the water environment. It monitors the water level in rivers, controlling the amount of water taken out and put back into them. It regulates the use of water resources for leisure purposes. It maintains sea defences, controls drainage of wetlands, replenishes fish supplies, builds flood barriers, and so on.

The first of these functions – supply of piped water – began in the nineteenth century with the development of the new industrial towns. Various private water companies and municipal corporations obtained permission through local Acts of Parliament to provide piped water to specific towns and cities, and this eventually prompted the central government in 1847 to impose upon them a statutory duty to supply with piped water all houses which demanded it. This legislation, together with the amendments of 1863, provided the basis for urban water supply for the next hundred years. Today, 99% of households in England and Wales are connected to the water mains – a higher proportion than in any other European country apart from the Netherlands (Jones 1987, p. 2).

Right from the start, water supply was organized by private companies as well as by public authorities, and the private sector has remained active in supplying water ever since. Although municipal ownership and control was progressively extended at the expense of the private water undertakers so that some 80% of water was being supplied by local councils by 1913, private enterprise was never entirely eclipsed, and twenty-eight private companies survived the era of 'gas and water socialism' and have continued to supply around one-fifth of England's water to this day. Until 1989, these private water utilities operated under statutes governing their rate of return and their mode of operations, but when the rest of the industry was privatized, the statutory water companies were also allowed to convert to limited liability company status, and a number of them were swiftly taken over by French water companies seeking a foothold in the English market.

In most parts of Britain, however, water supplies were provided until 1974 by local authorities. The system was fragmented and inefficient, for there were over 1,400 local authorities in England and Wales, most of which ran and jealously clung on to their own water undertakings. From 1945 onwards, governments began to enforce amalgamations in an attempt to increase efficiency, and over the next thirty years the number of municipal water suppliers shrank from 1,186 to just 150 as control of water passed in most areas from local councils to clusters of neighbouring councils organized as joint boards. By 1974, therefore, most local councils only indirectly controlled and managed the water supply in their areas through nomination of councillors to sit on these joint boards.

The second branch of the industry – effluent disposal – has a rather different history, for private enterprise was never involved in collecting and treating sewage. It was the municipalities which laid the sewers, emptied the cesspits and built and ran the sewage farms, and although the central government tried to encourage amalgamations as it did with the water undertakers, the local councils were generally successful in hanging on to these functions. By 1974 there were still no fewer than 1,393 different sewage authorities in England and Wales. Many of these were tiny and most lacked either the will or the resources to finance their operations adequately. Sewage farms were often old and overloaded, with the result that foul water was often returned into the rivers and the sea virtually untreated, and the network of sewers under the streets was generally neglected as money was spent on more visible and electorally advantageous public works (see Kirby 1979; Parker and Penning-Rowsell 1980). Nevertheless, this highly fragmented system still managed to connect 95% of households to the sewerage network, a figure that compares favourably with countries like France (56%), the USA (75%) and the former West Germany (86%) (Water Industry Unions Committee 1985).

The third branch of the industry was concerned with river management and land drainage. Obviously this function relates closely to the other two, for drinking water in most parts of Britain is drawn from the rivers while treated sewage and industrial waste is pumped back into them to be carried away to the sea. Nevertheless, river management has again historically been organized by a distinct and fragmented set of agencies. In 1948, thirty-two River Boards were created to assume responsibility for managing the water environment in England and Wales, and fifteen years later they were replaced by twenty-nine River Authorities which were given additional and important powers to regulate the use of the rivers. In particular, the River Authorities were authorized to license and charge for abstraction of water from the rivers by industry and water undertakers, and to give or withhold consents for discharges into rivers by industry, farmers and sewage authorities. From 1963 onwards, therefore, the River Authorities could in principle maintain river flows by refusing to allow water suppliers and users to take more water out of the rivers, and they could also clean up the rivers by refusing to allow more waste to be discharged than the rivers could handle.*

By the early 1970s, therefore, the water industry comprised around 180 water suppliers, 150 of which were joint boards of local councils with the rest private undertakers; nearly 1,400 sewage authorities, all under local authority control; and twenty-nine River Authorities with the power to regulate both abstraction from and discharges into the river system. Nearly all of these agencies were swept away as a result of the 1973 Water Act which set up just ten Regional Water Authorities (RWAs) to take over virtually all the powers of the joint water boards, the sewage authorities and the River Authorities (for detailed discussion of the reorganization, see Jordan *et al.* 1977; Okun 1977; Richardson and Jordan 1979). Only the twenty-eight private water supply companies survived this radical upheaval.

The 1974 reorganization

The 1973 Water Act introduced the important new principle of 'integrated river basin management'. This meant that just one body would take responsibility for the entire water cycle in each river basin region. Instead of one agency piping the water from the river to the user, another piping it back from the user to the river, and a third trying to regulate the level of abstraction and discharges, the new RWAs would take responsibility for the entire process from the sea to the tap and back again. In this way it was hoped that decisions affecting one part of the water cycle would be taken with due regard to their impact on all other aspects of management of the river basin system.

The scale and extent of this reorganization were dramatic. Porter (1978, p. 163) described it as 'fundamental and far-reaching' while Richardson and Jordan saw in it (1979, p. 47) 'as radical a policy switch as can be cited in post-war Britain'. Coinciding as it did with the simultaneous reorganization of local government and of the management structure of the National Health Service, it represented the culmination of a technocratic period in British politics when governments sought to modernize public administration by creating huge new bodies which would benefit from economies of scale and which would be run by technical experts freed from the petty concerns of local politicians.

Local authorities fought the proposals bitterly and their opposition did win them some initial concessions, for they were allowed to retain responsibility for sewerage provision under agency agreements with the new RWAs, and their representation on the boards of the RWAs was increased to guarantee them a majority of seats. In practice, however, their influence over the new authorities was always marginal, for the boards themselves were so large as to be ineffective, and in 1983 they lost such little influence as they had when the sewerage agency agreements were ended and all local government representation on the RWA boards was terminated.

From 1983 onwards, the ten RWAs in England and Wales were run more like nationalized industries than like the old local authority joint water boards. Each Authority had a chairman and a board of between nine and fifteen people, all of whom were appointed by central government. The chairman and the board members were in turn advised by a chief executive and a management team of professional experts. The press, which had been allowed to attend board meetings before 1983, was now excluded.

The only channel of local authority influence that remained after the 1983 reforms was through new Consumer Consultative Committees (CCCs) established by each RWA for each county in its region. The CCCs were made up of representatives of industry, commerce, agriculture, voluntary organizations and local authorities, and typically the district and county councils would between them have half the seats. But these committees were weak and could only make recommendations to the board. As we shall see in Chapter 5, few of those with representation on CCCs saw them as significant and even the RWA senior managements were often sceptical about their function. The committees were rather like the user groups in the nationalized industries, or the Community Health Councils in the NHS, and they were just as anonymous and just as powerless.

The weakness of the CCCs and the removal of local authority representation left the boards of the RWAs free to set their own policies, though, like the nationalized industries, their control over their own finances was increasingly restricted by central government cash limits on new capital expenditure. Every year their spending plans had to be submitted to the Department of the Environment and thence to the Treasury, and every year the government would revise the plans in accordance with its own financial priorities. It was the irritation caused by these financial restrictions which was soon to prompt the move towards privatization.

The problems of privatizing water

The privatization of the water industry was, in a sense, the logical end-point to the reorganization process begun in 1974. The amalgamation of many tiny authorities into just ten large, multi-purpose bodies; the removal of local government representation; the restructuring of the boards into smaller, more cohesive units of decision-making; the shift away from government subsidies to self-sufficiency; the move from historic cost to current cost accounting; and the price rises which accompanied these changes (prices rose by more than 40% in the first year following the 1974 reforms): all of this unintentionally laid the groundwork for the eventual sale of the industry into the private sector.

Although privatization could probably never have happened without the reforms of 1974 and 1983, it would be a mistake to see these earlier reforms as intentional stepping stones to privatization. In 1974, the decision to reorganize was technocratic – the government believed that big, new organizations would be more efficient, and the professionals within the industry seized their chance to be free of local government 'interference'. In 1983, the decision to reform was part of the government's broader strategy to enforce tighter financial controls on the public sector industries. As late as February 1984, the Under Secretary of State at the Department of the Environment went on record as saying that the government did not regard water as suitable for privatization. The idea of privatizing did not surface until 1985, and when it did, it came not from within government but from the industry itself (see Bowers *et al.* 1988; Richardson *et al.* 1992).

In February 1985, the Treasury ordered the ten RWAs to repay to the government a higher proportion of their debt and to raise their charges in order to finance this. Several of the RWA chairmen were outraged by what they saw as a blatant attempt by the government to use higher water prices as a means of raising revenue without increasing taxes, and the chairman of Thames Water, Roy Watts, made it clear that he would favour cutting the link with the government altogether. The junior Environment Minister then made a surprise announcement in the House of Commons that, mindful of Mr Watts's views, the government would 'be examining the possibility of a measure of privatisation in the industry' (Hansard, 7 February 1985, vol. 72, col. 292w).

So swiftly did the government respond to the Thames Water chairman's comments that the suspicion has arisen that ministers were already considering the possibility of privatization. In other public sector industries, it seems that the government deliberately tightened financial controls in order to prompt managers into endorsing privatization (Steel and Heald 1984, p. 17), and this may also have happened to some extent in the case of water. Whatever the truth of the matter, it is clear that Roy Watts was pushing against an open door, for although the Prime Minister, in a response to a Parliamentary question in January 1985, expressed some caution about the practical problems in privatizing an industry like water, it is clear that neither she nor her ministers had any principled objection to such a move.

As things turned out, however, the practical problems were indeed daunting. Six in particular may be noted.

Public distrust

The first was simply that water is such a basic and fundamental resource that neither the government nor the industry ever succeeded in overcoming a widespread public conviction that only government could be trusted to provide it. Clean water is an essential condition of life and water has a special emotional as well as biological significance for many people. Without clean drinking water, we die, and without a secure system of transporting and treating waste water we are threatened by the sorts of diseases which once decimated urban populations. While it is true that we can (and in increasing numbers we do) buy bottled water, we are for all practical purposes dependent for delivery of this crucial service upon a utility in whose integrity and competence we are obliged to place our absolute trust every time we turn on the tap or flush the lavatory. What the privatization of water revealed was that many people preferred to place this trust in a state-owned and state-run utility rather than in one located in the private sector. As we shall see in Chapter 6, much of the public opposition to the privatization of the water industry sprang from the moral conviction that it was in some way wrong to allow private interests to profit from delivery of so basic a resource.

Natural monopoly

A second problem, which the Prime Minister herself had recognized in her comments in January 1985, was that water is a natural monopoly. Indeed, it has been described as 'the natural monopoly par excellence' (Littlechild 1986, p. 5). A natural monopoly industry is one where the economies of scale are such that production can most efficiently be organized by a single agency. In the case of the water industry, it is, of course, possible for competing suppliers to lay pipes along the same streets, and Chadwick's survey of sanitary conditions in English towns between 1838 and 1841 found a number of cases where this did indeed occur (see Hanke and Walters 1987). But such competitive arrangements are clearly grossly inefficient. In an industry such as water, where an existing network of pipes and pumping stations makes it possible to increase the volume of supply without incurring a proportional increase in cost, it will always be inefficient and wasteful to have more than one utility company operating in any one area. The decision to privatize thus entailed transferring into private ownership an industry in which effective competition for customers could never realistically be expected to develop and in which permanent state regulation of prices and quality would have to be maintained if the interests of consumers were to be safeguarded.

It is possible to find instances of other privatizations which have also involved selling a monopoly business – we saw in Chapter 1, for example, that British Gas was privatized as a single monopoly and that the twelve electricity supply companies enjoy effective monopolies within their regions as far as domestic customers are concerned. But water is the extreme case. Unlike BT, where competition with Mercury and with the cable companies is now beginning to make itself felt, or even British Gas, where there is now some competition to supply gas through a common pipeline network, there will and can never be competition to supply piped water to people's homes, nor to take away their foul water (although sewage treatment could in principle be opened up to competition).

Environmental regulation

A third specific problem in privatizing water was that the RWAs had both utility and regulatory functions. As we saw earlier, they took over water and sewage functions from the local authorities while also assuming the management and control functions of the old River Authorities. A decision to transfer them to the private sector would therefore mean one of two things. Either the RWAs could be sold off as they were, thereby creating private enterprise companies with the responsibility of granting or withholding abstraction licences and discharge consents – a policy which would entail private firms regulating other private users and which was without precedent. Or government could restructure the RWAs prior to sale so as to separate the regulatory functions from those involving pure service delivery – a policy which would involve abandoning the principle of integrated river basin management and which would throw the industry into another bout of major disruption. As we shall see, this particular dilemma created major problems for the government, which started out by pursuing the first option and ended up having to switch to the second.

Underinvestment

A fourth major area of difficulty which again marked out water from most of the other privatizations was that it was by no means clear that the industry was actually saleable. Most of the RWAs had large debts, but these could be written off if need be. More problematic was the scale of future investment which they would be called upon to make. After decades of neglect under local government ownership, and a further fifteen years of government cash limits, many of the authorities were facing major problems requiring huge amounts of capital investment. Ever since the 1974 reorganization, capital expenditure had been falling in real terms (see Figure 2.2) with the result that the

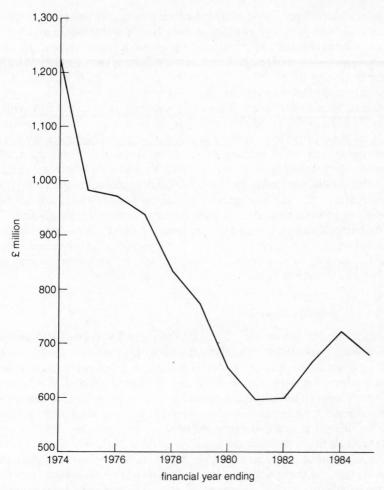

Figure 2.2   Capital expenditure by Regional Water Authorities, 1974–85 (in 1983 prices)

Source   Synott (1986, p. 15)

authorities had still not put right much of the neglect of earlier decades (see Rees and Synott 1988).

The results of this neglect were clear to see. At Anglian and Severn Trent there were problems of excessive nitrate levels in the drinking water caused by extensive use of fertilizers by farmers. At Northumbrian, ten out of nineteen bathing beaches were below official standards, and at Southern, where major new sea outfalls were planned, the cost of bringing all beaches up to EC standards was higher than for any other authority. At Yorkshire, rivers were heavily polluted and water quality was affected by discoloration, and at South West a series of accidents including the discharge of aluminium sulphate into the mains water supply had resulted in a poor public image and the prospect of costly litigation. Worst of all, though, was North West, where much of the sewer system, constructed during the Industrial Revolution, was decaying, rivers (especially the Mersey) were heavily polluted, the drinking water was contaminated by high levels of lead and twenty out of thirty bathing beaches were in breach of EC regulations.

Increasing public concern with environmental issues, coupled with an intensification of EC standards, was only likely to exacerbate the problems faced by these authorities, and the uncertainties regarding future investment needs made many of them look like poor prospects for privatization. Only Thames – by far the biggest of the ten, with no major problems and virtually debt-free – looked anything like an attractive investment prospect, and it was no coincidence that the management at Thames was the most enthusiastic in support of privatization. At the other extreme, authorities like North West seemed almost unsaleable, and the chairman of North West (who was later replaced) made it clear that he opposed the whole idea of privatizing water and doubted whether anyone could be enticed to buy his authority if it were ever offered for sale (see Speight 1985).

Differences between authorities

The fact that there were ten different authorities for potential investors to choose from presented the government with its fifth unique problem. Before 1989, privatizations had always involved single companies, but the state-owned water industry consisted of ten different businesses. Given the variations between them, there were obvious problems involved in any attempt to float them simultaneously, for who would buy North West in preference to Thames? City analysts also expressed doubts about whether the City could cope with all the paperwork involved in handling a simultaneous sale of ten different businesses. If, on the other hand, they were sold off piecemeal, Thames first and the others later as and when they were made ready for sale, it seemed doubtful whether all ten would ever successfully be transferred into private ownership since the planned sale of the electricity industry in 1990 and 1991 would eclipse any later water offers, and a general election after that could well result in the Conservatives losing office.

The existence of ten different authorities was problematic, then, although it also presented the government with a unique opportunity. There was, for example, the possibility of encouraging people to buy shares in their 'local' water company, thereby strengthening their identification with and interest in the enterprise in which they held their investments. More tangibly, while each authority enjoyed a natural monopoly within its region, the existence of the other nine could be used to stimulate some form of competition between them (see Littlechild 1986). There was, for example, the real possibility that an inefficient and poorly run business could be taken over by one of the others. There was also the opportunity for the government's price regulator to compare performance across all ten and to hold prices at the level at which the most efficient of them could operate profitably. And although competition in offering domestic water and sewage services could not occur, it was possible to envisage the ten businesses coming into direct product competition with each other in other areas such as commercial services, water engineering and provisions for leisure. Thus, despite the real problems involved, there were potentially some novel advantages to be had from selling ten separate water businesses.

Charging for water

The final problem to be confronted in any attempt to sell off the water authorities related to the method of charging. Nearly everywhere in England and Wales, major industrial and commercial users of water were metered, but households paid for water and sewage services through a 'water rate' levied, like local council rates, according to the notional rental value of the property they occupied. The result was that only one-quarter of RWA revenues was derived from unit pricing, while most of the services they provided were unpriced (Rees and Synnott 1988).

From the start it was clear that this system would have to change. Even without privatization, a new charging method would have had to be found because local authority rates were themselves being abolished to be replaced by the ill-fated community charge or 'poll tax' (which was itself later replaced by the council tax). This meant that domestic properties would no longer be rated, and that water rates would therefore have to be replaced by something else. In addition, the shift from public to private sector ownership seemed to many to necessitate a change in the existing system. Water rates were more like a tax than a service charge (Veljanovski 1987), and it seemed inappropriate for privately owned companies to charge for their commodity according to the imputed wealth of the consumer rather than the amount of the commodity consumed. As one financial analyst put it:

> To people learning about the water industry for the first time it is a shock to their preconceived notions of the way a business works to be reminded that in this industry revenues do not necessarily increase when you sell more of your product.
>
> (Challen 1987, p. 6)

The obvious solution to this problem was to introduce water metering for domestic households, but this was likely to be costly – as much as £4 billion – and could add as much as 15% to average household bills at a time when water prices were anyway likely to be rising (*The Independent*, 11 April 1991; 13 December 1991). Trials on the Isle of Wight and in eleven mainland towns have subsequently indicated that metering may reduce the demand for water (two-thirds of customers have actually ended up paying less than before as a result of economizing on water usage), and this could in turn reduce the need for new investment in reservoirs and other plant, but it is unlikely that such savings would come anywhere near balancing the initial cost of installing meters, and many critics continue to doubt whether this is the most cost-effective way to invest £4 billion.

There was also the impact on public opinion to consider, for surveys revealed some public opposition to metering (only one in five respondents to a *Which?* survey in May 1989, for example, favoured a switch from rates to meters), although a more recent and systematic public consultation exercise found that most people considered meters to be a fair method of charging for water (see Ofwat 1992). Opponents of privatization were also suggesting that metering would lead poor people to reduce water consumption to a point where their health could be affected – the water industry unions claimed, for example, that

> Users on low incomes could be forced to use less, especially as charges increase. It is not difficult to imagine isolated elderly people in particular being frightened into cost-cutting measures like not flushing the toilet regularly which would endanger their health and that of others.
> (Water Industry Unions Committee 1985, p. 24)

While such emotive claims are almost certainly without foundation – in most other European countries water supplies are metered without incurring additional health risks, and most people in Britain willingly pay much more to heat their water than they would ever have to pay for the water itself (Bird and Jackson 1967) – they nevertheless fed into the general public uneasiness about privatizing so basic an industry as water.

The problems, therefore, were daunting. Public opinion was opposed to privatization, the industry was a natural monopoly, the authorities performed regulatory as well as utility functions, several authorities looked virtually unsaleable, there were ten different businesses to dispose of, and the system of charging would have to be overhauled. Yet despite all this, it took just three months for the government to set in motion the process leading to eventual privatization. In February 1985 it announced that it would be investigating the possibility of privatizing at least some of the industry. In April it published a Discussion Paper.

The battle for water privatization

The government's Discussion Paper set out some general and familiar arguments about the advantages of privatization but drew attention to two specific issues regarding the privatization of water. First, it was concerned about the natural monopoly problem. Second, it raised the problem of whether the principle of integrated river basin management should be retained or whether it might be better to privatize the operational functions of the RWAs while transferring their regulatory functions to a new public sector agency.

In his response to the paper, the chairman of the Water Authorities' Association (representing all ten RWAs) made it clear that the industry was happy to proceed with privatization but was intent on retaining all existing powers and functions. 'It is essential', he warned, 'that if privatisation does take place it should be done on the basis of existing water authorities' (Jones 1985, p. 56). Just like the managements of BT, British Gas and BAA before them, the water industry chiefs were insistent that privatization should not break up their empires, and, as in the earlier privatizations, these warnings were heeded by ministers.

In February 1986, the government published its White Paper on the privatization of the water authorities (Department of the Environment 1986a). Ten reasons were given for the change, most of which were already familiar from other privatizations. Privatization would, first, free water industry chiefs from political pressures; second, release them from financial constraints; and third, give them access to the capital markets. Fourth, as private companies, the ten water businesses would be able to attract better-quality managers by offering higher salaries; and fifth, privatization would improve employee motivation. Sixth, customers would benefit because performance would improve as a result of comparative competition between the ten businesses, and this improved efficiency would lead, seventh, to lower prices and, eighth, to stronger incentives to find out what customers really want. Ninth, the sale would broaden share ownership; and tenth, would establish a clearer framework for protecting the water environment.

The White Paper made two important decisions clear. First, it sought to tackle the natural monopoly problem by establishing a new Office of Water Services (Ofwat) whose director general would regulate service standards and prices. In this, the government was simply following the precedent established in the earlier BT and British Gas privatizations, for there, too, prices were regulated by new agencies (known as Oftel and Ofgas), and the same sort of pricing formula used there was to be applied in the case of water (see Chapter 3). The director general of water services would also assume responsibility for the existing Consumer Consultative Committees which were to be simplified and strengthened.

Second, the White Paper established that the ten RWAs would not be restructured before privatization. Echoing the sentiments of the water chiefs themselves, it claimed that the system of integrated river basin management had 'worked well' since 1974 and that there was no reason to change it by separating the water supply and sewage disposal functions from the regulatory functions. The government therefore proposed to allow the new water companies to determine whether and how much other private companies would be allowed to abstract water from the rivers or to discharge waste water into them. The White Paper claimed that this should not cause a problem since those who felt aggrieved would have the right to appeal to the Secretary of State against a water company decision, and this procedure was spelled out in more detail in a later paper (Department of the Environment 1986b). As Rees and Synnott (1988, p. 188) have pointed out, these proposed arrangements represented a 'unique experiment with no precedent anywhere in the world' and they almost certainly reflected the government's desire to avoid confrontation with the ten RWA chairmen.

Having settled all the details, the government confidently expected to press ahead with the first privatization – almost certainly Thames – sometime in 1987. It had, however, completely miscalculated the extent and intensity of the opposition which its proposals would provoke. In particular, it seems to have been taken completely unawares by the hostility generated by its plan to allow the privatized companies to regulate the water environment, for this aspect of the White Paper brought it into direct conflict with organizations and interests which normally form the bedrock of support for Conservative governments.

One such set of interests was large private sector firms in sectors like brewing and chemicals. These companies relied upon abstraction of river water or discharges into the rivers as an essential aspect of their production process, and they were clearly dismayed at the prospect of their businesses being regulated by another capitalist enterprise, particularly one which was also involved in using the rivers for its own core business. Individually and collectively (through the Confederation of British Industry and through trade associations such as the Chemical Industries Association), these enterprises expressed their outrage at the proposal that the existing RWAs should simply be transferred as they stood into private ownership. In its submissions, for example, the CBI made clear its view that it was 'totally unacceptable' for privatized companies to be given statutory responsibility for prosecuting other companies (Richardson *et al.* 1992). Much the same point was also made informally at an individual level. As our CBI informant put it: 'It's certain that senior industrialists had a word in a few ears.'

Opposition also came from another source usually well disposed towards Conservative governments, the farmers and the landowners. The Country Landowners' Association (CLA), in particular, was vociferous in its open hostility to the White Paper, for like the industrialists, the big farmers were worried that private water companies with regulatory powers would attempt to meet tighter pollution requirements by cracking down on pollution of the rivers by farmers (silage, slurry, pesticides and nitrates all increasingly find their way into the water system) while continuing to pump their own sewage waste into the rivers with nobody to stop them doing it. As the CLA's water adviser told us:

> In our comments on the White Paper we said you must separate the regulatory functions and keep them in the public sector. The minister didn't like this, but we kept up the pressure. Almost to a man our county chairmen are Conservatives who are men of status in the community, and they've usually got the ear of their MP and are on Christian name terms. I suspect the minister got fed up with getting letters from MPs.

The combined opposition of the CBI and the CLA might alone have been enough to force the government to rethink – the senior Conservative minister, Lord Whitelaw, was apparently of the opinion, for example, that the Bill would never get through the House of Lords (*The Independent*, 12 August 1987). But on top of this came an effective campaign waged by the environmental lobby, and, in particular, by the Council for the Protection of Rural England which secured a legal opinion by a leading European lawyer to the effect that the government's plans were inconsistent with existing European Community law. This view later received support from the European Commission itself which warned that, although the issue would finally have to be resolved in the Court of Justice, it believed that the government's plans were probably in breach of EC directives to which it was bound (Richardson *et al.* 1992).

There were other problems as well. Public opinion was strongly opposed to water privatization, and the first sales were due to take place just around the time of the approaching general election. The water unions were also against the Bill and although their effectiveness was limited, one of them, Nalgo, was in the process of taking Thames Water to court for spending public money illegally by publicizing the case for privatization before Parliamentary authority had been given (*Financial Times*, 28 July 1986). Court action was also threatened by Labour-controlled local authorities which claimed that the government had no right to sell the water authorities since their assets had been taken away from local government without payment in 1974 and therefore still rightfully belonged to them (an argument which continued through to 1989 when six local authorities contested the legality of the sale in an unsuccessful attempt to stall or thwart it). And the government itself had still not worked out some of the major problems in privatizing the industry, not least how to reschedule debts and offset future investment needs so that all ten authorities might eventually find buyers.

Inevitably, in July 1986, the government beat a retreat and announced that it was shelving its privatization proposals. Nothing more was heard for nine months until the Conservative Party published its manifesto for the May 1987 general election. This proposed that all ten water authorities should be privatized during the next Parliament, but that their regulatory powers regarding licenses and discharge consents would to be taken away and vested in a new public body to be known as the National Rivers Authority (NRA). Put another way, the principle of integrated river basin management was being abandoned and the pre-1974 division between utility functions and river management functions was being reintroduced in a new guise.

The water industry chiefs were furious. The Water Authorities' Association, representing all ten RWAs, immediately complained that it had not been consulted about the new proposal, and in July 1987, when the victorious Conservatives published a Green Paper setting out their NRA proposals, the water authority managements mobilized their opposition. The WAA itself issued a statement in advance of the Green Paper describing the NRA plan as 'folly' (*The Independent*, 24 June 1987), and in its formal response to the plan it asserted that the proposals would 'no longer achieve the key objectives which privatisation was intended to secure' (*The Independent*, 10 September 1987). Even more worrying for the government, though, was the vociferous opposition of the Thames Water chairman, Roy Watts. He had originally been the person responsible for suggesting the whole idea of privatizing water, yet now he became the government's sternest critic. Describing the manifesto commitment as 'short on costs, short on vision and short on consultation'

(*Financial Times*, 17 May 1987), he led a deliberately public and bitter campaign to force the government to reverse its plans. Employing a professional firm of political lobbyists, Watts targeted the 140 London MPs in an attempt to mobilize Parliamentary opposition within the Conservative Party. In late July, the Secretary of State, Nicholas Ridley, tried to counter this campaign by writing to these MPs telling them to ignore Watts, and by writing to Watts himself warning him to shut up or risk being sacked (*The Independent*, 20 August 1987).

But Watts would not shut up. He based his opposition on the principle that the 1974 system of integrated river basin management was successful and should be retained, but what really explained his fury at the government's proposals was the prospect of losing that part of the business which had the greatest potential for profitable expansion after privatization. Around 6,000 of the industry's 50,000 workforce would be transferred to the NRA, and these would include many of the skilled managers and engineers who would be needed if the companies were to compete for lucrative overseas river management contracts. As Watts himself admitted in a *Sunday Times* interview (13 September 1987): 'It's the potential growth bits that the government is proposing to take away. It's the bits that will add the extra value when we are sold.'

The opposition of Watts and his colleagues to the break-up of their authorities was reminiscent of the campaigns waged by other chairmen to maintain their business empires on privatization, but if anything, this was the bitterest confrontation of all. As *The Independent* (18 July 1987) suggested: 'In none of the government's previous privatisations has it been faced with such reluctant managements'. Yet having already once changed its mind, the government could not climb down, and the prospect of being dragged to the European Court of Justice served to strengthen ministers' resolve. Gradually, the opposition from the water industry waned. In September, the chairman of Severn Trent broke ranks, welcomed the government's proposals, and suggested that his authority should be first in line to be sold. The following month, the chairman of Anglian Water somewhat less enthusiastically also endorsed the principle of establishing the NRA. And in December, the government published its White Paper. The decision would not be reversed and it was time for some quiet negotiation.

Through the first half of 1988, the ten RWA chiefs worked on exacting concessions from the government, including generous debt write-offs and provision for unforeseen future costs arising from tighter EC pollution controls to be passed on directly to customers. By July, when the government announced that all ten authorities would be sold simultaneously, the authority chairmen were able to present a united front in favour of the government's plans, and seven months later, as the bill was going through Parliament, they even went so far as to write to all MPs urging them to support it. By then, however, the government was bogged down in a number of other difficulties.

One was that the privatization of the water industry, which had never been popular, became increasingly unpopular as time went by, and particularly as people began to realize that water prices were due to rise sharply in future years. As we shall see in Chapter 6, by 1989 around three-quarters of voters disapproved of water privatization – a level of opposition unmatched by any other privatization before or since. Given that the government was in 1989 already deep in electoral trouble due to the implementation of the hugely unpopular 'poll tax', many Conservatives began to wonder whether it made political sense to press on with the equally unpopular sale of the water authorities, and even the Conservative media began to urge ministers to think again. The *Sunday Times* (12 February 1989), for example, described water privatization as 'a shambles, a threat to the much more important electricity privatisation the following year, and a political mess which Labour should be able to run with all year', while the *Spectator* (18 February 1989) warned: 'We are on the verge here of what may be the biggest and most embarrassing failure of official policy in the Government's present term of office . . . This is a privatisation which will earn nothing but blame and recrimination'.

Added to the concern about public opinion were continuing problems with the European Community, and, in particular, with the Environment Commissioner, Carlo Ripa di Meana. In 1980, the EC had issued a directive on drinking water quality which aimed to reduce the level of nitrates and other contaminants to 0.1 micrograms per litre of drinking water by 1985. By the late 1980s, Britain (and, indeed, most other EC countries) had made little progress in meeting this target, partly because many in the industry and in government apparently believed that it was neither practical nor necessary to achieve such a level of purity. In December 1987, however, the government publicly conceded that it was breaking the EC directive, and it committed the industry to meeting these standards by means of up to £6 billion of new investment in mains pipe refurbishment and water treatment works. For the Environment Commissioner, spurred on by British environmental pressure groups such as Friends of the Earth, this was too little too late, and it became clear that the newly privatized water businesses would still be in breach of the drinking water directive when they began trading and would therefore be liable to prosecution.

The threat of massive fines for non-compliance, coming on top of the huge bills for upgrading treatment plants and pipelines, would clearly threaten the future profitability of the privatized water companies, and in order to avoid this, the government inserted a clause into the Water Bill exempting the companies from legal action on water quality provided they could demonstrate that they were making reasonable progress towards meeting the standards in the EC directive.

Carlo Ripa di Meana was outraged at what he saw as a deliberate attempt to flout EC law, and in February 1989, just as the Bill was going through the House of Commons, he threatened to take the British government to the European Court unless it withdrew the clause. This put ministers in an extremely awkward position, for not only would the prospect of future prosecutions make the water businesses less easy to sell, but also a European

Court hearing would make the British government appear insensitive to environmental concerns at a time when environmental issues were becoming politically more and more important. The Green Party in Britain had polled an unprecedented 15% in the recent elections for the European Parliament and even Margaret Thatcher had felt obliged to pronounce herself in favour of more environmentally sensitive policies. Accordingly, ministers had begun to argue that water privatization was motivated by the government's desire to improve the environment, the argument being that establishment of a new National Rivers Authority separate from the water businesses would help enforce environmental standards more rigorously than before (we consider this argument in Chapter 5). This claim would, however, clearly be undermined if the government were now to resist EC pressure to enforce water purity standards on the privatized businesses.

At the same time as ministers were wriggling on the horns of this particular dilemma, they were also confronted by growing scepticism in the City about the financial viability of a privatized water industry. Given the level of future investment required and the existing level of debts carried by most of the authorities, financial analysts began to talk openly about the possibility that the flotation might fail. By February 1989, many cautious voices were urging the government to call a halt, and newspaper financial analysts were warning that the sale would flop if the government insisted on going ahead with it.

Gradually, however, the problems were sorted out, although it cost a lot of public money to do it. Backbench jitters were calmed, and in April, the Water Bill cleared the House of Commons with only four Conservative MPs defying the whip and voting against it. The threat of litigation was averted as, in May, ministers came to a compromise agreement with the EC under which the newly privatized companies need not be prosecuted for failing to meet water quality standards provided they maintained an agreed level of investment and demonstrated that they were moving as fast as possible towards compliance. Later in the same month, City anxieties were eased by the announcement that the government was writing off £5 billion of debt owed by the water authorities – this despite an assurance just three months earlier by the Secretary of State for the Environment that 'There is no question of writing off all the debt, or anything like it' (*Financial Times*, 13 February 1989).

Continuing worries about the future cost of complying with ever tighter EC standards were countered in two ways. First, as we shall see in Chapter 3, a system of price regulation was set in place which allowed for annual price rises higher than inflation to enable the companies to increase investment and which also allowed them to pass on to customers any unavoidable new costs arising after the price limits had been set. Second, having already written off the debts, the government in August announced an additional cash injection of £1.5 billion (the so-called 'green dowry') to help the companies meet their new investment requirements. As *The Economist* (5 August 1989) observed, the combined cost of the debt write-off and the green dowry cancelled out the revenue which the sale was expected to generate, 'leaving the government with a profit of about zero'.

The cost to the public of all of these concessions was increased still further during 1989 by a massive advertising campaign. The RWAs themselves spent £24 million on what they termed a 'water awareness campaign' designed to inform the public about the industry and its functions. During March and April, before the Water Bill had even cleared the House of Lords, water was the most expensively advertised product in Britain (*Sunday Times*, 30 April 1989). In addition, the government spent around £150 million in all on further advertising, underwriting and advisers' fees, and in financing customer inducements (*Daily Telegraph*, 4 April 1990). Those who registered in advance for shares in their local company, for example, were entitled to bonus shares or to discounts on the second and third instalments, and these costs were also borne by the Treasury. Although the exact costs of the sale are still disputed, it does seem that water was the most expensive privatization of all to market (*The Independent*, 15 January 1990).

All these advertisements and inducements did little to make water privatization any more popular with the public, but they do seem to have encouraged more people to invest in the issue. The flotation, which in February 1989 had seemed doomed to fail, was in December achieved with spectacular success: 2.7 million people applied for water shares and the offer was oversubscribed 5.7 times. The sale grossed £5.2 billion, though after the debt write-off, the green dowry and the other costs incurred in making the industry marketable, the government actually made a loss on the sale of nearly £1.2 billion. Investors, though, were happy. At the close of the first day's trading, when 30% of water shares had changed hands, the 100p part-paid shares were trading at between 131p and 157p, and were showing an average profit to those who stagged the issue of 44% (Price Waterhouse 1990).

The water industry after privatization

As soon as they escaped government control, most of the newly privatized water services PLCs (WSPLCs) began to reorganize, to innovate and to diversify. With the prices charged for their core sewage and water business tightly regulated by Ofwat, and the scope for expansion in the core services limited by the nature of demand for the product, it was always apparent that the search for growth and enhanced profitability would focus on new areas of activity. The more conservative businesses, such as Welsh and Yorkshire, aimed to achieve between 10% and 15% of their turnover from non-regulated activities within five years. The more audacious ones, such as North West and Thames, were aiming as high as 50% (*Sunday Times*, 5 November 1989).

Diversification took various forms. Sometimes new companies were established under the umbrella of a holding company. At Southern Water, for example, six new 'enterprise companies' were set up to deal with transport management, scientific services, engineering design and project management, information technology, estates management and plumbing services, and a seventh, handling security services, was added a year later. Each of these new companies is a separate profit centre and is expected to sell its services both to the core business and to external clients. Southern also made an early bid to break into the expanding bottled water market when it launched its Hazeley Down mineral water (again through a new company) in 1991 (see Southern Water annual reports).

Sometimes, diversification was accomplished swiftly by taking over existing companies in order to gain a foothold in new markets. At North West, for example, the aim was to develop as a major international water engineering company, and to this end, companies in Britain, Ireland and America were acquired in November 1990 while a Malaysian offshoot was also established to take responsibility for a contract which was won to manage the water treatment plant at Ipoh. In common with a number of other WSPLCs, North West also began investing in development of surplus land near its reservoirs, negotiating a joint housing development with Beazer Homes and planning various commercial deals (see North West Water annual reports).

Other companies have bought into plumbing, waste disposal or even telecommunications companies – Chapman (1990) identifies telecommunications and cable television as likely targets for investment, for fibre-optic cable must be laid underground alongside water mains and sewer pipes. Those companies, like Southern, which have smaller water utility companies operating within their areas, have often bought shares in them (although they have encountered competition in this from the three giant French water companies which started buying shares in these smaller companies in the late 1980s). Sometimes the WSPLCs have decided to invest in companies which are important suppliers or customers for them. Welsh Water, for example, took a stake in South Wales Electricity when it was privatized.

As we shall see in Chapter 4, all this reorganization and diversification has had important consequences for the workforce. Companies like Thames moved quickly to reduce the number of recognized trade unions and to replace collective wage bargaining with a system combining basic salaries with performance-related pay. Thames also abolished the old public sector demarcation between staff, craft and manual grades, and it reduced working hours for blue-collar workers to the norm for its white-collar staff. Other companies, too, took the opportunity to establish changed working practices at least within their new businesses where labour relations could be constructed anew free of the old public sector legacy (Ferner 1991).

Diversification also caused a headache for Ofwat, whose task it is to regulate water prices. Early on, the director of water services changed the licence provisions of the WSPLCs to ensure that investments in new areas of business did not pre-empt resources which should be going into the core business. Ofwat also made it clear that losses in the new businesses would have to be met by shareholders and could not be cross-subsidized out of revenue from the core business (see Byatt 1991). Indeed, the director general even went so far as to suggest that any substantial moves into new and unregulated areas outside the core business should be notified to him in advance, even though this exceeded the formal powers vested in him when the office was set up (*The Times*, 19 June 1991).

Profits, generally, were buoyant in the years immediately following privatization, and this, too, concerned Ofwat's director general. All ten WSPLCs recorded profits and dividends in the first three years of private sector operation much higher than had been forecast (see Chapter 3). To some extent, this reflected raised productivity and improved efficiency as well as returns on the unregulated parts of the business, for changes in work organization and the improved incentives for employees and managers reduced operating costs and therefore contributed to improved economic performance. North West, for example, cut its operating costs from 60% of turnover before privatization to 46% of turnover in the first year after privatization (North West Water *Annual Report*, 1990). Nevertheless, the suspicion also arose that price regulation was too lax, and that the WSPLCs were reaping the benefits of exploiting their captive markets. As we shall see in Chapter 3, water prices rose substantially each year after privatization, and this put pressure on Ofwat to tighten up company profit margins and led to increasing strains between the companies and the regulator.

Conclusion

If the water industry in England and Wales can successfully be privatized, then it is difficult to think of any public sector industry which could not also be sold off. The problems encountered by the government in selling the ten water businesses were daunting, but one by one they were overcome.

The industry was, for a start, burdened with debt, so in the run-up to privatization the authorities were forced to start paying off their debts and what was left – £5 billion – was then written off before the sale. The industry was also suffering from years of underinvestment, and its commercial prospects were blighted by the growth of a green agenda in Britain and in Europe which threatened to overwhelm future profits with demands for improved water quality and enhanced standards for rivers, sea and beaches. This problem was countered by handing over another £1½ billion to the companies to help them bring facilities up to standard, and by fixing future prices so that money would be available for all necessary improvements without eating into dividends. The sale was deeply unpopular, but a huge advertising campaign, together with the lure of anticipated first day profits, helped entice over 2½ million people to apply for shares.

Against all the odds, therefore, the sale was a success, although in the end it cost the government more to get rid of the industry than it received back in revenue. So far, investors seem happy, for dividends have been well above the stock market average. But what of the other objectives which water privatization was intended to fulfil? Looking back to the original White Paper of February 1986, for example, the government claimed that managers in the industry would benefit from improved incentives and greater autonomy, that ordinary employees would be motivated to work harder because they would own shares in their own company, that consumers would benefit from lower prices and from enhanced responsiveness to their wishes, and that the environment would be improved as a result of the clearer framework of protection and control. To this list we might also add the hope, expressed privately though never set down in any White Paper, that the privatization would win the Conservatives votes, and the belief that it would encourage the spread of a more entrepreneurial culture among those who bought shares in the offer.

Drawing on the results from our research on two of the privatized water businesses, Southern and North West, the following chapters consider how far these hopes and expectations have been fulfilled. In Chapter 4 we analyse how privatization affected the management and employees in the two companies. Chapter 5 looks at its impact on various interest groups, including the trade unions within the companies and those like farmers, big business and the environmental lobby who have a direct interest in the water system. Chapter 6 examines the claim that those who buy shares tend to switch political allegiance to the Conservatives, and Chapter 7 reviews the evidence regarding the emergence of a new entrepreneurial culture among those who have bought shares for the first time as a result of the privatization programme. We begin, however, with the consumers of water. How have the ordinary domestic customers fared as a result of the water industry's moving from the public into the private sector?

3 The consumers

One of the principal justifications for the privatization programme has been the claim that the shift from public to private ownership forces companies to pay more attention to what consumers want. In an article published jointly with Michael Beesley in 1986, for example, Stephen Littlechild (who was later to become the chief regulator of the privatized electricity industry) argued:

> Privatisation will generate benefits for consumers because privately-owned companies have a greater incentive to produce goods and services in the quantity and variety which consumers prefer. Companies which succeed in discovering and meeting consumer needs make profits and grow; the less successful wither and die.
>
> (Beesley and Littlechild 1986, p. 38).

Similarly, the minister responsible for the early privatization programme, John Moore (1983, p. 13), made it clear that 'the main prize' from the policy would accrue, not to employees, nor even to the company managements, but to the consumers.

The reasoning behind this is that state-owned enterprises are thought to be dominated by producer interests such as managers and trade union leaders. Because taxpayers have no choice but to continue financing these industries, those who run them and work in them are in a position to disregard their customers and to divert revenue into higher wages or subsidies for inefficient working practices rather than seeking to reduce prices or raise the quality of service they provide. In the private sector, by contrast, companies lose market share if they lose customer confidence, and private firms therefore have no option but to concern themselves first and foremost with the expressed demands and grievances of their consumers.

Consumers are said to gain from privatization in three specific ways. First, the quality of the good or service should improve. Privatized companies can raise more money for new investment and will be more concerned to innovate in order to attract new customers, and these changes should result in a better product. Second, prices should fall, again as a result of efficiency and productivity gains. Where firms operate in a competitive market they will be obliged to keep prices down in order to maintain or expand their market share, but even when they operate with little or no competition, price regulation should ensure that prices remain low and that customers reap the benefit of improved efficiency and the introduction of new technologies. Third, privatized firms should be more responsive to consumers, for they will be more concerned about their public image than the old nationalized industries ever needed to be. Complaints will therefore be dealt with more quickly, back-up services better organized, consumers' views more assiduously sought out, and so on.

This, then, is the promise: 'a much better deal on price, on service, on delivery, on the whole operation' (Redwood 1990, p. 2). Whether this promise has been fulfilled is the question at issue in this chapter.

Quality of product

Opponents of privatization often maintain that it lowers the quality of the product or service to consumers as profit-orientated companies forsake their old commitment to a 'public service' ethic and seek ways of cutting corners in order to maximize returns. In the case of BT, for example, fears were expressed that a private company would neglect essential but unprofitable services such as the network of public callboxes and the emergency 999 service, and in the early years following privatization it looked as if some of these fears were justified. By 1986, two years after privatization, 21% of public callboxes were out of order, and the volume of complaints to the Telecom Users' Association doubled between 1986 and 1987 (Thompson 1988). In 1987, the government regulator, Oftel (the Office of Telecommunications), reported that faults on exchange lines were taking longer to rectify, delays were increasing in providing new lines, and operator and directory enquiries services were unsatisfactory. In 1988, Oftel found that only 74% of faults were being repaired within one day, as compared with 85% or 90% a few years earlier, and in 1989 it received 32,000 complaints about BT, an increase of more than a third over the previous year (Chapman 1990).

The suspicion was that BT was cutting the quality of its service in order to maximize its profits, although Oftel found that the deterioration of service around 1987 had more to do with a strike and 'teething problems' following the introduction of new technology (Carsberg 1989). Since then, perhaps because competition from Mercury has intensified, BT has made stringent efforts to improve on all the quality-of-service indicators (see Ferner 1991). The poor publicity has been countered and connections and repairs have speeded up. The director general of Oftel, writing in 1989, professed himself reasonably well pleased:

> The range of services now available and the range of apparatus are much wider and much better than in the days before privatisation and

liberalisation. Some improvements would no doubt have come about anyway, as a result of improved technology, but I do not believe they would have matched the scale of what has actually happened.

(Carsberg 1989, p. 94)

The early BT experience has nevertheless left its mark on a sceptical public, and by the time water came to be privatized there was widespread concern that the private sector could not be trusted to maintain quality standards in so vital a service. In the run-up to privatization, consumer bodies like the National Consumer Council began to warn that provisions for consumer protection were inadequate (Gordon 1989), and leading Labour Party politicians such as John Smith claimed that pursuit of profit by privatized water companies would prove incompatible with concern for quality standards (*The Independent*, 4 February 1989). In May 1989, the magazine *Which?* reported that nearly 60% of people disagreed with the government's claim that privatization would lead to improvements in water quality. In our survey of members of the public in the southern and north-western regions in autumn 1989, we also found that less than a quarter believed that privatization would improve water quality while half believed it would not (see Table 3.1).

Table 3.1   Views on the relationship between privatization and water quality

'Water privatization will improve/has improved water quality'	Before privatization		After privatization	
	No.	%	No.	%
Agree strongly	22	3	1	0
Tend to agree	172	21	31	4
Neither agree nor disagree	170	21	292	35
Tend to disagree	302	37	268	32
Strongly disagree	109	13	186	22
Don't know	50	6	50	6

$N = 828$ (missing = 3 in 1989; 0 in 1991)
Source   Survey (reweighted data). See Appendix for details of the survey design.

Since privatization of the industry in 1989, quality standards have been policed by a number of different government agencies. Three new agencies established in 1989 are the key ones. First, the Drinking Water Inspectorate (DWI) monitors the water coming through the tap to ensure that it meets public health standards. Second, the Office of Water Services (Ofwat), whose main job is to regulate prices in the industry, also keeps a check on the quality of the service being offered by the water companies and seeks to ensure that they carry out all the requirements of their licences. Third, the National Rivers Authority (NRA) is responsible for managing and controlling the water environment. In addition, the water services PLCs are also subject to regulation by Her Majesty's Inspectorate of Pollution (HMIP), the Office of

Fair Trading and the Monopolies and Mergers Commission, government departments such as the Department of the Environment (DoE) and the Ministry of Agriculture, Fisheries and Food (MAFF), and the EC. As Michael Carney (1992, p. 43) observes: 'The most obvious point about . . . the regulators is that there are an awful lot of them'.

Many in the industry believe that this regulatory system is too complex and too cumbersome. The managing director of Thames Water warned before privatization that 'the emergence of a proliferation of regulatory agencies' was threatening to create 'overlap, duplication and confusion' (Harper 1988, p. 223), and the chairman of the Water Authorities' Association similarly warned that 'over-regulation' was threatening the benefits of privatization (Jones 1987). Such fears have been repeated since 1989. The chairman of Southern Water complained in the 1991 *Annual Report*, for example: 'The extent of the regulatory regime now far exceeds anything that existed in pre-privatisation days and its growing costs and demands on our resources are causing concern'. At the time of writing, there are government plans to establish a new environmental agency combining HMIP, DWI and at least part of the NRA, a move which is aimed to reduce some of the overlap and confusion which currently exists between all these different bodies.

One consequence of all this regulation and monitoring is that there is generally good information on various quality standards since privatization. Indeed, in the water industry, as in a number of other privatizations, it seems that the switch out of the public sector has increased the amount of information available and the amount of publicity about it. This is true for both the quality of the water provided and the adequacy of the service.

Drinking water quality

Table 3.1 showed that few members of the public believed in 1989 that privatization would improve the quality of drinking water. Many, however, believed that improvements were required. In the May 1989 *Which?* survey, for example, more than 20% of people said that they were not satisfied with water quality, most of them complaining about discoloration or taste. In a Harris survey for *The Observer* (2 July 1989) nearly one-third of respondents were dissatisfied with drinking water quality. And our survey in September 1989 generated very similar findings to the *Which?* report, 21% of respondents being either 'dissatisfied' or 'very dissatisfied' with the drinking water delivered to their taps (Table 3.2).

These levels of dissatisfaction have increased slightly since 1989, and virtually nobody believes that privatization has done anything to improve matters. Sales of mineral water and water purifiers indicate a rising level of public dissatisfaction with drinking water quality over the last ten years. In 1990, 355 million litres of mineral water were drunk in Britain, an increase from just 110 million litres ten years earlier, and a much faster rate of increase than elsewhere in the world. A survey conducted in 1991 by Ofwat found that

Table 3.2 Satisfaction with drinking water quality before and after privatization

	Before privatization		*After privatization*	
	No.	*%*	*No.*	*%*
Very satisfied	239	29	216	26
Fairly satisfied	384	46	368	44
Neither	32	4	40	5
Fairly dissatisfied	89	11	105	13
Very dissatisfied	81	10	93	11
Don't know	3	0	6	1

$N = 828$ (missing = 0)
Source Survey (reweighted data)

39% of the population was buying bottled water, or was using a water filter, or was boiling tap water before drinking it (Ofwat 1992, p. 26).

The objective indicators, however, suggest that the quality of tap water is better than many consumers judge it to be. According to the DWI's first report, drinking water quality in England and Wales was 'generally of a high standard and much was of an exceptionally high standard' (*The Times*, 15 August 1991). In over 3 million tests carried out during 1990, the DWI found that all of the quality criteria established at the time of privatization were met in 99% of water samples. Water quality is good, but many consumers do not believe it.

There are various reasons for this. One is the well-publicized failure of the British water industry to achieve the high drinking water standards laid down in the EC directive of 1980 which sought to reduce the level of nitrates and other contaminants in the water supply. In January 1992, the European Court found the British government guilty of failing to comply with this directive, although Britain is not alone in this transgression, for none of the twelve EC states currently achieves the extremely low levels of contamination which the EC lays down. Britain was prosecuted, not so much because it is any worse than the others, but because British pressure groups like Friends of the Earth have been particularly active in campaigning in Brussels.

The problem of contamination arises mainly because fertilizers and pesticides used by farmers end up in the water system. It is an issue which has received enormous publicity, but there are many in the industry in Britain who argue that the £2 billion now being spent by the water companies to reduce contamination, and the billions more likely to be spent in the future, represent a misuse of resources. EC standards on pesticides, for example, have been set at or even below the lowest concentrations which can be detected (0.1 micrograms per litre, or one part in 10 billion, equivalent to just 2 litres of any pesticides in the entire daily water supply of England and Wales). Effectively this is a zero target, and it is some twenty times more stringent than the levels deemed safe to drink in the USA or, for that matter, in Britain before the directive came into force (*The Independent*, 22 July 1991). Even Friends of the Earth accepts that British drinking water is perfectly safe and that there is no need for anyone to buy mineral water or water purifiers (*The Times*, 15 August 1991).

Whether or not some of the EC standards are unrealistic or unnecessary, many domestic consumers are clearly worried by constant reminders that their water supplies fail to comply with them. In addition, public expectations have also risen over the years. While many of us may still accept that our tap water is safe to drink, we object to the taste of chlorine, or we find the water somewhat discoloured, and something which was accepted without comment at one point in time thus becomes a cause for complaint at another. There is no evidence that water quality is any worse than it has ever been, and there are certainly no grounds for believing that privatization is reducing water quality, but consumer expectations are rising, and privatization has contributed to this by drawing people's attention to an industry which they previously took very much for granted. Over the next few years, the quality of drinking water in Britain will rise, but it may not rise fast enough to match the growing expectations of those who consume it.

Quality of service

While the quality of drinking water is the main concern of most consumers, the performance of the privatized water companies can also be evaluated on a range of other criteria which are now closely monitored by Ofwat. These include, for example, imposition of hosepipe bans, incidence of interrupted supplies, reductions in mains water pressure, and incidence of flooding due to inadequate sewer provision (see CRI 1992).

Statistics are collected on each of these indicators for each water PLC, and this enables Ofwat to draw comparisons between the different companies and to judge whether standards of service are rising or falling over time. The figures show that there are problems, notably in London and the South-East where a series of unusually dry summers has reduced river flows and depleted water tables to a point where hosepipe bans have become common and some households have been forced to rely for supplies on standpipes.

These, however, are problems of long standing and can hardly be blamed upon privatization. On the key question of whether things have been getting better or worse since 1989, Ofwat reports 'a mixed picture with some improvements but in some cases a deterioration of service' (Ofwat 1992, p. 11). It is, of course, early days, and all that can really be said with any confidence at this stage is that quality of service is now being rigorously monitored for the first time. With more and better quality-of-service indicators being added (for example, Ofwat intends to measure levels of water leakage from 1993 onwards and to penalize those companies with the worst records), it is clearly going to be difficult for the companies to increase profits by allowing the service to deteriorate, even if they wished to do so.

Much the same conclusion can probably be drawn for the other privatized utilities as well. In 1992 Parliament passed the Competition and Service (Utilities) Act. This gave all the regulators of privatized companies the same powers to obtain information on service quality and imposed on them the responsibility to ensure that companies did not sacrifice service quality in an attempt to expand profits. It also introduced automatic payment of penalties to customers in the event on non-performance (an idea which has been in operation in the water industry since 1990–1). Judging from experience in the water industry, compensation schemes may not be very effective, for the amounts that can be claimed are tiny, and Ofwat (1992, p. 30) believes that perhaps only 1–2% of those water customers who could have claimed compensation in the first year in which the scheme operated actually did so. Indeed, only 15% of water customers even knew such a scheme existed.

While there are undoubtedly problems in measuring service quality, in collating all the data which are needed in order to judge it, and in devising effective compensation where quality is found to be substandard, it is nevertheless fair to conclude that privatization has created for the first time a framework of regulation from which consumers should begin to benefit. A government survey of public and private sector consumers conducted in 1993 found that the privatized utilities were thought to have improved their service by nearly 90% of users (*Independent on Sunday*, 22 August 1993).

The system of price regulation

Price regulation of monopoly industries can in principle be achieved in one of two ways. The first, commonly used in North America where there is a long experience of privately owned utilities, is to peg prices with reference to rates of return on investment (for details, see Veljanovski 1987). Under this system, companies are allowed to levy charges which are sufficient to earn them an agreed rate of return on their capital employed. The problem with this system is that it provides little incentive for a company to raise efficiency and it can induce companies to overinvest in order to increase the amount of capital employed and thus increase the returns they are permitted to make.

The second possibility, which has been used in Britain since BT was privatized in 1984, is to impose price caps. The principle of price capping is very simple, although the details of how it is operated can become very complex. A regulator is appointed which from time to time adjusts the total amount by which the company is allowed to raise its charges. The cap itself is fixed relative to the overall rate of inflation in the economy and is expressed by the formula, 'RPI $-$ x' where 'RPI' is the retail price index (that is, the inflation rate) and x is a figure determined by the regulator as a reasonable target for efficiency gains. If the company achieves better efficiency gains than this target, then it is allowed to retain the resulting profit, but if it fails to achieve these efficiency gains then it has to make do with lower profits and may even have to take a loss. If, over a long period, the company achieves efficiency gains better than the value of x, then the price cap formula may be tightened, but frequent adjustments obviously should not occur since this would prevent the company enjoying the fruits of its own endeavours and would therefore erode the incentive to achieve greater efficiency in the future.

When BT was privatized, the government set x at 3%. In other words, BT was expected to keep its aggregate annual price rises at 3% below the prevailing rate of inflation. This figure was set for a ten-year period with the provision that either BT or its regulator, Oftel, could call for a revision in the light of experience after five years. The company also had the right to ask for a reference to the Monopolies and Mergers Commission (MMC) if at any time it was unhappy with the way it was being regulated by Oftel.

As things turned out, BT was able to meet this initial price cap fairly comfortably, for new technology enabled it to reduce costs by shedding labour. Higher than expected profits then led Oftel to tighten the formula at the first opportunity in 1988 by raising x from 3% to 4.5%. In 1991, three years before the next review was due, Oftel asked for the formula to be changed again and it raised the value of x from 4.5% to 6.25%. Then, just one year after that, Oftel intervened yet again. This time it not only changed the value of x (raising it to a remarkably stringent 7.5%), but also enforced a cut in installation charges and laid down certain stipulations regarding the company's capital programme, setting targets for the installation of fibre-optic cable and the extension of the digital telephone service. The company issued a statement complaining at what it termed this new form of 'interventionist regulation' (*The Guardian*, 10 June 1992), but in the end it complied with Oftel's ruling rather than appeal to the MMC and risk an even more adverse judgment.

By 1992, it was clear that Oftel had effectively moved away from the original spirit and intention of the 'RPI − x' system of regulation. Whereas it was originally intended that x should be set for ten years, with the possibility of review after five, and that BT should be able to retain the fruits of any efficiency gains achieved over and above this figure, Oftel in fact revised x upwards three times in four years in response to evidence that the company was making high profits. The 1991 review was prompted by the political controversy provoked by the company's £3 billion profits that year, and it suggests that the regulator was in effect capping profits rather than prices. Undoubtedly BT's customers have benefited from this successive tightening of the price regime, at least in the short term, but it does now seem that what is notionally a price cap system of regulation has evolved into something suspiciously like the American rate-of-return system.

Much the same pattern has been repeated in the other utilities privatized since BT. When British Gas was sold in 1986, a new regulator, Ofgas, was established on the same lines as Oftel, and much the same system of price regulation was established for domestic customers, although in this case provision was also made for the company to pass on in its prices any changes in its own costs of buying gas from the North Sea fields. The value of x for British Gas was originally set at 2%, but, as in the case of telecommunications, the regulator took the first opportunity for review (in 1991) to raise this to 5% following a 46% profits rise in 1990.

In both of these industries, the regulators have proved vigilant, perhaps even aggressive, in enforcing price cuts and efficiency gains – when they were in the public sector, neither British Telecom nor British Gas ever came anywhere near to holding price rises year on year to 7.5% and 5%, respectively, below the rate of inflation. But in both, the result has been growing tensions between the company and its regulator (see Veljanovski 1993).

Part of the problem is that the regulators have increasingly tried to influence detailed aspects of company policy-making which the companies believe is none of their business – Oftel's demands regarding the speed at which BT was laying fibre-optic cable, and a recent claim by Ofgas that British Gas was 'brainwashing' its customers into buying expensive service contracts, both generated heated complaints and resistance from the companies concerned. Underpinning this issue, however, is the fundamental problem of regulators attempting to limit profits between the periodic reviews. In the case of British Gas, mounting tensions eventually led to a complete breakdown in its relations with the regulator in August 1992 over the question of how much the company should be allowed to charge other suppliers for using its pipeline, and the company took the unprecedented and highly risky step of appealing to the Monopolies and Mergers Commission to rule on the rate of return which it should be allowed to make on its assets. The MMC report in August 1993 resisted calls to break up the company in order to encourage competition, but it did recommend that the company's monopoly over the supply of gas to domestic consumers should be ended.

In the water industry, too, the system of price regulation has come under increasing strain. Ofwat (and, indeed, Offer, the electricity industry regulator) differs from Oftel and Ofgas in that it regulates more than one company. With 134 staff, Ofwat oversees the ten privatized WSPLCs as well as the remaining twenty-three former statutory water supply companies (WSCs). The regulator is responsible only for the 'core business' – water supply, sewage disposal and recreation and amenity uses of rivers and reservoirs. Where companies diversify into other forms of activity such as engineering, construction, computing or consultancy work, their activities and profits are not subject to regulation since in these areas the companies are exposed to effective competition. When they do diversify, as most have, the WSPLCs are prevented from using revenue from their core business to finance such activities, and they are under an obligation to ensure that the core business does not suffer as a result of diversification.

The existence of more than one company in these industries means that the electricity and water regulators are in principle in a position to compare performance, costs and prices across different companies in the same industry and therefore to establish realistic regulatory targets with reference to the results achieved by the most efficient company. This comparative performance evaluation or 'yardstick competition' is particularly significant in the water industry, where it is being used to determine new price cap levels for each company when the first price review takes place five years after privatization in 1994. The idea is that companies which have been performing well will be set a price at which they can record higher than average profits while those which have been performing badly will be penalized (Yarrow 1989).

Given the very different problems faced by the different companies, it will, of course, be extremely difficult for Ofwat to gauge which companies are performing well and which badly (Wright 1992), and some analysts doubt that such comparisons are even practicable (Hill 1989). How, for example, can the regulator judge the comparative performance of Southern Water, with its problems of sea and beach pollution and its reliance on underground water sources, with that of North West, with its decaying urban sewerage system and its reliance for water supply on rivers and reservoirs?

Such issues are currently under consideration prior to the 1994 review. What is already clear, however, is that the principle of yardstick competition is acting as a spur to improvement and innovation in all companies. As the deputy chairman at Thames has explained:

> It is a reality if somebody says that North West is doing something better than we are or Severn Trent. That gets the board up on their feet and moving around. That is the reality of competition. That sort of thing has got a real impact on the business.
>
> (Harper 1992, p. 104)

While they enjoy monopolies in their own areas, the WSPLCs can therefore in a very real sense be said to be competing with each other through the mediation of Ofwat's price regulation regime.

A further distinctive feature of price regulation in the water industry, as compared with other privatized industries, is that prices have been rising rather than falling in real terms. The price cap formula for the WSPLCs is 'RPI + k' where k represents a company's projected future capital expenditure requirements less an x factor for increased efficiency. In 1989, following protracted bargaining and negotiation between ministers and the relevant chairmen, the ten privatized companies were given different k factors reflecting the different amounts of money they needed to spend over the following ten years on improvements to treatment plants, sea outfalls and other infrastructure in order to meet EC standards governing drinking water, bathing water, and so on. In every case, the anticipated future investment requirements outstripped any efficiency gains which could be expected during the same period with the result that the initial value of k was positive for all ten WSPLCs, varying from a low of 3.0% for Yorkshire Water to a high of 7.0% for Northumbrian (see Price Waterhouse 1990). In every case except Southern (whose k falls to zero after 1995), substantial price rises were therefore anticipated when the industry was privatized, with average prices set nearly to double in real terms over the ensuing ten years (Carney 1992).

Provision was also made at the time of privatization for a so-called 'cost pass-through' or 'interim adjustment' mechanism which would allow price caps to be varied if company investment costs suddenly changed as a result of, say, increased prices in the construction industry or new regulations from Brussels imposing higher quality standards. In the event, only one company (South West Water) has so far made an application under this provision, and in this case Ofwat agreed to raise k from 6.5% to 11.5% for three years to enable the company to meet new EC bathing water quality regulations.

As in the telecommunications and gas industries, Ofwat has not invoked an interim review, but it has twice in the first five-year period pressed the companies into lower price increases. In 1991 the director general requested 'voluntary' price cuts on the grounds that construction costs had fallen and profits were higher than expected, and he backed this with a threat to conduct an interim review (*The Independent*, 2 October 1991). All bar two of the thirty-three companies responded by agreeing, reluctantly, to keep their price rises at about 1% lower than was permitted by their k factors. Exactly one year later, the director general demanded that the earlier cut should stay in place and that a further 1% reduction should be made. These modifications of the price regulation formula have made the water companies increasingly concerned that the regulator is rewriting the rules. By insisting on reducing prices after just one or two years of good results, rather than waiting for the full five years before a formal review was due, Ofwat seems to be moving to a system of annual reviews described by the chief executive of Thames Water as 'short-termism worse than ever' (*The Independent*, 2 October 1992).

Underlying these moves to reduce the price cap is a fundamental issue regarding profit levels. Because the water industry required a huge investment programme in order to meet its water quality and pollution targets, it was explicitly recognized at the time of privatization that Ofwat should fix price caps at a level which would allow the companies to make profits big enough to pay dividends which would attract the amount of new investment they would need. Alone among the regulators, Ofwat was therefore given the duty to ensure that the companies could make a reasonable rate of return on their capital. This, however, left open the crucial question of how big profits needed to be in order to attract sufficient investment funds (their so-called 'cost of capital').

In the ten years to 1989, average real dividend levels of companies quoted on the Stock Exchange grew at a rate of 5.7% per annum, so when water was privatized, the government tried to set k levels at a point which would allow the new PLCs to sustain a real dividend growth of around 5% which would allow them to compete for funds (White 1992). After 1989, however, dividend growth on the Stock Market slowed down to just 1% real in 1990 and −2% real in 1991. In this context, the dividends declared by the WSPLCs in their first year or two of operation began to look very attractive, for in 1991 none of the companies declared dividends below 14% (or 4% in real terms). Predictably, Ofwat saw this as excessive.

In July 1991, Ofwat suggested that dividends were higher than was necessary, particularly since water was a low-risk investment, and it proposed that the 'cost of capital' was probably no greater than 5–6% after tax. The companies responded with a figure 4% higher than the Ofwat estimate and argued that, if their profits were reduced in line with the Ofwat recommendations, they would be unable to attract sufficient funds to pay for the investments which the EC and others were demanding. This argument over the 'cost of capital' still continues, and it will be crucial in the determination of new values of k in the 1994 review. In one sense it is a highly technical argument which need not concern us, but in another it provides a highly significant illustration of one of the fundamental problems in the whole system of price capping.

The basic problem, as in the other utilities, is that the regulator is unwilling or unable to resist pressures to change the price cap formula in the five-year period between reviews. This has created a climate of uncertainty among potential investors who have come to see these industries as risky. Ofwat argues that water and sewage businesses are a safe investment and need not, therefore, make high profits in order to satisfy their shareholders. The companies, however, argue that, far from being seen as 'safe', investment in water shares is increasingly being seen as risky precisely because the regulator has been intervening so frequently to peg back profits. As one stockbroker has argued:

> Regulators are very very risky . . . we saw British Telecom and British Gas floated and then, sure enough, along came the regulator and the MMC and changed the goal posts . . . the risk of interference from the regulator drives these share prices.
>
> (White 1992, pp. 57–9)

Ofwat, therefore, is caught in a painful dilemma. If it resists the temptation to interfere with prices in the periods between reviews, the companies can make high profits without any requirement to reduce their charges to customers. If, on the other hand, Ofwat orders them to cut their prices whenever profits appear to be becoming excessive, this undermines investor confidence in the future stability of the price regime and makes higher profits and dividends necessary in order to compensate for the increased risk. Ofwat justifies its attempts to limit dividends on the grounds that water is a low-risk investment, but every time it does this it makes investment riskier!

All this, then, raises the question of why the various regulators have failed to operate the price-capping system in the way that was originally intended. Effectively they have moved away from price-capping towards the American system of fixing prices according to the rates of return which the companies are making (Wright 1992), but it was never intended that the regulatory regimes should work in this way. In theory, the companies were to be permitted to make whatever profits they could while staying within their price ceilings, but in practice – in telecommunications and gas as well as in water – high profits have provoked swift revisions to their pricing formulae.

The explanation for this is political rather than economic. Put simply, it has proved politically impossible for the regulators to permit these companies to make high profits and to pay high dividends, irrespective of whether or not this is the result of efficiency gains. Particularly in the water industry, where real prices are rising rather than falling, where there is no effective competition from alternative suppliers, and where privatization was and remains very unpopular with most of the electorate, big profits swiftly provoke a hostile reaction in the media and among opposition politicians and the pressure builds on Ofwat to 'show its teeth'.

There is little understanding in the general public about how the price-capping system in any of these industries works, and there is widespread ignorance about the specific arrangements for controlling prices in the water industry. Few members of the public seem to understand the complexities of the 'RPI + k' formula, few are aware of the investment programmes which the companies have embarked upon, and many apparently therefore believe that increased prices are a direct result of the privatization of water and the subsequent exploitation by the companies of their monopoly position. According to an Ofwat (1992) survey, over a quarter of the population attributes increased water bills to privatization, and the Southern Customer Service Committee (1991) found that 'customers are largely unaware' of the massive investment programme which is the cause of their increasing bills. What the public sees is big profits and substantial salary increases for top executives in the industry (see Chapter 4), and this translates into an irresistable pressure on Ofwat to keep prices and profits down. Privatization, it seems, cannot insulate these industries from political pressure.

Price levels since privatization

Despite Ofwat's success in keeping price rises in 1992 below the level of k, average (non-metered) water bills still rose from £119 to £169 between 1989 and 1992. In our two case-study regions, average annual water bills had risen by 1992 to £174 in Southern and £156 in North West. In international terms, these are not high figures – consumers in Germany, Belgium, France and the Netherlands all pay higher water charges than in Britain (*The Independent*, 23 September 1992) – and relative to the cost of other commodities, it may still be argued that water supply and sewage treatment represent good value at around £3 per week. The fact remains, however, that the rate of increase in water prices is much faster than that of most other commodities, for, as Figure 3.1 shows, price rises have been steep and have far outstripped the general rate of inflation. On average, water bills increased 20% in real terms in the first three years after privatization (see CRI 1992).

These increases are, as we have seen, due mainly to the massive new investment programmes forced upon the companies by EC directives and by the dilapidated state of much of the sewerage system, and there are some signs from our survey that customers are beginning to understand this and are perhaps becoming rather less inclined to blame price rises on privatization *per se*. The figures in Table 3.3 indicate that while a substantial majority (91%) believed in 1989 that privatization would increase prices, only 68% believed in 1991 that it actually had done so. The uncertainty and confusion surrounding this issue, however, is reflected in the rise from just 4% to 18% in those who did

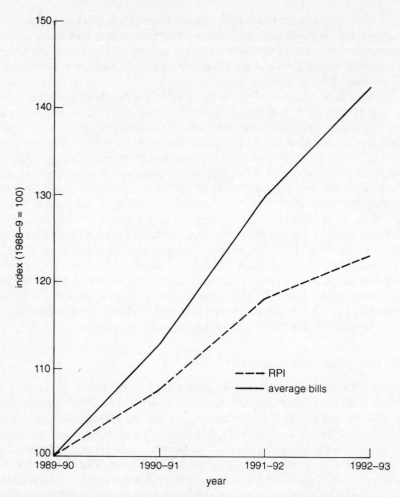

Figure 3.1 The rate of increase of unmetered domestic water and sewerage charges compared with the Retail Price Index, 1989–93

Source   CRI (1992)

not know how best to respond to the question. People know full well that prices have risen, but they are now less certain than they were that privatization is the culprit.

Customers also apparently remain reasonably satisfied that they are getting value for money. In 1989, two-thirds of our sample described the charge they were paying for water as 'very' or 'fairly' reasonable, with around a quarter thinking it was unreasonable. Eighteen months later there had certainly been a shift in attitudes following the price rises, but half of the sample still felt that charges were reasonable, while 38% thought they were not.

Table 3.3 Views of the relationship between water privatization and increased charges

'Water privatization will increase/ has increased water charges'	Before privatization		After privatization	
	No.	%	*No.*	%
Agree strongly	508	61	288	35
Tend to agree	243	29	273	33
Neither	28	3	73	9
Tend to disagree	33	4	99	12
Strongly disagree	6	1	18	2
Don't know	9	1	76	9

$N = 828$ (missing $=1$)
Source Survey (unweighted data)

Drawing together all the evidence, it seems that, even where privatized companies have enjoyed effective monopoly or near-monopoly markets, consumers have objectively gained as regards the prices they have to pay. The fear has often been expressed that prices will rise when an enterprise is privatized since it will need to pay dividends to shareholders. Yet the experience in Britain over the last ten years or so suggests that any additional costs incurred by having to pay dividends are more than cancelled out by the gains from efficiency savings. In the case of BT and British Gas, price rises are now pegged in both cases substantially below inflation. In the water industry, the picture is more complicated, given the rising real charges and the concern of Ofwat that the companies are enjoying too high a rate of return on their capital, but it is important to remember that here, too, an x efficiency factor is being imposed.

Price regulation by Ofwat has succeeded in creating a quasi-competitive environment in the industry, and the use of yardstick competition to fix the values of k after 1994 will reinforce this. If anything, Ofwat, like the other regulators, is erring more on the side of the consumer than on the side of the companies it is regulating, and there is no evidence to support the views expressed by critics of water privatization that the regulator would prove too weak or would be 'captured' by the companies. On price as on quality, it is hard to avoid the conclusion that consumers do seem objectively to have benefited from privatization.

Accountability to customers

Formally, private sector companies are accountable and responsible not to their customers but to their shareholders. However, it is often argued by defenders of privatization that such companies will seek to please their customers in as many ways as possible in order to win more business, and that in practical terms this is likely to enhance rather than undermine their accountability to their public. Such an argument is less plausible in the case of monopoly companies, however, for they have no need to defend or extend their market share. Like public sector monopolies, private sector monopolies enjoy a captive market and therefore presumably have little incentive to pay attention to what their customers want.

There are four measures which may be taken to judge this aspect of the companies' performance: the knowledge which customers have about the company; the viability of watchdog bodies operating on behalf of consumers; the volume of complaints received from customers; and the way the companies handle customers with problems.

Company visibility

In most industries, privatization seems to have had the paradoxical effect of removing enterprises from the public domain of politics while at the same time publicizing and politicizing their affairs to a greater extent. This process was particularly marked in the case of water, an industry which attracted very little public attention before privatization yet which has had a high profile ever since (Chapman 1990).

Increased visibility should be of benefit to consumers, for the glare of publicity not only enhances their knowledge and understanding about a service for which they are paying, but also acts as a safeguard against bad practice by the companies themselves. However, there are grounds for believing that the post-privatization water industry is not well understood by many people despite the publicity and despite the attempts by the companies themselves to project a corporate identity through expensive advertising campaigns. As one senior manager in the industry has candidly admitted: 'If you do market research, and ask them who provides their water service and who provides the drainage, quite a high proportion of the population are not totally clear about it' (Harper 1992, p. 100).

Part of the problem is that very few people have any direct contact with those who provide them with water and take away their sewage. In our survey, only around 1% had contacted their water company to pay a bill (for most pay by post or standing order), less than 1% had made contact in order to query a bill, between 1.4% (before privatization) and 1.5% (after) had made a complaint, and only around 2% had requested a repair or other service. For most people, before and after privatization, the water and sewerage undertaking is a remote institution with which they will never have personal contact.

A further factor promoting the anonymity and obscurity of the water industry is that there is no direct link between the amount of its product which people consume and the amount they pay. This will continue to be the case unless and until meters are installed. It is difficult to think of any other industry which is so detached from its customers that it never normally sees them and that it sends out bills to them irrespective of how much of its product they have consumed.

The companies have tried to raise their visibility to their customers, partly by advertising and partly by innovations such as public open days and the publication of 'customer charters'. In its customer charter, for example, Southern Water (1992) tells its customers: 'We listen to customers all the time. It is one of the parts of our job we enjoy most . . . We are always interested in your views.' Despite this, however, many people seem to have only the haziest idea about the company which provides them with this most basic of services.

Consumer watchdogs

We saw in Chapter 2 that the principal channel of mediation between consumers and producers before privatization was the Consumer Consultative Committees. However, the CCCs were generally extremely weak and ineffective and were seen as such by both the RWA managements and the organizations invited to participate in them (see Chapter 5). Since privatization, responsibility for the defence of consumer interests has fallen to Ofwat and its ten new regional Customer Services Committees (CSCs). These are committees of twelve people each, all of whom are appointed by Ofwat from among consumer organizations, welfare groups, women's organizations, trade and professional associations and groups representing the disabled. These committees hold various consultation exercises and are responsible in the first instance for handling customer complaints. Ofwat (1992, p. 15) believes they 'play a vital role in customer protection', and since 1993 this role has been strengthened through the establishment of a National Customer Council consisting of the director general and the various CSC chairpersons.

Unfortunately, however, few customers seem to know about the CSCs. A survey commissioned by Ofwat in 1991 found that few people even knew of their existence and activities, let alone the role of the CSCs. While 37% of the population was apparently aware that an organization had been established to regulate prices and look after the interests of customers, only 6% of them (or just 2% of the population as a whole) could actually name it (Ofwat 1992, p. 68). This low level of public awareness seems no better than the situation before privatization – Customer Services Committees have replaced Consumer Consultative Committees, but there are few people outside the industry who know about either!

This is confirmed by our survey, in which we asked consumers to whom they would complain if a grievance was not resolved by their water supplier. In 1989, before the industry was privatized, just 3% of consumers thought of approaching the CCCs which had by then been in existence for six years. Most people put their faith in the political process – 28% said they would contact their MP and 5% mentioned their local councillor – or in government bureaucracies such as the Environmental Health Officer (10%) or, fifteen years after water was removed from local government, the town hall (15%). Twenty-two per cent admitted that they did not have a clue.

Eighteen months later, notwithstanding Ofwat's efforts to publicize complaints procedures through a leaflet sent to every household, just 4% of customers mentioned the CSCs, with another 1% each mentioning Ofwat or its director general. People do seem to have become aware that water has been removed from the public arena, for resort to explicitly political channels such as MPs and councillors had decreased significantly (to 20% and 3%, respectively), but so, too, had the proportion of respondents having any idea at all where they might complain (the percentage who could not answer the question rose from 22% to 27%). Ofwat and its CSCs may or may not be doing an effective job in safeguarding the interests of consumers, but it is clear that many consumers themselves are blissfully unaware of what is being done on their behalf and are by and large as ignorant of complaints procedures as they were before privatization.

Number of complaints

An important measure of how well companies are meeting the expectations of their customers is the number of complaints received against them. Because an independent complaints procedure with computerized records was only established after privatization, it is difficult to gauge how far complaint rates have changed as compared with when the industry was in the public sector, but it is obvious from the rate of increase in complaints since 1989 that many more people are formally expressing grievances today than ever did before water was privatized.

This may partly be explained by the very existence of a new complaints procedure. Ofwat (1992) itself believes that a rising tide of complaints should be taken not as an indicator of increasing problems and dissatisfaction, but rather as the product of a growing public awareness of Ofwat and its role. Give people a means to complain, and that is exactly what they will do.

There is undoubtedly some truth in this argument, although three factors suggest that it cannot be the full explanation. First, as we saw earlier, customers are actually less satisfied than they were with the quality of service they are receiving. To take but one example, with nearly a quarter of the population now unhappy about the quality of its drinking water, the scope for increased complaints is enormous. Second, we have also seen that most members of the public are still completely ignorant about Ofwat's existence, and it is therefore difficult to explain away the rising tide of complaints simply as the product of the increased visibility of the complaints procedure. And third, customers do not themselves believe that it is any easier for them to make their views heard than it ever was. As Table 3.4 demonstrates, the public has become increasingly disenchanted with the accountability of the industry, with far fewer customers believing that things have improved than anticipated improvement before privatization.

One factor which undoubtedly does help explain the growing number of complaints is the increased publicity and controversy surrounding the water industry. All the press and media attention which has been paid to water quality and environmental issues, together with the sharp rise in charges, has almost certainly prompted many more people to express their anger and

Table 3.4 Public perceptions of accountability in the water industry

'Privatization will increase/has increased accountability to customers'	Before privatization		After privatization	
	No.	*%*	*No.*	*%*
Strongly agree	74	9	44	5
Tend to agree	234	28	188	23
Neither	96	12	154	19
Tend to disagree	301	36	223	27
Strongly disagree	90	11	98	12
Don't know	33	4	121	15

$N = 828$
Source Survey (unweighted data)

frustration. Things may not have grown any worse since 1989, but privatization has made people much more alert to them. In this sense, it can be argued that privatization has enabled the expression of grievances, not so much because it has led to the establishment of formal complaints procedures, but because the very act of privatizing the industry itself focused public attention on it and therefore prompted people to complain when things went wrong.

As companies like BT and British Gas have also found, there is a deep level of distrust of private sector monopoly among the British public, and it is this which helps create an atmosphere in which consumers take more care to ensure that they are not being exploited or shabbily treated. As we shall see in Chapter 7, people seem to trust the government to deliver basic services in a way that they do not trust capitalist enterprises. Paradoxically, perhaps, this means that industries in the public sector can probably get away with things that they cannot get away with when they are privatized, for people expect the service to deteriorate and are therefore on the look-out for any sign that this may be happening.

Ofwat (1992) records that, in their first year of operation (1990–1), the ten Customer Services Committees received 4,613 complaints – a rate of 1.7 for every 10,000 connections. Just one year later, this had increased to 10,635, or 4.0 per 10,000 connections. These are not huge figures, although it should be remembered that they refer not to the total number of complaints made, but rather to the numbers of people who complained to the CSCs. Given that the complaints procedure requires that customers first take up their grievances with their local company, and only approach their CSC if the company fails to satisfy them, the total number of initial complaints in the industry as a whole is therefore likely to be much higher than the level recorded by Ofwat.

In our survey, 1.5% of customers interviewed in 1991 claimed to have contacted their water services company to complain about some aspect of the service over the previous twelve months – a much larger proportion than that officially recorded as having contacted a CSC. It is also interesting to note, however, that this figure for the total number of initial complaints is virtually unchanged since before privatization, for in 1989 we found that 1.4% of customers had complained to their RWA during the previous year. This would seem to give some support to Ofwat's claim that the rising number of complaints brought to its attention should not be taken as an indicator of declining service quality, but is rather a reflection of more people learning how to use the official channels.

Of the complaints dealt with by CSCs in 1991–2, most concerned either charges (38%) or billing (25%). Clearly, a large proportion of the increase in complaints is explained, not by any deterioration in service, but by the rise in water charges (and, indeed, in water company profits) which many customers resent or do not understand. Some complaints, however, do relate to service quality. In 1991–2, 13% of complaints concerned water supply, 9% concerned water quality (usually taste or colour), 4% concerned water pressure and 2% were to do with sewerage, and in every category the number of complaints received had nearly doubled as compared with the previous year.

Dealing with problems

With the substantial increases in water charges since privatization, the problem of arrears and non-payment has been increasing. In June 1992, the Citizens Advice Bureau reported that more people were now seeking help with 'water debt' than were approaching it with problems of tax, telephone debt or social fund payments (*The Times*, 5 June 1992). In order to protect customers from arbitrary abuse of monopoly power, water services companies are obliged to seek a court order before proceeding to disconnect households who fail to pay their bills. In 1991, a staggering 900,000 court summonses were issued (Ofwat 1992, p. 39).

The number of households disconnected from the water supply actually fell substantially at the time of privatization – from 5,902 in the six months to September 1989 to just 2,524 in the six months to March 1990. Since then, however, the figure has been rising again, and by September 1991 it stood at 7,662, considerably higher than the pre-privatization level. The rate of disconnection varies widely between different companies and seems to reflect differences in company policies. In 1991, Ofwat published a set of agreed guidelines designed to reduce the number of disconnections, but some companies seem to be observing the letter of the Code of Practice while continuing to offer their customers little help or advice in paying off debts (see Southern CSC 1991, p. 5), and in June 1992 the director general publicly condemned the dramatic rise in the number of customers cut off (*The Guardian*, 10 June 1992).

The companies, of course, have a right to payment for the services they provide, and there is a view held by some that much of the arrears is the product of a refusal to pay rather than an inability to do so. Nevertheless, the issue of nearly 1 million court summonses is a massive indictment of the companies' failure to make contact with their customers, explain why prices have risen, and investigate genuine cases of hardship, and the steady increase in the rate of disconnections is a disturbing sign that some companies at least are less concerned with their customers' welfare than they claim to be in their propaganda.

Conclusion

In the privatized industries like gas, electricity and water, the fate of the consumer depends very largely on the effectiveness of the regulator. In this chapter we have seen that, by and large, the regulators appear to be doing a good job on behalf of the millions of consumers who effectively have little or no choice between competing suppliers.

This is particularly true as regards price levels. The system of regulation in the privatized industries is in two crucial respects different from that which operated when they were in the public sector. First, the regulators are always looking to keep prices down and to force greater efficiency savings. Whereas ministers might push prices down one year only to push them up the next, the pressure from regulators is always in the same direction. It is for this reason that prices have fallen so sharply in British Gas and BT. There can be few other companies whose real prices fall each year by as much as 5%, still less 7.5%, and such achievements were never matched when these industries were under direct state control. As regards water, where real prices are rising, efficiency gains are still being imposed by the regulator and the increased charges are being used to finance a massive new investment programme whose costs would in any case have fallen on water users, taxpayers, or both.

The second difference is that the regulators are nominally independent of government and can therefore look after the interests of customers without having to worry about the shifting concerns and priorities of ministers intent on winning the next election. This independence is a crucial safeguard for the consumer, and it is important that it should not be eroded (which is why the evidence discussed in this chapter, that regulators may be responding to political pressure by moving away from price-capping towards regulation of short-term profit margins, is disturbing).

On prices, therefore, our conclusion is that the consumer has gained from privatization. On quality and accountability, however, we must remain more circumspect. The obvious temptation of price-capped companies will always be to short-cut quality standards in order to raise profit margins. The government has belatedly attempted to plug this gap with the 1992 Competition and Service (Utilities) Act, and regulators like Ofwat have made important progress in identifying measurable criteria of quality against which different suppliers can be evaluated both against each other and against their own past performance. All that can be said at this stage is that quality seems not to have fallen and that it is now being monitored more carefully than before.

On accountability, the case of the water industry at least suggests that customers have gained little if anything from privatization, and that some may have lost. The companies are still experienced by most customers as remote agencies about which they know little or nothing. Despite considerable publicity by the companies and by Ofwat, most people still have no idea about the regulatory regime, nor about how to pursue complaints. The number of complaints has risen, though two-thirds of them have to do with charges rather than service quality, and the companies are generally seen by their customers as unaccountable – an impression likely to be reinforced by heavy-handed actions against those in arrears.

The privatization of the utilities, and especially water, was hugely unpopular. Now they are privatized, the public still seems sceptical about their performance. It is this scepticism which may help keep prices down and quality up in the future, for these companies are aware of their poor corporate image and of the need to improve it by developing a strong customer service ethic. This at least marks a positive change from the era of nationalization.

4 The employees

We saw in Chapter 1 that the Conservative government came to the conclusion quite early in its first period of office that 'public ownership' of major industries benefited producers at the expense of consumers. The nationalized industries were seen as irremediably inefficient when compared with their private sector counterparts. Managers lacked initiative, for in the monopolized public sector there were few incentives to innovate and the government was always there to bail them out with taxpayers' money. Furthermore, a heavily unionized workforce meant that wages could be forced up, inefficient working practices could be safeguarded and consumer preferences could generally be ignored. The result was that consumers and taxpayers were increasingly obliged to put up with low quality services at ever higher costs.

Privatization was seen as the way to redress the balance between producers and consumers. Transferred into the private sector, managers would be forced to seek economies in order to attract private investment and to secure a market for their products, and employees would be forced to work harder and to abandon their restrictive practices. Consumers would benefit from all this as costs were lowered and greater choice was offered between competing suppliers. Even in the case of 'natural monopolies', such as the water industry, it was believed that regulatory regimes could be established which would function as 'surrogate market mechanisms', forcing down costs and improving levels of service.

Seen in this way, privatization represented a potential threat to managers and employees alike, and from the outset the public sector trade unions consistently opposed the government's programme precisely because it was interpreted as an attack on the interests of their members. As the Labour Research Department (1983, p. 1) claimed: 'Above all, privatisation is carried out at the expense of the workers'. The government, however, argued that while privatization should benefit consumers, it could also bring advantages for producers. For managers, privatization offered the opportunity to escape from political control. Managers would be 'freed to manage' and high rewards in terms of both salary and job satisfaction could flow from this new-found autonomy. For ordinary employees, privatization offered the chance to share in the prosperity of the companies for which they worked. For the first time, they could own shares in their company, and if managers and workers 'pulled together' to make these companies successful, then ordinary workers would benefit both from increased pay and from dividends based upon rising profits. Old attitudes based upon an outmoded 'them-and-us' confrontational mentality would then soon be jettisoned as employees came to understand the link between the success of their company and their own material rewards.

Privatization, pay and job security

In an attempt to evaluate these claims, we interviewed a sample of employees working in the North West and Southern Regional Water Authorities three months before the industry was privatized and again eighteen months afterwards (see Appendix for details). Although the size of this sample ($N = 107$) is too small to allow for much detailed analysis (and the final sample underrepresents the number of manual workers in the industry), the patterns of change in the way different categories of employees answered our questions at the first and second interviews can provide us with some interesting insights into the impact which privatization has had upon managers and lower-level employees.

The first point to make about the findings from these interviews is that privatization was and remains unpopular among most grades of employees. In 1989, only 27% of our total sample approved of the privatization of water, while 50% disapproved (the remainder expressed no opinion). Enthusiasm for privatization was strongest among managers, where around half expressed approval and about a quarter disapproved, and was lowest among manual and clerical workers, where these proportions were reversed. Employees in lower managerial and supervisory (LMS) grades were slightly less hostile than those below them, but were markedly less enthusiastic than the managerial grades.

By 1991, opposition to the privatization of the industry had eased somewhat among our sample of employees, with roughly equal numbers now supporting and opposing it (44% and 42%, respectively). However, this reduction in the total number of opponents is a reflection of a shift in opinion which occurred only among managers and those in LMS grades. By 1991, virtually all of the managers had come to approve of the change and many of those in the LMS grades had also been won over (the proportion approving having all but doubled from 30% to 58%). Among manual and clerical workers, however, there was no detectable change in attitudes, for around half of them still disapproved of the privatization of the industry, with only a quarter in favour. Indeed, while all of the managers in our sample and two-thirds of the LMS grades opposed the idea of returning to the public sector when they were interviewed in 1991, only a quarter of manual and clerical workers disapproved of such a move while around half of them supported it. Thus, not only do many employees in the lower grades still feel unhappy about the decision to privatize the industry, but many also express the view that the decision should be reversed.

These are important findings, for they point to the possibility that the workforce as a whole may be polarizing in its attitudes following the privatization of the industry. Consistently with other studies (for example, O'Connel Davidson *et al.* 1991), we find that managers and LMS grades are becoming more enthusiastic about life in the private sector, while clerical and manual workers are still frequently committed to the principle of public ownership. This apparent polarization of attitudes and opinions between higher and lower grades suggests that rather than overcoming the division between management and workforce, 'them' and 'us', privatization may actually be hardening it.

Many of those who objected to the privatization of water did so on ethical grounds. The most common reason for opposing the privatization, cited by 57% of opponents in 1989 and by 64% in 1991, was simply that essential services like water should not be owned and exploited by private enterprise. Most, however, were also concerned about its effects on their own livelihoods, and in particular the future security of their jobs.

In a previous study of water authority employees, Nelson and Cooper (1993) found that employees were worried that privatization threatened their pay, hours of work, job descriptions, job security and future career opportunities. They also found in interviews conducted six months after privatization that levels of satisfaction on most of these items had fallen, indicating that for many employees their earlier fears were being realized.

Our survey of employees similarly considered four key dimensions of their work – their earnings; prospects for promotion; scope for showing personal initiative; and job security – but we did not find the same generalized level of concern as in the Nelson and Cooper study. Indeed, on three of the four dimensions, there was considerable optimism in 1989 across all grades of employees that privatization would either improve things or at worst make no difference (Table 4.1). Only on the question of job security did we find any widespread concern that privatization might prove a real threat.

On earnings, Table 4.1 reveals a remarkably high degree of satisfaction across all grades prior to privatization, and in all grades the number of people who believed that their earnings would improve as a result of privatization exceeded the number who believed they would deteriorate by a factor of at least 2.75. Satisfaction with promotion prospects was much lower than satisfaction with pay among all grades other than managers, but again, there was little sense that privatization would make matters any worse, for most non-managerial employees believed that things would probably stay much the same while managers tended to believe that they would improve. As for the scope for showing personal initiative and responsibility in the job, there were surprisingly high levels of satisfaction across all grades, for even among manual and clerical workers, two-thirds said they were contented, and here, too, there was little sense that privatization might create problems – although manual workers did tend to be rather pessimistic, while managers were extremely optimistic.

Table 4.1   Satisfaction and expectations regarding pay and conditions, 1989

	Current satisfaction				Future expectations					
	Satisfied		Dissatisfied		Improve		Worsen		No change	
	No.	%	No.	%	No.	%	No.	%	No.	%
Pay										
Manual	10	83	3	17	5	42	1	8	5	42
Clerical	32	82	8	18	11	28	4	10	22	57
LMS	31	72	12	28	21	49	3	7	14	33
Managers	9	100	0	0	7	78	2	22	0	0
Promotion										
Manual	4	33	5	42	2	17	1	8	8	67
Clerical	22	56	13	33	10	26	6	15	18	46
LMS	21	49	20	44	15	35	7	16	18	42
Managers	8	89	1	11	6	67	0	0	3	33
Initiative										
Manual	8	67	4	33	1	8	5	42	1	8
Clerical	25	64	13	33	15	39	·6	15	15	39
LMS	38	88	5	12	25	58	3	7	13	30
Managers	9	8	1	11	8	89	0	0	2	22
Security										
Manual	9	75	2	17	2	17	7	58	3	25
Clerical	22	84	3	8	1	3	19	49	13	33
LMS	39	91	1	2	1	2	19	49	10	20
Managers	8	89	0	0	1	11	3	33	4	44

$N = 103$, missing $=4$ (don't knows excluded but included for calculation of percentages)
Source   Employees survey (see Appendix for details). Small expected frequencies preclude the use of significance tests in this and other contingency tables in this chapter.

It was on the question of job security, however, that widespread and deeply felt fears for the future surfaced. Public sector employment has traditionally been associated with relatively high levels of job security, and this is reflected in the high levels of satisfaction expressed by all grades on this aspect of their jobs. The rhetoric of privatization clearly threatened this, however, for talk of improved efficiency and higher productivity was easily interpreted by trade unions as well as by workers themselves as a potential attack on their traditional job security. As the chairman of Yorkshire Water warned when privatization was first mooted: 'Many of the employees in the water authorities come from reasonably sheltered water authority backgrounds and may be apprehensive about their future in a privatised and more commercial environment' (Jones 1985, p. 57). Subsequent events have proved him right.

What is particularly interesting about Table 4.1 is that all grades, including managers, seemed 'apprehensive' about the security of their jobs in the run-up to privatization. Around one half of those in manual, clerical and LMS grades thought that their job security would get worse following privatization, but so, too, did a third of the managers. This is not surprising when we remember that privatization was intended to affect managers as much as lower-level employees. In the words of the chairman of Thames Water, Roy Watts (1987, p. 19): 'Executives will have to learn to live without comfort . . . executives judged on action not promise, and rewarded accordingly'. All grades, therefore, saw privatization as a potential threat to their jobs; when we asked our sample of employees to identify what the disadvantages of privatization were likely to be for them personally, the most common answer, given by 39% of all employees, was the loss of job security.

Eighteen months later, these same employees were reinterviewed to find out whether their hopes and fears about their future in the private sector had been justified. The first point to make about these follow-up interviews is that, for all grades other than managers, the general sense of optimism seems quickly to have disappeared after 1989. For managers, privatization has been a very positive experience, for none of them identified any personal disadvantages resulting from it when we reinterviewed them in 1991. For other grades, however, privatization has proved less beneficial than many employees had apparently anticipated.

In 1989, for example, only around a third of those in lower grades (35% manual, 39% clerical and 35% LMS) had believed that they would derive no benefit from the privatization, but eighteen months later, three-quarters of manual employees and around a half those in clerical and LMS grades reported that privatization had in fact been of no benefit to them. Outside management, the only benefit which most employees could identify was in the form of the free and subsidized shares which they had been offered (see below).

While those outside management could identify few benefits to themselves, most did recognize that privatization had nevertheless brought changes which were affecting them. All managers, 86% of LMS grades, 85% of clerical workers and 67% of manual employees said that things had altered at work, and in many cases they reported that the pace of work had quickened – three-quarters of the sample said that they were now working harder while only one in twenty felt that their jobs had become easier. This finding, which is consistent with the study by O'Connel Davidson *et al.* (1991), may be explained by the introduction of new performance-related payment systems at managerial levels and by the pressures felt at all levels as a result of continued efforts at cost cutting.

On the issue of promotion, things seem to have turned out (with a few notable exceptions) much as people anticipated they would. In 1989, levels of satisfaction with promotion prospects were not very high, and few people outside of management expected things to improve or deteriorate with privatization. Eighteen months later, most employees above the manual grades have found that little has changed. Managers have, however, been disappointed, for while six out of nine of them thought prospects would improve after privatization, only two reported in 1991 that this had actually come about.

Table 4.2   Reported changes in pay and conditions, 1991

	Improved		Worsened		No change	
	No.	%	No.	%	No.	%
Pay						
Manual	3	25	4	33	5	42
Clerical	12	31	2	5	25	64
LMS	11	26	4	9	28	65
Managers	7	78	1	11	1	11
Promotion						
Manual	1	8	7	58	4	33
Clerical	8	21	9	23	22	56
LMS	7	16	12	28	24	56
Managers	2	22	0	0	7	78
Initiative						
Manual	6	50	2	17	4	33
Clerical	15	38	6	15	18	46
LMS	19	44	3	7	21	49
Managers	8	89	0	0	1	11
Job security						
Manual	0	0	5	42	7	58
Clerical	2	5	19	49	18	46
LMS	3	7	17	40	22	51
Managers	0	0	2	22	8	89

$N = 103$, missing $= 4$
Source   Employee survey

Manual employees, too, seem to have been over-optimistic in 1989, for while they generally expected things to stay the same, more than half of them reported in 1991 that things had actually grown worse.

Managers have fared much better as regards job enrichment, however, for the period since 1989 has been an exciting one for many managers. One told us that whereas before he 'just had to get the job done', now, as the head of a profit centre, it is 'all down to me. If it goes wrong it's my responsibility, if it goes well and we make a profit I get a pat on the back . . . [and] it shows in my pay packet.' Most managers feel empowered by privatization. Two-thirds of them reported in 1991 that their jobs had become more stimulating and all but one of them found that they were now able to exercise greater initiative in decision-making. For the managers, therefore, water privatization has brought precisely the benefits which they had hoped for and expected, while for other grades, any change in the scope for using personal initiative has been rather less marked.

The third aspect of change which we investigated was pay. We have seen that in 1989, satisfaction with earnings was high among all grades and that all grades were optimistic about the future. Eighteen months later most of our respondents (83% of manual workers, 82% of clerical workers, 72% of LMS grades, and all the managers) remained satisfied with their pay, and in most cases their earlier expectations appear to have been fulfilled, for they report that their earnings have stayed much the same (the majority view among clerical and LMS grades) or have improved (the majority view among managers).

As with promotion prospects, so too with earnings, it is only among manual employees that we detect any sign that things may actually have deteriorated, for although most of them are satisfied with their earnings, one-third of this group nevertheless report that their pay has fallen since privatization. The reason for this lies in the reduction in opportunities for overtime and weekend working for manual grades. Since privatization, the water companies have been keen to cut back expenditure on what are seen as inefficient working practices, and this has involved reductions in the amount of non-emergency work carried on 'out of hours'. A number of our manual worker respondents commented on this in interviews, and the phenomenon appears to be widespread among the water PLCs (see O'Connel Davidson *et al.* 1991).

On average, however, pay rates in the privatized water industry have held up well since 1989. Figures supplied jointly by NALGO and NUPE, two of the biggest unions in the industry, show that the 1991 wage settlements were above the rate of inflation and in line with average earnings. More tellingly, wages and salaries paid to water employees in the PLCs have risen faster than those paid to their erstwhile colleagues who were transferred in 1989 to the public sector National Rivers Authority. In 1990, the first year following privatization, the difference was marginal – an average increase of 9.68% in the PLCs compared with 9.25% in the NRA. In 1991, however, the gap widened appreciably, for wages increased by 8.63% in the PLCs but by only 6.5% for those employed by the NRA. It is not unreasonable to deduce from this that average pay rates of workers in the privatized companies have almost certainly risen faster than would have been the case had the industry remained in the public sector.

The group which has undoubtedly benefited most from increased earnings has been those at the very top. In virtually every privatization, top executives and directors have sought swiftly to raise their pay levels to those pertaining in comparable private sector firms, and this has resulted in huge (and often contentious) salary increases. Bishop and Kay (1988) found in a study of eleven privatized companies that top salaries were raised by an average of 78% in the first year, and Dunn and Smith (1990) claim that salaries of senior managers in privatized firms rose by an average of 250% in real terms over the period from 1979 to 1988.

The water industry was no exception. In the first thirty months following privatization, the average salary of the chairmen of the ten water PLCs rose by 166% (see *Sunday Times*, 13 May 1992). In addition, all ten chairmen took out substantial 'executive share options' at the time of privatization, and the subsequent increases in water share prices meant that by 1992 the chairmen were holding share options worth on average £180,000 each. These could be sold after a minimum of three years.

Other top managers have also benefited from large salary increases and from generous share option schemes. The *Sunday Times* estimated that in 1992, across the ten water PLCs, some thirty-three executive directors stood to make an average of £130,000 each from share options while another 450 top managers would make an average of £30,000 each. The lower down the management hierarchy we go, of course, the less dramatic are the financial benefits which have accrued. Nevertheless, managers in general have done well out of privatization, and salaries have been boosted in most companies by the move towards personal contracts and performance-related pay (PRP). By 1993 at least eight of the water PLCs had introduced a PRP scheme for managerial grades.

The final factor to consider is job security. We saw earlier that all grades felt relatively secure in their employment in 1989, but that all of them, including the managers, were troubled by the prospect of job losses following privatization. As part of their opposition to water privatization, the trade unions had warned that it would destroy jobs, and the experience of earlier privatizations such as BT seemed to bear this out (by the end of 1992, BT had shed 40,000 jobs and another 30,000 were due to go over the following two years). Union leaders such as the general secretary of the GMB, John Edmonds (1987, p. 4) saw this as a portent for the privatized water industry: 'Employees in the industry now fear that they will face the same future as their colleagues in British Telecom where numbers have been cut . . . water workers have performed well and deserve better treatment'.

The situation in the water industry was, however, very different from that at BT. Many of the redundancies at BT were created by the extraordinary pace of technological change in the telecommunications industry, rather than as a result of privatization as such. In the water industry, however, the scope for productivity gains through the introduction of new technology within the core business was very limited after 1989, and 'overmanning' had been tackled through 'natural wastage' and early retirements during the 1970s and 1980s long before the industry was privatized.

Indeed, as things have turned out, employment by the ten water PLCs has actually *increased* substantially since privatization and has more than compensated for the loss of 6,000 jobs to the NRA in 1989 (Figure 4.1). This increase in employment was largely a function of the expansion of the new PLCs into a range of subsidiary activities rather than of any growth of employment in the 'core' water and sewage businesses (see Chapter 2). Nevertheless, there have been few job losses in the core businesses since privatization, and for those who were still employed in the industry in 1989, privatization has not posed any significant threat to jobs.

Such evidence has, however, done little to reduce the worries of employees, for the concern about job security in 1989 was still present in 1991. Of all four of the dimensions of job satisfaction we investigated, this one produced by far

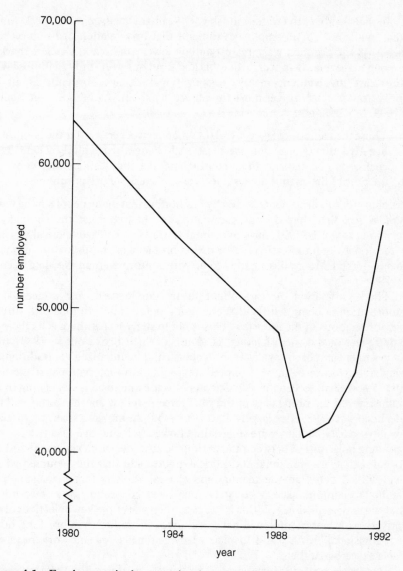

Figure 4.1   Employment in the ten regional water services companies, 1980–92
Source   NALGO and NUPE (1992)

the highest proportion of people reporting that things had grown worse over
the preceding eighteen months. Over 40% of manual, clerical and LMS grades
believed that their jobs had become less secure and virtually nobody in these
grades ventured the opinion that security had improved. The exception is,
once again, the managers, for eight out of the ten managers we interviewed
believed that their jobs were no less secure in 1991 than they had been before
privatization.

In their study of the water industry, O'Connel Davidson *et al.* (1991) found that, while 60% of all employees thought that privatization had reduced job security, the problem was greatest among lower grades and was less marked among managers. It appears from this and from our own study that those with the least involvement in the organizational changes brought about by privatization tend to feel most threatened by them. As Nelson and Cooper (1993, p. 17) suggest:

> Those in positions of less control (i.e. manual workers) suffer the greatest negative effects of major organisational change, particularly when the change is one outside their control and the implications and consequences of the change are less clear, as in the case of privatisations.

Support for this argument is given by our finding that many people in the lower grades feel that they do not know and are not told what the company is planning to do. In 1991, 60% of manual workers and 40% of clerical workers cited 'poor communications' as a major problem in the industry, although many in the LMS grades claimed to be better informed than they had been in 1989.

The combination of fears about future employment and concern that information is being withheld represents a potent mixture for the future of labour relations in the industry. This is not to suggest that there is likely to be any repeat of the sort of industrial conflict which broke out in 1983 when government-imposed cost limits provoked a highly unionized yet traditionally moderate workforce into an unprecedented month-long national strike over pay. As we shall see later and in Chapter 5, trade unionism is weakening in the industry and the propensity of the workforce to follow another strike call has declined since 1989, due largely to worries about the impact a strike might have on job security. What we are suggesting, however, is that there is evidence of a growing polarization between the optimistic attitudes of management and the pessimistic fears of manual and clerical grades, and that this, coupled with a widespread belief among manual and clerical workers that management is failing to communicate adequately, may well be producing a lowering of morale in the workforce. If this is the case, then one of the key objectives of the privatization programme will have backfired, for rather than breaking down any divisions, hostility and suspicion between managers and workers, it will have exacerbated them.

Our sense that this polarization is growing is reinforced by the answers we received to a general yet fundamental question in which respondents were simply asked whether they thought of their company as a 'good' or 'bad' employer. Prior to privatization, there was a strongly held view among more than 80% of employees at all levels that Southern and North West Water were 'good employers'. Eighteen months later, much of this goodwill seems to have evaporated outside the management grades, for around one-third of manual, clerical and LMS employees believed that their company had grown worse. Comparing these findings with those of a Scottish 'control group' of workers in a water industry which had not been privatized and where over 80% of respondents denied that their employer had become noticeably better or worse since 1989, it does seem that it is privatization itself that has contributed to this reduction in goodwill.

Again, the exception to this pattern is the managers. Managers denied that there was a communication problem, and they denied that their company had worsened as an employer. Indeed, all of the managers we interviewed believed in 1989 that their company was a good employer, and all but two of them believed in 1991 that it had become even better! As on so many other indicators, therefore, there appears to be a wide discrepancy in evaluation of the experience of privatization between manual and clerical workers, on the one hand, and managers, on the other.

Employee share ownership and the case of NFC

We have seen that a gap seems to be opening up between management and lower grades. They have different opinions about whether the industry should have been privatized; their expectations in terms of the likely benefits of privatization were divergent; they report different experiences in terms of the benefits which they believe privatization has brought to them personally; lower grades bemoan a lack of communication with management of which managers themselves seem unaware; and while managers are now optimistic about the future, lower grades remain fearful for their jobs. On top of all this, a remarkable fund of goodwill towards the companies as employers seems to be dissipating among lower grades, while managers have become even more positive.

The appearance of this 'gap' seems to belie the government's claims that privatization can benefit workers and managers alike, let alone that it can forge a new sense of common purpose between them. Yet a key claim advanced by advocates of privatization is that the opportunity which it offers for extending worker share ownership will positively influence employee motivation. The argument is partly that worker shareholding will encourage employees to identify more closely with the company they work for, and partly that it will change their attitudes about the capitalist system of wage labour by giving them a material stake in the enterprise. As the water privatization White Paper explained: 'Employees will benefit from . . . closer identification with their businesses, greater job satisfaction, better motivation, and the prospects of the rewards that enterprise has brought to those who work for the industries that have been privatised' (Department of the Environment 1986a, para. 7). Or as Brennan (1988, p. 7) puts it: 'Employees who are owners of the firms for which they work will identify more closely with the success of those businesses, working more efficiently and cutting costs diligently'.

The example which is often given to illustrate this argument is that of the privatization of the road haulage consortium, the National Freight Corporation (now NFC), in 1982. As we saw in Chapter 1, the Conservative manifesto of 1979 had promised to return road haulage to the private sector, but in 1980 the government postponed the sale on the grounds that the company was not then marketable. A group of senior executives in the company responded with a proposal for an employee buyout. After a vigorous and successful campaign to persuade the employees to participate in the buyout, 10,000 workers, former employees and relatives of employees were persuaded to invest an average of around £600 each to buy the company from the government at a subsidized price of £53.5 million. NFC employees, former employees and their families raised 82.5% of the share capital, and the balance of the purchase price was subscribed by a syndicate of banks (NFC 1989). It was Britain's biggest ever employee buyout.

In order to keep control within the company, ownership of ordinary shares was restricted to past or present employees, pensioners and their families and to certain institutional investors authorized by the Board. Shares could only be bought and sold through an internal share market operated by a trust. Dealings took place on a quarterly basis, with prices being set by an independent valuer. By December 1988, the original investors had been joined by 35,000 other company employees and their relatives, and together these individuals owned 82% of the issued share capital.

Before the buyout, the company's trading record had, on its own admission, been 'disappointing'. In the late 1960s the company had been making losses as high as 80% of turnover. During the 1970s labour was shed and new management was installed, but profits still remained very low. According to the *Sunday Times* (20 October 1987), NFC had been known for its 'unreliability, low morale and lacklustre results'.

Since the buyout, however, the company's financial performance has improved dramatically. Profits rose by 50% in the first full year after privatization and by a further 70% the year after that (Letwin 1988). Pre-tax profits increased ninefold between 1981 and 1986. By 1988–9 the operating profit was £114.4 million, compared with just £27.6 million in 1983–4. The subscription price of an ordinary share at the time of the buyout was 2½p. On 25 November 1988, shortly before the company announced a share issue on the stock exchange, this price had risen on the internal share market to 185p. Ordinary workers found that their shareholdings were now worth thousands of pounds. NFC was valued at the time of the share issue in 1989 at £729 million – almost fourteen times the price originally paid for the company. According to *The Independent* (18 January 1989), more than 400 workers – including lorry drivers and secretarial staff – became 'quarter millionaires' and several became full millionaires. Even those who had originally invested only £200 now had holdings worth £15,000.

NFC represents a remarkable privatization success story – Vickers and Yarrow (1988, p. 164) describe it as 'one of the greatest successes of the privatisation programme'. Its success is all the more remarkable when we remember that the company has had to operate in a highly competitive market in which it was performing badly before the buyout. It is little wonder, then, that government ministers have regularly cited the case of NFC to justify their commitment to extending employee share ownership through the privatization programme (see, for example, Moore 1986a; and Redwood 1990). As the

Sunday Times (20 October 1987) commented: 'When a concern . . . sweeps to the sort of market leadership that National Freight now commands, the whole privatisation argument seems justified'.

There are, however, some obvious and crucial differences between the privatization of NFC through a management and worker buyout, and the privatization of other nationalized industries through a public flotation. Most of NFC was bought by those who worked in it. They controlled the company. Even after the company's flotation on the Stock Exchange, employee shareowners retained unique voting rights designed to safeguard their rights of control.

The situation is very different in other privatized companies. Whereas NFC employees originally owned 83% of the company, BT employees at the time of privatization were allocated just 10% of the issued share capital, and at British Gas just 5% of the shares were reserved for employees. In huge companies like these, there has never been any possibility of employees owning more than a tiny fraction of the total share capital. Nor have workers in these other industries enjoyed the same sorts of voting rights. Indeed, the free shares which have been allocated to employees in most of the big privatizations have restricted voting rights attached to them. The NFC pattern of effective worker control through share ownership has not, therefore, applied in other privatizations.

It is this lack of effective employee influence or control which has led critics to deny that employee share ownership can have anything more than the most marginal impact on efficiency and labour relations in the privatized industries. In their campaign against water privatization, for example, the water industry unions recognized that workers stood to benefit from a few free shares, but they argued that employees would own too small a proportion of their company to be able to influence decision making in any positive way (Water Industry Unions Committee 1985).

Although they own only a tiny fraction of the total share capital, rates of share ownership by employees in privatized industries such as BT, British Gas and the water PLCs are very high – around 95%. This has been achieved through various giveaways and inducements. In the case of water, for example, employees were offered £140 of free shares plus another £2 of shares for every year of service. In addition, two free shares were offered for every share purchased up to a maximum of £200. Furthermore, a discount of 10% was offered on share purchases up to £2,350, and employees were also given priority over applications from the general public on up to £14,350 worth of shares. Unlike the free and matching shares, both discounted and priority purchases could be sold immediately. Finally, and most significantly, employees could join a Save As You Earn (SAYE) scheme entitling employees with at least one year's service to buy ordinary shares on preferential terms. Those joining this scheme were required to take out an SAYE contract to save a specific amount each month for a minimum period of five years. At the end of this period the employee can either take the case accumulated in savings plus a bonus, or the savings can be used to buy company shares at a unit price agreed

Table 4.3   Participation in company share schemes

	Matching shares		Discounted shares		SAYE share scheme		Average monthly outlay
	No.	%	No.	%	No.	%	(£)
Manual	7	58	2	17	5	42	42
Clerical	31	80	5	13	16	41	36
LMS	38	88	12	28	34	79	58
Managers	8	89	6	66	8	89	94
All	84	82	25	24	63	61	56

$N = 103$, missing $= 4$
Source   Employee survey

at the start of the contract. As we saw earlier, top managers were also given access to an executive option scheme.

Ninety-six per cent of employees in our samples at Southern and North-West accepted the offer of free shares (those who declined did so for reasons of principle). Over 80% purchased some matching shares, and a quarter bought shares in the discounted general offer (all but three of whom still owned them in 1991). Over 60% of our sample had joined one of the company SAYE share schemes, although the underrepresentation of manual workers in our sample has slightly inflated the actual proportion of employees belonging to these schemes which is a little over half. The main reason given by respondents for not having bought matching shares, or for failing to join the SAYE scheme, was simply lack of cash. This was particularly the case among the lower grades – four of the five manual workers who had not bought matching shares said they could not afford it, as did four of the seven manual workers who stayed out of the SAYE scheme.

Table 4.3 reveals that it is in the higher grades that participation in the various share schemes is most heavily concentrated. Most significant here is the polarization by grade in the SAYE scheme, for participation in this implies a long-term commitment to remaining with the company and a degree of faith in the company's future prosperity. Significantly, the proportion of managers and LMS grades participating in the SAYE scheme is, at around 80%, double the participation rate of clerical and manual grades. Not for the first time, we see here clear signs of the polarization which has been developing since 1989 between higher and lower grades.

Employee share ownership, vertical identification and 'entrepreneurship'

When it was in the public sector, the water industry was characterized by a rather conservative and consensual workplace culture. Partly because of its roots in the pre-1974 system of municipal governance, partly because so many employees have traditionally worked in small-scale environments such as sewage farms and pumping stations, and partly because of the craft tradition among manual grades and the traditional dominance of engineers among higher grades, there was in this industry a rather pragmatic and technocratic workplace culture which was at least to some extent underpinned by a shared ethic of public service. Although the industry was heavily unionized, this was not a militant or politicized form of trade unionism. In 1989, 40% of the clerical workers and half of the manual and LMS grades were Conservative voters.

This was a conservative culture which emphasized routine and security over innovation and enterprise. Widespread satisfaction with pay levels, for example, reflected the fact that most employees valued their job security and were not especially motivated by the prospect of high earnings – asked to choose between a job offering good security but a low income, and one offering high earnings but little security, 81% of our sample went for the former. It was also a consensual culture for the water authorities were, in the eyes of most workers, 'good employers', and there was little sign of any real antagonism between workers and management. Asked whether workers and management are like a team or are on opposing sides, nearly three-quarters of the sample opted for the team analogy (Table 4.4).

All of this has been shaken up by privatization. New chairmen recruited from the private sector were appointed to most of the authorities in the years preceding flotation, the PLCs have restructured themselves and have begun to diversify into new activities, new pay and incentive schemes have been introduced, the intensity of work has been stepped up, and old inefficient working practices have been curtailed. The public service ethic of the old utilities has been replaced by a new ethic of 'customer service' emphasizing economic efficiency. The unions have been marginalized as higher- and middle-grade employees have been encouraged to negotiate their own personal contracts and national wage agreements have been terminated (see Chapter 5). At the fulcrum of these changes is the metamorphosis of workers into employee shareholders expected, as we have seen, to identify more strongly with the company and to embrace a new spirit of enterprise and individual advancement.

Vertical identification

Addressing first the question of whether employee share ownership has encouraged vertical identification between workers and management, we may note the paradox that worker shareholding in the water industry was intended to create many of the values which already existed before the industry was privatized and which privatization itself has begun to undermine. It is true that this was a rather conservative workforce, averse to risks, but we have seen that it was also a workforce which already identified quite strongly with management and its objectives. It can be argued that there was never any need to give workers shares in order to create the vertical identification with the company

Table 4.4   Perceptions of the relationship between management and workers

	Employees in SAYE scheme		All employees			
			1989		1991	
	Like a team	Opposite sides	Like a team	Opposite sides	Like a team	Opposite sides
	No.	%	No.	%	No.	%	No.	%	No.	%	No.	%
Manual	2	40	3	60	7	58	5	42	5	42	7	58
Clerical	8	50	8	50	29	74	10	26	20	51	19	49
LMS	26	76	8	24	32	74	11	26	32	74	11	26
Managers	8	89	1	11	7	78	2	22	8	89	1	11
Total	44	69	20	31	75	73	28	27	65	63	38	37

$N = 103$, missing $=4$
Source   Employee survey

which the White Paper on water privatization sought, for this identification was already there. Most workers thought the water authorities were good employers and most were happy to think of their relations with management in terms of teamwork. Since privatization, however, fears about job security have intensified and the attitudes and values of managers and lower grades have begun to polarize.

The question, therefore, is not whether employee share ownership can create a corporate consensus, but whether it can effectively substitute for the old public sector ethos which nurtured and sustained this consensus before privatization. The indications are that it cannot.

Conservative politicians like John Moore and John Redwood who claim that employees in privatized industries can be positively motivated by the new climate of competition and monetary incentives ignore the psychology of industrial change. As Vickers and Yarrow (1985, p. 14) point out: 'It is not always clear that increased stress on financial returns will actually improve performance . . . where an organisation has a well developed public service ethos, privatisation, by destroying the pre-existing atmosphere, may reduce some non-monetary work incentives'. We have already seen that the main concern of most employees was to ensure their job security rather than to maximize their earnings. A dramatic change which seemed to many to undermine job security in return for the chance of higher earnings was always likely to undermine the old ethos but was never likely in a workforce like this to produce positive responses. Rather, it could be predicted that such a change would be seen as threatening and would produce defensive rather than positive reactions. Woodward (1988, pp. 97–8), one of the few commentators on privatization to have recognized this, identifies a psychological problem associated with radical change in organizations: 'Fear of the unknown, fear of the unfamiliar . . . provokes defensive behaviour, rationalisation, denial and projection.' As we shall see, this is exactly what seems to have happened in the water industry.

Research on employee share ownership lends little support to the claim that it strengthens vertical identification and reduces industrial militancy. The evidence is mixed – Estrin and Wilson (1986), for example, found that share ownership does seem to reduce industrial conflict, while Meade (1986) suggests that it might actually increase it – but on balance the research that has been completed on this issue indicates that the impact of employee share ownership schemes is either very limited or non-existent.

In their study of a manufacturing firm in which a minority of employees had joined the company SAYE scheme, Dunn *et al.* (1991 p. 11) concluded that there was 'no evidence to suggest that share schemes had any perceptible impact on attitudes, either generally among the workforce or differentially among the joiners', and they speculated that the 'them and us attitudes said to plague British industry could be further institutionalised between the share-oriented minority and the rest'. Other studies have been no more optimistic. Nichols and O'Connel Davidson (1992) questioned employees in two privatized utilities and found that attitudinal differences between those who bought shares and those who did not were marginal. And using four companies as case studies, Fogarty and White (1988) found that employees in share schemes looked upon them favourably but that fewer than 30% felt that the schemes had caused any reduction in 'us and them' attitudes in the company. They concluded that such schemes can achieve little unless they are reinforced through high degrees of consultation and participation. There is, then, little evidence to indicate that share schemes alone can fundamentally shift attitudes or behaviour.

Our own study supports this conclusion. It is true that there is some indication from our results that willingness to strike may have declined somewhat since 1989. We asked all employees whether they would obey a union strike call even if they did not personally agree with the decision to strike. In 1989, 28% said that they would, and by 1991 this had fallen slightly to just 19%. This change was concentrated mainly among manual grades, for while more than half of the manual workers in the sample said in 1989 that they would obey a strike call on principle, this had fallen to only a quarter by 1991.

There are two important points to make about this finding, however. The first is that ideological commitment to the principle of trade unionism, as measured by this question, was low even before privatization, and this again indicates the prior existence of a rather consensual and conservative workplace culture. The second is that, although changes since 1989 probably do account for the slight change in people's responses (for in our control group of Scottish water workers, manual workers became more rather than less militant over this same period), this almost certainly has nothing to do with their receipt of shares, but is probably better explained by their growing fears for the security of their jobs.

That this change probably has little to do with share ownership among workers is shown by the breakdown in responses between those who joined and those who did not join the SAYE share purchase scheme. As we have already noted, membership of this scheme is almost certainly the most meaningful indicator of employee commitment through share ownership since it is long-term and voluntary. Yet there is no clear association between membership of this scheme and a change in willingness to obey a strike call. Of course, it has to be repeated that the numbers in this sample are very small. Nevertheless, there is nothing here to suggest that employee share ownership undermines trade union collectivism, and in our view the change in manual workers' responses to this question is almost certainly a product of their increased fears about job security rather than their exposure to share ownership.

Our belief that share ownership has done little to encourage corporate solidarism is also reflected in the views expressed by the employees themselves. In 1989 many workers expected that the introduction of employee share ownership would lead to stronger corporate loyalty and identification – only one-third thought that it would fail to have such an effect. When we returned to these same people eighteen months later, however, we found that only about one-third of them now believed that share ownership among workers had strengthened corporate identification while half of them believed that it had not. The manual and clerical grades had become particularly disillusioned while managers and LMS grades tended to believe that the initial promise had been fulfilled. In 1989, eight out of twelve manual workers anticipated that share ownership would make a difference to how people saw the company, but by 1991 eight out of twelve believed that it had not in fact done so. Similarly, three-quarters of clerical workers thought that share ownership had had no impact, although only half of them had anticipated such a negative result in 1989.

It is true that those who had joined the SAYE scheme were much more positive than those who had not in believing that share ownership had encouraged stronger identification with the company. Sixty-two per cent of those in the scheme answered this question in the affirmative, as compared with only 21% of those who were not in the scheme. However, participation in the SAYE scheme was, as we have seen, skewed by grade, for only just over 40% of manual and clerical workers joined the scheme as compared with over 80% of managerial and lower managerial grades, and when we control for grade, the effect of participation in the SAYE scheme all but disappears.

In their study of employee share ownership in the water industry, Nichols and O'Connel Davidson (1992) found that employee attitudes are more a function of grade than of whether or not workers buy shares. Higher-grade employees are the most actively involved in company share schemes, and the higher the grade, the more positive the attitudes about the effect these schemes have had. This, too, is our conclusion, for participation in the SAYE scheme is largely an effect of the stronger identification with the company among higher-grade employees.

This conclusion is further supported by the findings in Table 4.4. As we noted earlier, around three-quarters of our interviewees in 1989 felt that workers and management were like a team, while only a quarter believed that they were on opposite sides with opposing interests. By 1991, this commitment to the metaphor of the company as a team had declined among manual and clerical grades but was still strong among higher grades, and, as the table shows, participation in the SAYE scheme seems to have had little or no effect on people's answers. Manual and clerical grades became less committed to the concept of teamwork after privatization irrespective of whether or not they were active shareholders (by 1991, 55% of the manual and clerical workers who were not in the SAYE scheme saw their relationship with management as oppositional, but so, too, did 52% of those who were in the scheme). By contrast, managerial and LMS grades remained as strongly committed to the teamwork concept as they had been before privatization – in 1989 and in 1991, some 80% of LMS and management-level employees saw the relationship between management and workers in terms of teamwork – and this was so irrespective of whether or not respondents were in the SAYE scheme.

Much the same pattern emerges on other indicators of employee attitudes. Those in the SAYE scheme were less inclined to believe that the company had become a worse employer since privatization. They were also less likely to believe that privatization of the industry had been a bad thing or that it should be renationalized. But in all of these cases, the difference in attitudes turns out to be a function of grade rather than of share ownership.

The extension of employee share ownership in the water industry has not, therefore, led to stronger vertical bonds between management and workforce. Indeed, if anything it has weakened such bonds as previously existed, for the differential take-up of the SAYE scheme among different grades of employee has arguably exacerbated the growing polarization between them by creating one additional discriminator.

Encouragement of 'enterprise'

The second benefit which the extension of employee share ownership was intended to produce was a more 'enterprising' workforce. Here, as we have seen, there was scope for change, for this was a rather conservative, cautious and risk-averse workforce before privatization. The evidence suggests, however, that little has changed.

Most employees in all grades below management level were in 1989 strongly inclined to value job security more highly than the opportunity to increase earnings. In 1991 the great majority of manual and clerical workers, in particular, were still more concerned with security than with increasing their income. Nor does participation in the SAYE scheme have any effect on such attitudes. It is true that participants in the scheme were slightly less risk-averse than non-participants (22% of the former opting for higher earnings as compared with 15% of the latter), but this difference is entirely accounted for when we control for grade.

On other measures, too, we fail to find any appreciable impact of share ownership upon 'enterprise values'. In both sets of interviews, we gave employees three normative statements concerned with income distribution – one 'egalitarian' (that income inequalities should be reduced by increasing taxation on higher earners), one 'meritocratic' (that people's incomes should depend upon how hard they work), and one *laissez-faire* (that incomes should be determined by the demand for people's services in the market). As in our sample of the general public (see Chapter 7) we found that many respondents saw merit in all three of these logically incompatible positions – in 1991, 93% of all employees agreed with the meritocratic statement, 52% agreed with the *laissez-faire* view, and 49% agreed with the egalitarian position – but, more importantly, these proportions had remained virtually unchanged since the earlier interviews in 1989. Nor did participation in the company SAYE scheme reveal any independent association with answers to this question. Neither the move into the private sector nor the opportunity to buy shares in the company has had any impact on employees' basic values regarding income determination.

The same finding is repeated when we look at responses to four other attitude questions – one on the role of trade unions, one on taxation and individual incentives, one on the role of government in determining living standards, and one on the relative efficiency of the public and private sectors – all of which may be seen as indicators or measures of commitment to an 'enterprise culture' (the same questions were repeated to members of the public and are outlined in more detail in Chapter 7). If privatization had made the workforce more 'enterprising', we should expect the results to show up in the answers to questions like these, but with one interesting exception we find very little change between 1989 and 1991, and again participation in the SAYE scheme has no effect.

The one exception is in the answers to the question on the relative efficiency of the public and private sectors. Here, although there is little change in the overall answers for the sample as a whole, there is an interesting change within it, for while manual and clerical grades have become less convinced of the superiority of the private sector (a decline from 67% to 48%), managerial and LMS grades have become more convinced of it (an increase from 50% to 60%). Yet again, therefore, we find evidence here of a polarization of attitudes between higher and lower grades, for while the former have become more committed to a private enterprise culture, the latter have become more disillusioned with it.

One final indicator of whether employees have become more 'enterprising' as a result of participation in share ownership is the interest they show in their holdings. Both of our case-study companies displayed the current share price (and often the relative performance of the company's shares in comparison with other water PLCs) on screens and noticeboards throughout their main offices. If share ownership really did create a stronger culture of enterprise among employees, we should expect them at least to show an interest in and awareness of how their shares were performing. In fact, however, even those who joined the SAYE scheme were often ignorant of current share performance.

Eighty-eight per cent of SAYE members, and 50% of non-members, claimed regularly to check the company share price. However, only 71% of members and 24% of non-members could offer an estimate of what the current share price was, and half of those who offered an estimate gave a figure which was at least 30% wide of the mark. Nor were employees particularly active shareholders. Most employees – 89% of those in the SAYE scheme and 67% of others – did claim that they had read the company's annual report, which is mailed to every shareholder. Only a minority, however – 37% of SAYE members and 17% of non-members – had attended the special AGM for employee shareholders. Given that, even among those in the SAYE scheme, fewer than half could accurately estimate the company share price and fewer than half bothered to attend the special AGM, it would be surprising if concern about the company's profitability featured significantly in the thoughts and actions of many of even the most committed employee shareholders. In contrast with the situation at NFC, where share ownership vested effective control of the company in the workforce itself, the introduction of employee share ownership in the water industry has not given workers outside management any sense that they can control or influence the direction of company affairs.

Conclusion

As regards its impact on the workplace, privatization of the water industry has achieved two of the results which were intended. First, it has freed managers, many of whom feel that their jobs have been enriched, that rewards for initiative have been enhanced through profit-related pay, and that they enjoy greater autonomy than before. Second, it has probably reduced the willingness of workers to follow a strike call from their union. This latter change does not, however, reflect any shift in employees' attitudes away from traditional collectivism and towards a new enterprise culture, but is rather a function of fear. A workforce which always was concerned about job security has been made to feel insecure as a result of the move into the private sector, and it is for this reason alone that industrial action may have become less likely.

These two trends – the enhancement of managerial autonomy, on the one hand, and the increased sense of insecurity among lower grades, on the other – are indicative of the polarization which is now taking place between higher and lower grades. In this chapter we have seen evidence for this polarization on a wide range of indicators. Higher grades have become more supportive of the original decision to privatize water, while lower grades remain largely opposed to it; higher grades can identify ways in which they personally have benefited from privatization, while lower grades can point to no benefits other than the initial handout of free shares; managers believe that their pay has improved as a result of privatization, while manual workers think theirs has deteriorated and others think nothing has changed; lower grades often believe their company has become a worse employer as a result of privatization, while higher grades believe it has improved; lower grades complain of a communication problem where higher grades see no problem; lower grades deny that share ownership has encouraged corporate identification, while higher grades believe that it has; lower grades have become less convinced about the relative superiority of the private over the public sector, while higher grades have become more convinced of it; lower grades have become increasingly likely to see the relationship between workers and management as one of opposed interests, while higher grades remain strongly committed to the belief that this relationship is based upon teamwork; and, reflecting all of this, twice as many people in higher grades as in lower grades have become committed employee shareholders by joining the SAYE share option scheme.

This polarization of attitudes, beliefs and experiences consequent upon the privatization of the industry militates against the likelihood that either of the two main objectives outlined in the White Paper on water privatization can be achieved. The belief that employee share ownership would foster stronger vertical bonds of identification between workforce and management has proved to be illusory – indeed, the relatively strong bonds which already existed in the industry before 1989 have almost certainly been weakened rather than reinforced by the move into the private sector. And the hope that employee shareholding would in some way release a new spirit of enterprise throughout the workforce, such as happened at NFC, has been undermined by the intensification of workers' traditional concerns about job security.

If it really was a key objective of the government's privatization programme to overcome the 'them and us' division between management and workforce in British industry, then the evidence from this study suggests that the result is likely to be quite the reverse. A relatively conservative and consensual workforce in the water industry is becoming disillusioned, alienated and frightened, for as management becomes increasingly optimistic about its future in the private sector, the lower grades become ever more detached and disenchanted with the changes they are experiencing.

5 Land, labour and capital

We saw in Chapter 2 that the water industry was fundamentally reorganized in 1974 when a confusing mêlée of unelected regional river authorities, indirectly elected joint water boards and elected local authority sewerage undertakings was integrated into just ten multi-purpose Regional Water Authorities. Further changes followed in 1983 when direct representation of outside interests on the boards of RWAs was ended, and, just six years after that, the industry went through another major upheaval as the National Rivers Authority was carved out of the ten water authorities while the remainder of the industry was transferred into the private sector.

These changes had major implications for a range of organizations with interests in the provision of water services. These fall broadly into three clusters. One, organized around the use of land, consists of the representatives of those (like farmers and landowners) who own or work the land and of those (like environmentalists and amenity groups) with an interest in the water environment. A second, organized around the use of labour, consists of the trade unions representing those employed within the water industry itself. The third, organized around the use of capital, consists of organizations (like the Confederation of British Industry) which represent companies which use water in the production of goods or provision of services.

Before 1974, these three sets or organized interests had to deal with 29 river authorities, 187 water boards and a staggering 1,393 sewerage authorities. They then had to adjust in 1974 to a new policy context in which just ten multi-purpose regional bodies (in addition to the 28 single-purpose statutory water companies) controlled virtually every aspect of water management, initially under the control of large boards of management meeting in public and containing many coopted representatives of outside interests, and latterly (from 1983) under the direction of much smaller boards meeting privately and with no outside representation on them. Finally, since 1989, they have had to adjust again as they have learned to deal with two new regulatory quangos (the NRA and Ofwat) and ten large new companies operating within the private sector.

This chapter traces the impact of these upheavals on each of the three sets of interests – land, labour and capital – which constitute the three 'factors of production' of classical political economy and the three main pillars of the contemporary capitalist system.

Land as property: the farmers and landowners

Most of the rivers, reservoirs and boreholes in England and Wales are found in the countryside, and most of the countryside is owned by private individuals – although some is also owned by corporate investors such as insurance companies or pension funds, by charitable organizations such as the National Trust, or by the Crown (see Massey and Catalano 1978). The interests of traditional landowners are represented by the Country Landowners' Association (CLA) which has some 47,000 members, among them some of the oldest, wealthiest and most famous titled families in Britain.

Some of these people also belong to the National Farmers' Union (NFU) which represents large and small farmers, some of whom own land, others of whom rent it, but all of whom use it principally to produce crops or livestock rather than simply as a source of rent or a means for sustaining activities such as shooting. If the CLA is the voice of the traditional landowning class in Britain, the NFU is the voice of the agricultural industry.

Both of these organizations have a clear and direct interest in the activities of the water industry, and both employ officers in their national headquarters who specialize in issues concerning water. The CLA's specialist water adviser told us that water affects the interests of his members more than any other single area of state or private sector activity. On a wide range of issues – including water charges, rights of abstraction from rivers and boreholes, the control of pollution, provision for flood defences and land drainage, compensation for pipe-laying, and the management and regulation of fisheries and rod licences – both farmers and landowners are vitally affected by the activities of the water industry.

Before 1989, these concerns were safeguarded and expressed through a combination of institutional arrangements and informal liaison with the water authorities which is best characterized as a 'corporatist' form of interest representation and mediation (Saunders 1985). The 1974 reorganization of the industry had worked to the advantage of the CLA and NFU because they found it much easier to establish regular contact with just ten multi-purpose bodies organized at regional level than it had been to try to stay in touch with hundreds of much smaller and more limited authorities organized mostly at a local level (see Saunders 1984).

Between 1974 and 1989, the CLA and the NFU enjoyed a special relationship with both the Ministry of Agriculture (which had overall responsibility for land drainage and flood defence) and with the ten RWAs, and this effectively gave them an 'inside track' on policy-making and implementation. Stafford (1980), for example, identified an 'extensive consultative chain' involving the NFU, the CLA and the RWAs, while Parker and

Penning-Rowsell (1980, p. 242) saw agriculture as enjoying a 'dominant influence on water planning' through membership of strategic committees, regular consultation, use of informal contacts and the existence of a set of sentiments and values held in common by water planners and the land and agriculture lobby.

Of particular significance in this relationship were the institutional arrangements governing land drainage. The regional and local land drainage committees and internal drainage boards were dominated by farmers and landowners, and every regional committee in England was chaired by a farmer or landowner. This often led these committees to support policies – such as drainage of pasture land to enable cereals to be planted – which were fiercely opposed by the environmentalist lobby with its concerns to protect wetlands and the wildlife which they contained (see, for example, Pearce 1982).

Both organizations were also represented on the Consumer Consultative Committees, established in 1983, although neither found them a particularly significant channel of interest mediation. Much more important were less formal means of liaison which developed from 1974 onwards as the NFU and CLA forged close personal contacts with key officers in the regional headquarters and the divisional offices of the various water authorities. 'Once you know the people you're talking to and they know you,' explained one CLA informant, 'then you get helpful answers'. Similarly, an NFU official explained that 'I can speak to the Chief Executive . . . In relation to matters of principle, they are generally very receptive' (interviews reported in Saunders 1984).

Through these informal and personal contacts, the NFU and CLA pursued concerns such as the need to strengthen sea defences to protect farmland threatened by coastal erosion, the modification of tariffs for supplying water to cattle troughs, the proportion of the cost of a new pipeline to be borne by the recipient of the service, disputes over abstraction licences and discharge consents, and so on. The NFU and CLA did not always get their way, but discussions and negotiations always took place in a context described on both sides as positive, helpful and amicable.

The privatization of the water industry in 1989 meant that all of this had to be renegotiated and reconstructed. When we spoke with the NFU and CLA immediately before the privatization, they were uncertain about how effectively they would be able to defend their members' interests under the new arrangements, and when we returned to them in 1991 it was clear that much had changed.

Both organizations saw the new Ofwat Customer Services Committees as playing a more important role than had ever been the case for the old Consumer Consultative Committees, and both had taken steps to secure representation on them, although in the case of the CLA this was achieved in only two of the ten regions. The old, close and personal relationships enjoyed with the water authorities themselves, however, have gone. A large part of the reason for this is that so many of the concerns affecting the NFU and CLA are no longer the responsibility of the privatized water companies, but now lie in the sphere of responsibility of the NRA. There is less need than before to maintain contact with the companies themselves, and the relationship has therefore withered to a point where farmers and landowners are simply two groups among many with whom the companies deal when and as necessary. In 1991 the CLA told us: 'We've lost the regional contacts we had with the old water authorities. When there are things to take up, we've lost the regular contact that we used to have with them.' Similarly, the NFU recognized that its 'relations with the PLCs are patchy to say the least. Some were clear that they didn't want to maintain the relation as before.'

Far more important for both organizations is the National Rivers Authority and its various regional committees for flood defence, fisheries and (most importantly) rivers. But here, too, the NFU and CLA have lost the favoured status which they previously enjoyed through their control of the land drainage committees and boards which used to report directly to the Ministry of Agriculture. Now the land drainage committees (in their new guise as flood defence committees) report not to MAFF but to the NRA, and unlike MAFF, the NRA sees its first priority as the protection and improvement of the water environment rather than the protection of the interests of the agricultural industry.

The NRA's concern with safeguarding the natural water environment, coupled with the reduced need for cereal farming consequent upon the EC's grain surpluses, has meant that government funding for draining or protecting farmland has all but ceased. And although they enjoy representation on the crucial Rivers Advisory Committees of the NRA (which deal with key issues affecting their members such as water quality, pollution and abstraction), the NFU and CLA now find that their influence has been diluted by substantial representation of other groups (including environmentalists and the newly privatized water PLCs) and by the fact that these committees meet in public session with the media present. Furthermore, the NRA (prompted by the tightening of EC environmental standards) is proving much tougher on environmental issues than the RWAs ever were, and its approach is much more formal and legalistic.

This does not necessarily mean that farmers and landowners always lose out in the new system. For example, the CLA and NFU had for years been concerned that the water authorities were taking too much water out of rivers and were failing to maintain an adequate rate of flow. In some cases, authorities had granted licences to themselves to abstract more water from rivers than was actually flowing in them (*The Independent*, 16 June 1992). Precisely because the RWAs were responsible for regulating levels of abstraction, yet were also themselves doing much of the abstracting, it had always been difficult for the NFU and CLA to secure effective action on this issue, but in 1992 the NRA acted on it by demanding that the water companies reduce their levels of abstraction in forty rivers where the problem was most pressing. This measure met with the wholehearted support of the CLA, in particular, for many private landowners use the rivers on their land for fishing and other pursuits.

The shift to a more formal and bureaucratic system of management and regulation since 1989 has, however, caused farmers and landowners some problems in other areas of the NRA's activities, and this is nowhere clearer than in control of pollution, where the NRA is increasingly being seen by farmers, in particular, as a punitive enforcement agency. The CLA told us, for example:

> The farmer knows that when the NRA man comes he's got a summons in his back pocket. You see an NRA van park on your land and you think, 'Oh God!' . . . The relation between us and the NRA is a bit difficult on this issue of pollution.

Similarly, the NFU confirmed that:

> The NRA is a much more effective enforcement agency than the water authorities were, so that's not necessarily a good thing for farmers. The water authorities were polluters and this inhibited them from prosecuting others for pollution. The number of prosecutions of farmers has risen.

In fact, the rate of prosecutions brought on pollution charges has escalated fairly dramatically since the NRA took over responsibility for river management from the former RWAs, and it is not only farmers who have been targeted. In its first full year of operation the NRA brought 309 successful prosecutions for pollution, and in 1990–1 this figure rose to 484 and resulted in fines totalling over £400,000. Included in this list of polluters were 17 cases brought against the water PLCs themselves (National Rivers Authority, *Annual Report and Accounts*, 1991). Figures on prosecution rates before 1989 are difficult to compile, although the NRA itself claimed in its first *Annual Report and Accounts* (1990, p. 18) that 'enforcement activity has increased significantly compared with previous years', and this would seem to be borne out by statistics for by far the largest of the RWAs, Thames Water, which in 1988 brought only 32 prosecutions, an unspecified number of which were successful (*The Spectator*, 1 April 1989, p. 13).

This increase in the rate of prosecutions is viewed critically in some quarters, not least by the CLA, which feels that the new drive against farm pollution is threatening some of its members with bankruptcy: 'Of course pollution is a problem, but my fear is they're being far too restrictive without bringing common sense to bear . . . I fear the NRA at the end of the day may force people out of business.' According to the CLA, the NRA's intention is to turn every livestock and dairy farm into a sealed unit so that no slurry or silage can seep out into the water system. The cost of this is likely to prove prohibitive for some farmers, who will therefore end up being prosecuted and going out of business.

This sort of complaint about the NRA's stringency on pollution control is echoed by the water companies, who now find their own practices being regulated by an independent body for the first time since 1974. Michael Carney of the Water Services Association (the organization representing the old statutory water companies) spoke for many in the industry when he recently argued that the NRA is pursuing unnecessarily high standards of river purity and that the cost of compliance far exceeds the marginal improvement in environmental quality which is likely to be achieved (Carney 1992).

Carney's complaint was essentially that a rising level of prosecutions is too easily taken by the NRA and by commentators in politics and the media as a yardstick against which to judge progress, and he suggests that the NRA is in danger of uncritically accepting the ideal standards proposed by environmental lobbyists such as Friends of the Earth while ignoring the practical question of balancing the costs of higher overall standards against the real benefits which they will bring. He believes that the NRA tends to err on the side of overregulation since it bears no responsibility for the escalating costs of compliance but may be criticized as too weak if it fails to pursue very high environmental standards, and he concludes that 'the costs of environmental improvement do not have a sufficiently large place in the NRA's thinking' (Carney 1992, p. 34). Most consumers, he says, will remain oblivious of reductions in nitrate levels in drinking water, improved bacteriological counts in bathing waters, or improvements in river quality, yet these things often entail huge expenditure.

Although important on its own terms, this argument is also significant for what it tells us about the way the water industry is now being regulated. Clearly a major agenda shift has taken place. Before 1989 there was little trace of complaints from farmers or landowners about the ways in which the RWAs were regulating their activities, and the overall impression was of a relationship grounded in a basic consensus. Since 1989, however, there is a sense that the concerns of farmers and landowners are no longer receiving the priority once accorded them and that other interests are now forcing the pace. In particular, environmentalists seem, since 1989 and the formation of the NRA, to have come in from the cold.

Land as a natural resource: environmentalists and amenity interests

Environmental neglect before 1989

Those concerned with the various environmental aspects of the water industry never were entirely without a voice under the old arrangements. Following the 1983 Act, many of the Regional Water Authorities established special consultative committees on which organizations concerned with amenity and nature conservation – among them the Council for the Protection of Rural England (CPRE), the Royal Society for the Protection of Birds (RSPB) and various local societies – were invited to sit. These new committees were not without influence, but they enabled these organizations to achieve only a limited impact through consultation rather than effective participation. Groups like the Nature Conservancy Council had a right to be told what the RWAs were planning, but the authorities themselves could (and often did) ignore any objections which might be raised against their proposals. Furthermore, the range of opinion included in the consultative procedures was fairly narrow. This was true both in the type of organizations which were consulted and in the range of issues on which they were consulted. The Nature Conservancy Council was generally seen by water authorities as the key corporate voice of the environmental and conservationist lobby, and this meant that less established (and perhaps rather more radical and 'awkward') groups were effectively sidelined or ignored altogether. This then had the effect, intentionally or otherwise, of restricting the agenda of consultation to a very narrow band of issues. While authorities might consult with the Nature Conservancy Council over questions of wildlife and its natural habitats, for example, they rarely consulted with anybody over issues such as the disposal of raw sewage into the sea, or the declining quality of rivers, or the level of nitrates and pesticides in drinking water. Indeed, information on such issues was often hard to find. For much of the 1970s and 1980s, environmental questions were reduced simply to issues of nature conservation.

By the time the industry was privatized in 1989, it had become obvious to many observers that years of relative neglect of the water environment had resulted in a major build-up of problems which would require huge sums of new investment to rectify. The problem of neglect had been widespread and serious in the days before 1974 when the industry had been under local authority management – the 1970 Jeger Report, for example, showed that half of all sewage treatment plants were substandard and overloaded and that 3,000 of them were failing to meet their discharge conditions (Rees and Synnott 1988). But the 1974 reorganization failed significantly to reverse the decline, especially when the RWAs came under the increasingly restrictive regime of government cash limits. As we saw in Chapter 2, real capital spending by water authorities was virtually halved between 1974 and 1985, and this was reflected in growing environmental problems such as nitrate and lead pollution of drinking water, fouling of bathing waters and beaches and widespread pollution of the river system. By the time they were privatized, most authorities were in breach of EC environmental standards.

In 1988, there were over 23,000 recorded incidents of water pollution (Gordon 1989). More than one-third of these were caused by industry, and one-fifth were caused by agriculture, but a further 20% of them were caused by water authorities themselves. The UK was, for example, the only country in the EC which was still disposing of raw sewage at sea, and this resulted in the failure of 23% of the designated bathing beaches in England and Wales to comply with the EC Bathing Water Directive (NRA, *Annual Report and Accounts*, 1991, p. 13). Pollution by the water industry was also the result of neglect and chronic underinvestment. There was a 22% failure rate at sewage treatment works, often resulting in pollution of rivers, and increasing numbers of sewage treatment plants were failing to meet their consent conditions (Rees and Synnott 1988). Although the 1974 Control of Pollution Act gave members of the public the right to sue water authorities for such failures, only one successful prosecution was ever brought (*The Independent*, 22 July 1988).

River quality, which improved during the 1960s and 1970s due mainly to the replacement of dirty industries by cleaner ones (*The Economist*, 25 February

1989), deteriorated during the 1980s. Despite well-publicized triumphs such as the reintroduction of salmon into the Thames, a report on freshwater quality by the standing Royal Commission on Environmental Pollution shows that river quality deteriorated between 1980 and 1990 and that there is now extensive pollution of aquifers, the underground sources of water (*The Times*, 11 June 1992). The NRA's map of river quality published in 1991 also showed a deterioration between 1985 and 1990, although it does indicate that 65% of river length in England and Wales is still of 'good' quality (class I) with a further 33% classified as 'fair' (cited in Carney 1992); these proportions compare favourably with the EC as a whole where only 39% of rivers are class I (*Financial Times*, 18 March 1989). Nevertheless, during the 1980s more lengths of rivers were downgraded than were upgraded with a net deterioration of 1200 km of rivers or more than 3% of the total (*The Economist* 25 February 1989).

The effect of privatization

We saw in Chapter 2 that government ministers attempted (belatedly) to represent water privatization as a 'green' policy designed to improve this overall situation by enabling the industry to raise the cash to tackle its environmental problems. Neither the environmental lobby nor public opinion believed that privatization would make things any better, however, and many argued that it would only make things worse.

There was, for example, widespread concern about the level of commitment which privatized water companies would show to conservation matters. In particular, the conservation lobby feared that the companies would try to raise revenue by selling or otherwise commercially exploiting environmentally sensitive land such as the sites around reservoirs – Thames Water, for example, was said to own a land bank worth 'several billion pounds' (*The Independent*, 21 February 1989). These fears were exacerbated by a report commissioned jointly by the CPRE and RSPB which concluded that both wildlife and landscape were endangered by the likelihood of the new PLCs deciding to sell off or otherwise exploit much of their 455,765 acres of land holdings. According to the report, these included some 300 sites (amounting to one-third of a million acres) of conservation or recreational value where the new PLCs might decide to promote schemes like timeshare log cabins and private boating (*The Independent*, 5 December 1988).

This worry about future exploitation and 'asset-stripping' was echoed by many other organizations including the ramblers, the National Trust, the Countryside Commission and water sports groups (see *The Independent*, 25 January 1989). It was also expressed in several of the interviews we conducted in 1989, including not only conservation groups, but also groups like the National Angling Council (concerned that low-value activities like angling could be displaced by higher-value ones such as speedboats) and the Nature Conservancy Council (worried that a privatized water industry might sacrifice conservation in order to intensify commercial exploitation of reservoirs).

Indeed, while the conservationists feared that the reservoirs might be turned over to anglers, the anglers were equally worried that fishing might be forced off reservoirs by a move to more lucrative recreational uses such as powerboats!

A less specific worry, expressed by the Labour Party and by pressure groups such as Friends of the Earth and echoed in public opinion surveys, was that privatization would result in less concern generally for the environment than had been shown by water authorities when they were in the public sector. According to this view, public authorities are more trustworthy than private ones, partly because they are likely to be motivated, at least in part, by a public service ethos, and partly because they are indirectly accountable to the public through the medium of elected government.

In our survey of members of the public, 55% of those questioned in 1989 agreed with the view that the environment was likely to suffer as a result of water privatization, while only 26% disagreed. Clearly, therefore, the government's claim that privatization was in part a 'green' strategy convinced few people, most of whom agreed at this time with the environmentalists and conservationists who saw it more as a threat than as a salvation.

As things have turned out, however, fears that privatization would result in a further decline in environmental standards appear to have been misplaced, and it was noticeable in our 1991 repeat interviews that this particular worry had diminished significantly among the general public in the eighteen months following the sale. The 1991 responses from our survey revealed that, while 55% of people had expected things to get worse as a result of privatization, only 28% now believed that this had happened.

This decline in public fears regarding the impact of privatization on the environment is consistent with evidence suggesting that the early concerns expressed by the environmental lobby were largely unfounded. There is, for a start, little sign that the companies have systematically been asset-stripping by selling off environmentally sensitive sites. There has, of course, been a depressed period in the property market and the rate of sales may therefore have been lower than might otherwise have occurred. Nevertheless, there were just 122 sales (worth some £35 million) in the financial year 1991–2, and 100 of these were simply transfers of land assets to different subsidiary companies within the same group (Ofwat 1992, p. 60).

Organizations which in the run-up to privatization expressed worries about the possible exploitation of land currently devoted to conservation or low-value recreational uses were by 1991 reasonably happy that their fears had appeared groundless. Our informant from the National Anglers Council told us in 1991: 'I feel much easier on this. The fears weren't justified.' And at what had been the Nature Conservancy Council, now English Nature, the verdict was much the same: 'Exploitation of reservoirs hasn't happened. A lot of the companies don't want people on their reservoirs. We've had no problem.'

Nor is there any evidence that environmental issues are being handled any less sensitively now than before privatization. If anything, the reverse seems to be true. Of course, all the PLCs are now engaged on a massive spending programme to improve water quality in rivers, at bathing beaches and through the tap. Southern Water, for example, makes much of the fact that it is now spending nearly twice as much to clean up the water system than it was when the industry was in public ownership (see, for example, *Southern Water News*, April 1992). This investment programme has, however, been forced upon the companies by the EC. What has changed as a direct result of privatization, however, is the stringency with which such standards are being enforced, and the professed concern of the companies themselves to be seen to be doing something to improve environmental quality. Both of these factors have been important in the move to improve environmental standards.

Before 1989, the RWAs both provided water and sewerage services and regulated them. The result was that regulation was generally lax. As we have seen, the water authorities themselves were responsible for 20% of all incidents of water pollution – mainly as a result of leakage from sewage treatment plants (Gordon 1989). They not only often condoned their own polluting activities, but were also on very shaky ground when it came to prosecuting farmers or industrialists for doing the same thing. The result was that environmental standards were often not enforced and the quality of the water environment continued to decline.

It was this confusion of responsibilities which government ministers claimed would be resolved by the removal of the utility functions into the private sector while retaining the regulatory functions in a new public sector agency, the NRA. The argument, simply put, was that the NRA would effectively enforce standards against both the water PLCs and other polluters in a way that the former RWAs had proved incapable of doing. Privatization was the means by which the water utility poachers could be separated from the water regulation gamekeeper, and the environment would benefit as a result.

At the time, this argument encountered considerable scepticism among the government's critics, and understandably so, for we saw in Chapter 2 that improved environmental standards were more an eleventh hour rationalization for the government's desire to privatize than an explanation of it. The NRA was forced upon the government; it did not choose it. Nevertheless, while improvement of the water environment through better regulation may not have been the original objective behind privatization, it has been one of its major benefits. Part of the evidence for this can be seen in the rate of prosecutions brought by the NRA since it was set up in 1989, for as we saw earlier, the NRA has been showing its teeth and has increased the number of actions brought against farmers and industrialists as well as initiating prosecutions for the first time against water companies themselves. But the NRA does much more than simply prosecute polluters.

One of its key responsibilities, in addition to issuing discharge consents and prosecuting those who break or disregard them, is to license abstraction from rivers. Licensing was previously in the hands of the RWAs which were, of course, themselves by far the largest volume abstractors. As we saw earlier, the NRA has attempted to improve river flows by reducing the amounts taken by water companies from rivers which are in danger of drying up. In this it has won the support of anglers and landowners as well as environmentalists. It also introduced in 1993 a national charging scheme for abstraction of water, and this has resulted in charges being levied on many private users who previously abstracted water without payment. This measure has, needless to say, upset groups like the CLA, many of whose members are now paying for abstraction licences for the first time, but it is likely to reduce the overall volume of water abstracted, particularly during drier parts of the year and in the most vulnerable parts of England and Wales since charges are heaviest in these cases.

The NRA's functions also cover land drainage and flood protection and its creation has therefore gone some way in undermining the hegemony previously exercised by farming interests through their domination of the previously autonomous regional and local land drainage committees. Interviewed in 1991, our informant at English Nature felt that the threats to wildlife posed by drainage of wetlands were now, as a result of the establishment of the NRA, much less worrying than before.

In addition, the NRA also has a responsibility for fisheries, navigation, conservation and recreation. Here it works by a code of practice agreed by the DoE at the time of privatization and designed to safeguard existing recreational uses while balancing them against the conservation of wildlife and its habitats and the need of the water PLCs to make a return on their assets. According to the National Anglers Council, this code is working well as regards the safeguarding of existing recreational uses. There has, for example, been no deterioration in fish stocks since privatization, nor have the water PLCs dramatically raised their charges (as was feared before 1989) to those using rivers or reservoirs for fishing or other leisure pursuits.

The NRA, then, has an overall responsibility for the management of the whole water environment, but unlike the RWAs before 1989, its regulatory and management role is not confused since it does not itself function as a major user of the resources for which it is responsible. The result is that environmental issues now receive a higher priority than before, while the infuence of farmers and landowners (as well as of the PLCs themselves) has been leavened by the increased significance accorded to environmental groups. As our English Nature informant put it:

> I don't like to say it, but I think it's been a great improvement over the previous system. One reason is that the water companies have got someone to control them now which they didn't have before . . . [Another is that] the NRA is more sympathetic to us than the RWAs were. We didn't have anyone nationally to talk to before.

Not only does the NRA appear more receptive to the environmental lobby than the RWAs tended to be, but the new water PLCs also seem more concerned to respond to environmental concerns than was the case with their predecessors. As private sector companies, it seems that they are more sensitive to criticisms than they were when they were in the public sector. This was again noted by our English Nature informant:

> Now they can say to their shareholders that it's bad publicity to be seen drying out rivers through overabstraction or polluting rivers from

sewage works. The water PLCs certainly seem to want to present a caring image towards the environment.

As we noted in Chapter 3, privatization was so unpopular, and public distrust of the new PLCs is so widespread, that the companies have had little choice but to do all they can to improve their public image. Privatization has raised the public profile of their activities and has therefore pushed environmental questions higher up their scale of priorities.

There is also a very real sense in which the water companies themselves have a vested interest in improving the water environment. As Michael Carney (1992) of the Water Services Association points out, cleaner rivers mean that the industry has to spend less time and money on purifying the water which it supplies to its customers. Furthermore, environmental improvements mean an expansion of business for the companies with increased turnover and increased investment, and the pricing regulations under which they operate mean that the companies can cover these costs through increased charges without losing customers. Seen in this way, there is little reason for believing that a private water industry will be any less assiduous in raising environmental quality than a public one.

Summarizing all of this, we can conclude that nature conservation is now accorded a higher priority than before 1989, that the activities of the water industry in overabstracting or polluting rivers are now much more closely monitored and tightly controlled, that pollution by other users is also now more stringently regulated, that recreational users are no worse off than before, and that the environmental lobby has strengthened its position relative to that of producer groups like the NFU and CLA.

It is possible, of course, that all of this could have been achieved by reforming the water industry rather than privatizing it, but it would probably have been much more difficult to achieve. The establishment of the NRA has been crucial, but such a radical reform might have been politically impossible in the absence of privatization, for most water professionals were strongly committed to retaining the 1974 principle of integrated river basin management, and the strength of opposition by the RWA chairmen to splitting their regulatory powers from their utility functions would have been even more difficult to counter without the move into private ownership. Even if the NRA could have been established while leaving the rest of the industry in public ownership, there is also the lingering doubt whether a public sector regulator would have pursued its objectives quite as keenly against other public sector agencies as it has done against the private sector water PLCs which enjoy little public sympathy and which remain so acutely concerned about their corporate image. It is difficult to believe that the Treasury would happily have sanctioned the expenditure of millions of pounds of public money to meet conditions imposed by a public sector NRA on a public sector water industry.

These considerations lead us to conclude that the success of the NRA must be attributed at least in part to the privatization of the rest of the industry, for while the 1989 privatization cannot alone take the credit for the gradual improvement in environmental quality which has now been set in motion, it is unlikely that it could have been achieved to an equivalent extent without it.

Organized labour: the marginalization of the trade unions

We saw in Chapter 1 that the nationalized industries and public services were by the 1970s the most heavily unionized sectors of the British economy. The water industry was no exception. Although the closed-shop agreement in the industry was terminated in 1983, union membership remained high. At the time of privatization, the pathfinder prospectus estimated that 82% of manual workers (represented variously by the GMB, TGWU, NUPE, CSEU and building unions) and 76% of white-collar grades (represented by NALGO, MATSA, NUPE and FUMPO) belonged to trade unions.

According to its left-wing critics, privatization is a strategy for 'scrapping existing working arrangements [and] getting rid of workplace trade union organisation' (Whitfield 1983, p. 55). This threat to trade unions may materialize in any of three ways. First, company restructuring and diversification in the wake of privatization can dilute the density of union membership. Second, and related to this, union negotiating rights may be curtailed or even withdrawn as a result of a move from national to local wage determination. And third, unions may be bypassed as employers encourage employees to enter personal contracts in which pay reflects individual performance indicators.

Company restructuring

We saw in Chapter 3 that the 'core' activities of the water PLCs are tightly regulated by Ofwat, and that although returns on the core water and sewage businesses have exceeded expectations in the early years following privatization, the scope for expanding profits on the basis of efficiency gains in the core activities alone is clearly limited. Activities outside of the 'core' are, however, unregulated, and this has prompted the water PLCs both to diversify into new areas (see Chapter 2), and to reorganize their existing functions in order to create autonomous enterprises or 'profit centres' distinct from their regulated 'core' actitivies. For example, Southern Water has established separate enterprises for engineering design, laboratory analysis, waste management, vehicles and plant, and systems technology, and these all now function independently of the 'core' business, selling their services back to the 'core' while also competing for business elsewhere.

The significance for the trade unions of this simultaneous process of diversification and internal reorganization is that many of these new activities and 'profit centres' are only weakly unionized or even not at all. Within the core business there is as yet little sign of any major erosion of membership, for in our sample of 107 employees, trade union membership remained virtually unchanged at around 82% between 1989 and 1991. Only two of our interviewees had left their union over this period, and both of these were managers. Since privatization, however, there has been a marked decrease in union density in the companies as a whole: diversification and the creation of non-regulated subsidiaries have increased the total number of employees by 20%, many of whom are non-unionized. At Southern Water, for example, total employee numbers rose by something like 25% between 1989 and 1992, but union density in the company fell during this same period from 75% to 62% (company figures). Corporate restructuring and diversification have therefore created the possibility for different conditions and pay rates to be established within different profit centres within the same company, and in some of these centres the unions have effectively been sidelined.

Local-level bargaining

The second trend which has weakened union power within the industry has been the move away from national-level bargaining. Before privatization, pay and conditions would be settled nationally within three negotiating bodies which brought together representatives of the ten Regional Water Authorities, the twenty-nine statutory water companies and all of the different unions in the industry. Although the 1983 Water Act went some way towards decentralizing this process, nearly all negotiation prior to 1989 was still done through these three national joint councils which between them determined pay rates, the grade structure, hours of work, overtime rates, standby and callout payments, notice periods, holidays, sick leave, and provisions governing arbitration procedures and union recognition for the entire industry (see *IRS Employment Trends*, no. 516, July 1992).

In the run-up to privatization, however, the ten water authorities, led by Thames Water, began to distance themselves from this national bargaining system, and, national-level bargaining has now been abandoned throughout the industry with the result that the different companies can and do now negotiate different pay rates and conditions.

In most cases, the national system has been replaced by 'single-table negotiations' within individual companies. Single-table bargaining means that, where there is more than one union representing workers, they negotiate together rather than individually with the company. All the recognized unions in a company are therefore obliged to negotiate as a single bargaining unit representing all their members. Such a system shifts 'the responsibility for reconciling the different interests within a workforce from management to unions' (*IRS Employment Trends*, no. 463, May 1990, p. 5) and makes it difficult for the unions to maintain comparability across different companies. As an official at NALGO head office told us: 'National bargaining was controllable, but now it's difficult pulling it all together.'

By 1993, seven of the water PLCs had moved towards single-table bargaining. In four of them (Welsh, Northumbrian, Yorkshire and Thames), a radical attempt has been made to sweep away the old demarcations between manual and non-manual staff so as to enable a single set of negotiations to cover all employees in just one forum. Thames Water has gone furthest in this by abolishing altogether the demarcation between 'manual', 'staff' and 'craft' grades. The working week for blue-collar workers has been reduced to bring it into line with that of higher grades, and the company has put everybody on a basic salary plus performance-related pay (*The Times*, 2 December 1990). All negotiations at Thames are now done through a single company council. Throughout the industry there is now a commitment to reduce the traditional 38-hour week worked by 'manual' and 'craft' employees to the 37 hours worked by 'staff'.

There are three main reasons why these companies have been keen to move to single-table bargaining. First, it enables harmonization of the terms and conditions of both manual and non-manual grades. This then allows a single pay and grading structure to be established covering all employees and makes it easier to move towards a situation where eventually manual and non-manual staff can be represented by a single union. Second, it allows negotiations to be conducted more efficiently. As a personnel officer at Southern Water told us: 'We only see the unions once a year now.' Third, by blurring the boundaries between manual and non-manual workers, it creates the possibility of developing a more flexible workforce while reducing the likelihood of demarcation disputes (Margisson and Sisson 1990).

The unions have accepted these changes simply because they are preferable to the alternative of single-union agreements or total derecognition. As the NALGO representative at Southern Water put it: 'Single-table bargaining is the only way forward for us. It means that in a situation where we are being marginalized we at least have some guaranteed input.' Yet single-table bargaining may simply prove to be a stepping-stone to single-union agreements, for once separate negotiations for different categories of employee have gone, and the traditional demarcations between different groups of workers have disappeared, it is but a short step to withdrawing recognition altogether from the smaller or weaker unions which no longer have any specific role to play within negotiations.

There are signs already that this is beginning to happen. At Northumbrian Water, NALGO acts as the sole union representative on the company council which negotiates pay and conditions, while the other seven unions have not been given a seat. At Welsh Water, NUPE is no longer recognized, and Yorkshire Water no longer negotiates with the TGWU and UCATT. Wessex Water has recently announced that it does not see Unison (the new merged union combining COHSE, NALGO and NUPE) as appropriate and has therefore decided to withhold recognition. There is, as our NALGO informant accepted, a 'growing move to derecognize trade unions in the water industry'.

Personalized pay deals

The third development which has threatened the unions has been the move towards personal contracts and peformance-related pay (PRP). By 1993, at least eight of the water PLCs had moved towards some form of PRP scheme for some members of staff, although such schemes are still uncommon outside white-collar grades.

The significance of these schemes for the unions is that they shift the determination of pay from a collective to an individual level and minimize the role that unions can play. At Southern Water, for example, the local NALGO representative plus one steward are allowed what are known as 'slot discussions' with management where they can make submissions regarding the system of rewards under PRP, but their negotiating role has been drastically undermined by this change. As the Employee Relations Manager at the company explained in a written statement to us, it has 'reduced the necessity for trade union involvement'. At some other water PLCs, union involvement has been ruled out altogether – South West Water, for example, does not permit the unions any role in negotiating PRP schemes.

Among managerial grades, therefore, unionization in the water industry is now effectively dead. Many managers are now perfectly happy to negotiate their own terms. As one manager at North West Water told us:

I feel confident now that I can negotiate with my boss what are the appropriate pay and conditions for me. So I don't really feel that I need to rely on the unions anymore to sort this out for me. I much prefer the personal, one-to-one approach to negotiating.

Even for those who still have reservations, union membership is becoming increasingly inappropriate. As a middle manager at Southern Water explained:

I've always believed in unionism, but I'm having to question the efficacy of staying in the union for my career's sake. I feel that it is now seen as more appropriate for me to leave, which means I probably will.

It remains to be seen whether the extension of PRP to lower grades will have the same result. We have seen that personal contracts have so far been confined to white-collar 'staff', but this is changing. Severn Trent Water, for example, is planning to move to some form of performance assessment for craft and manual employees, and there is little doubt that in the future other water PLCs will follow suit. Among these lower grades, commitment to the principle of trade unionism remains strong at present. In our survey of employees, around two-thirds of manual, clerical and LMS grades agreed in 1989 with a statement that trade unions are an 'essential safeguard' for employees, and this proportion had not changed when they were reinterviewed in 1991. Taken together with the evidence in Chapter 4 of a growing polarization of attitudes between higher and lower grades, this suggests that the unions may still find a role to play in representing lower-grade employees for some time to come.

The three developments we have reviewed in this section nevertheless indicate that the role for the trade unions in the privatized water industry has declined sharply and is likely to become increasingly marginal as time goes on. The unions themselves are clearly aware of this – an official at NALGO head office told us, for example, that the union could 'no longer take the membership for granted' – and they have responded by trying to change their image and the basis of their appeal by emphasizing benefits of membership such as insurance services, personal loans and financial advice. Like Sapper

(1991), however, we are sceptical about the effectiveness of these services in holding or recruiting members, for we found no evidence from our sample of employees that they were particularly interested in these services, nor even that they knew that they existed. The employees we interviewed (and particularly the blue-collar workers) were far more concerned about the ability of the union to secure a good pay rate and conditions of service, yet, as we have seen, it is precisely here that the unions are losing many of their traditional functions.

Capital: why the CBI did not want water privatized

We saw in Chapter 2 that the Confederation of British Industry, the largest single pressure group in Britain representing the interests of industrial capital, played a key role in 1986 in opposing the government's original plans for privatizing the water industry. Its concern at that time was mainly that private sector water companies should not be allowed to retain the regulatory powers enjoyed by the RWAs, since this would result in one capitalist firm having the right to regulate another. Having won this battle, the CBI then fell silent as the government changed its plans and sold off the water utilities after first transferring their regulatory powers to the new NRA.

Its silence, however, did not signify consent. In 1989, just three months before it finally happened, the CBI was still unhappy about the decision to privatize water. As one CBI officer told us:

> The CBI can't oppose the principle of private industry – there's no way we could oppose water privatisation. Yet most of those in industry who deal with the water industry would have said 'no'. Even today CBI members wouldn't want water in the private sector. Our members don't mind being at the hands of a public monopoly, but they don't want to be at the mercy of a private monopoly. They know, being in the private sector themselves, how the profit motive can work.

Even in 1991, CBI officers still privately believed that the privatization was misjudged: 'Given the choice, companies would still rather water was in the public sector.'

Why should an organization committed to the defence and advancement of private enterprise be so unhappy about this particular privatization? The answer is that capitalist enterprises have lost money as a result of water privatization.

The amount which any given industrial user pays for its water and sewage services is determined by a standing charge, which varies according to the size of supply pipe, plus a metered charge for the volume of water used. These water charges have been rising steeply since privatization. The average charge to industrial users in the ten regions covered by the privatized water companies rose by 13.4% (a 5.7% real increase) in the first year of privatization, by 16.9% (7.2% real) in the second, and by 8.9% (4.5% real) in the third (figures computed from CRI 1992, Table 3.9). For some major users, this represents a significant increase in production costs, and the compound effects over the next ten years or so will be substantial for many of these companies. This is already beginning to cause friction. As the deputy chairman of Thames Water has recently admitted:

> We are getting more problems with our large customers . . . They are giving us a very hard time indeed because for them the amounts of money are really quite significant and they are in a recession and times are hard, and there the dialogues do get very difficult indeed.
>
> (Harper 1992, pp. 116–17)

The growing restlessness of big capitalist enterprises is reflected in the results of a 1991 survey of the 200 biggest users of water, gas and electricity which found 87% opposition to the 'RPI − *x*' price regulation formula and which showed even greater dissatisfaction with regulation of water prices than with the gas and electricity price regimes (*The Times*, 2 July 1991). As the CBI told us on our second visit in 1991: 'Water has become more of an issue because the charges are going up, therefore, it's more of a cost to industry.'

Of course, the CBI knows, and most major companies know, that the key reason for water price rises lies in the major investment programme now being undertaken in the water industry. The complaint, however, is that a major part of the cost of this is being borne by other industries. Had water remained in the public sector, the cost of this programme would have fallen primarily on individual taxpayers, not on private sector business. By privatizing it, an avowedly pro-business Conservative government ensured that big industrial users would pay a larger proportion of the total cost.

Perhaps because the Conservatives did not want to admit to harming private enterprise, and the Labour opposition did not wish to draw the attention of the public to the fact that part of its tax burden was being transferred on to big companies, this was an implication of the privatization which went little noticed at the time. It was, however, picked up in a particularly hostile editorial in *The Spectator* (12 August 1989, p. 5):

> What is happening, albeit in a violent fashion, is that all the costs of the business are being transferred to the price of the product, rather than being partly swallowed up in general taxation . . . What this means is that the individual consumer is, relatively, the gainer in the privatisation of water and electricity, at the expense of the industrial user. Because, for as long as the cost of such industries was partly recovered through general taxation, the general public, rather than industry (relative to its use of water and power a tiny contributor to the Exchequer) were the fall guys. This effect of water and electricity privatisation has gone completely unnoticed.

It was also picked up by the CBI, which is precisely why the organization representing private enterprise in Britain would have preferred water to remain in public ownership. As a CBI officer explained in 1991:

> It's true that we didn't want privatization, mainly because it's exposed our members to much higher charges than when it was a public

monopoly. If you're meeting improved environmental standards and it's a public monopoly then the government has to foot the bill. If it's a private company, all they can do is pass it on to the customer rather than share it with the taxpayers.

This logic provides a fascinating illustration of an argument developed forcibly by a number of Marxist political theorists in the 1970s. Developing Marx's own characterization of the bourgeois state as an 'ideal collective capitalist', writers like Nicos Poulantzas (1973) argued that the capitalist state may aid capital accumulation in the economy as a whole by socializing some of the 'running costs' of enterprises so as to boost their margins of profitability. Policies such as nationalization of basic industries, which on the face of things appear antithetical to the development of capitalism, can therefore turn out to be quite 'functional' or even 'indispensable' for the continued survival of a strong capitalist sector.

But if nationalization socializes some of the costs of private enterprise and thereby boosts profitability, then it would seem to follow that privatization might well transfer these same costs back to private sector producers and therefore depress profitability. This does seem to have been the case with water privatization, where a government intent on supporting capital accumulation in the private sector might have been better advised to retain ownership of an industry requiring a massive injection of new capital which was going to entail increased charges to other industries. In the late 1980s, the unsentimental analysts at the CBI saw the force of this argument quite clearly, but the government had other fish to fry and chose to ignore them.

The CBI was not entirely ignored, however. The organization itself claims that the massive debt write-off of £5 billion before privatization was the product of its lobbying: 'It is said that people would not have bought shares if the debts [had not been] written off, but they would have done. All that would have happened is that the water companies would have raised their charges to us' (CBI interview in 1991). In other words, the debt write-off prevented even higher charges being levied on industrial water users to service interest payments. Whether or not the CBI's claim to have influenced the government over this is valid is impossible to judge (and virtually every pressure group we contacted made some claim to have fundamentally altered the privatization White Paper), but it certainly is the case that the write-off saved the rest of industry a lot of money over the medium term.

Like the NFU and the CLA, the CBI was certainly an effective lobbyist in the pre-privatization water industry. My 1984 study of Southern Water found that, like the NFU, the CBI was well organized at regional level and managed to maintain regular liaison with the authority on both a formal and informal basis. As a CBI informant at the time put it: 'We influence their ideas and they influence ours – in the nicest possible way. There's nothing underhand about it' (quoted in Saunders 1984). And, of course, the CBI enjoyed representation on the Consumer Consultative Committees, although it did not regard these as important channels of communication.

These arrangements enabled the CBI to influence crucial decisions in areas like water charges and pollution control. Metering agreements at Southern Water, for example, were completely renegotiated with the CBI in 1976, despite the authority's initial reluctance to make any changes. Similarly on pollution controls, the two sides came to 'practical compromises' on levels of permissible chemical effluent and other issues concerning waste disposal. As my CBI informant put it in 1984: 'Certain requirements were too stringent . . . You have legislation which becomes impossible and then you have . . . a compromise which may be outside the terms of the legislation itself.'

With privatization, this situation has changed significantly. The companies can still discuss charges, although even here Ofwat has made clear its disapproval of discounts for large users and is pushing for a common tariff (a policy which the national CBI supports). On pollution controls, the CBI has now to deal with the NRA. The CBI's regional Water Liaison Committees have been redefined as environmental committees and they now meet with the regional officers of the NRA approximately three times a year. Our CBI informant described relations as 'excellent – very frank and constructive'. In addition, CBI representatives sit on the Ofwat Customer Services Committees in each region (which are described as 'more purposeful' than the old Consumer Consultative Committees) and on the NRA Regional Rivers Advisory Committees.

The biggest change noted by the CBI is that enforcement (for example, on industrial discharge consents) has become much more vigorous now that responsibility for it has passed to the NRA. As with the farmers and the landowners, so, too, with the industrialists, the NRA is imposing standards over which the RWAs had been much more casual: 'The NRA is very professional, easy to talk to, but at the end of the day it will enforce to the limit' (CBI interview in 1991). The compromises of 1984 are, therefore, a thing of the past. The CBI claims to favour this rigorous enforcement policy since it enables the best companies to prosper.

The CBI maintains that its relations with the different parts of the water industry, and particularly with the NRA, are as good after privatization as they ever were before. This is quite possibly the case. But it is also undeniably the case that relations have become more formal. This is partly because of the approach taken by the NRA itself which is willing to talk but seems unwilling to engage in the sorts of negotiations and compromise which the RWAs got into. And it is partly because the CBI has now to organize liaison across three bodies in each region – the NRA, Ofwat and the PLCs – rather than just one. The 'personal rapport' mentioned by my CBI informant in the 1984 interview seems much less in evidence in the changed circumstances of 1991.

Conclusion

Privatization has created clear winners and losers among the various organizations with an interest in the water industry. The biggest winners have been environmentalist interests, which have found an effective champion for their cause in the NRA. The biggest losers have been the trade unions within the industry itself.

Through changes such as the introduction of performance-related pay, the move to single-table bargaining and the growth of subsidiary operations which are only weakly unionized, if at all, the trade unions have been most severely affected by privatization. In 1979, the water industry was a bastion of public sector union strength. Today, the unions are becoming increasingly marginalized. In its impact on the trade unions, if nowhere else, the government's privatization strategy does seem to have hit its target.

The key new player in the water industry since 1989 has been the NRA. It has so far successfully avoided 'regulatory capture' by any of the powerful producer interests with which it deals. It has also replaced the rather cosy relations which existed between the RWAs and groups like the NFU, the CLA and the CBI with a more formal and rigorous climate of enforcement and regulation of environmental standards. Despite initial wariness, the environmental lobby has been pleasantly surprised by the effects of this change, and there is clear evidence that privatization is leading to improvements in the water environment as government ministers in 1989 claimed it would.

The main reason for this success is that government regulation has become effective, perhaps for the first time. The history of the water industry clearly demonstrates not only that private companies (even big and powerful companies which enjoy effective monopolies) can be regulated effectively by state agencies, but also that state agencies seem particularly bad at regulating themselves. Whatever else one thinks about the benefits and costs of water privatization, the division which it forced between those who provide the water and those who regulate its use must count as an unambiguous bonus.

6　The voters

Since the privatization programme began in 1980, the government has developed many different arguments to support it, but there is one which is rarely mentioned by ministers yet which has played a crucial role in sustaining Conservative enthusiasm for continued sales. Like the policy of selling council houses to sitting tenants, the offer of shares in newly privatized companies is believed by most Conservatives (and, indeed, by most of their political opponents) to be a vote winner.

Journalists and academics have generally concurred with this assessment. Writing of the third Thatcher administration, for example, the *Financial Times* claimed that 'Privatisation has become one of the strongest sources of its political appeal' (quoted in Pirie 1988, p. 16). Writing for an Australian audience, Kenneth Wiltshire (1987, p. 108) has argued that 'a whole army of little capitalists' has been created in Britain by the privatization programme and that this has helped the Conservatives to remain in office. And pointing to the windfall gains made by most buyers in privatization issues, David Marsh (1990, p. 25) believes that 'Those who have benefited from the "yuppy football pools" . . . have often rewarded the Conservatives with a vote'.

Such arguments have been used to help explain why the Labour Party lost an unprecedented four consecutive general elections between 1979 and 1992. In his review of Labour's 1987 general election defeat (*The Independent*, 17 June 1987), for example, Peter Jenkins was in no doubt that the spread of share ownership was playing a significant part in eroding Labour's traditional support base:

> The old class religion has lost its appeal to the home-owning working classes, even more so to the share-owning working classes. . . . Working class shareholders may be to 1992 what working class home-owners proved to be to 1987 and 1983.

Similarly, the Labour MP, Frank Field, clearly believed that Labour's heavy defeat in 1987 owed much to the spread of share ownership: 'Canvassing in the last general election taught me just how significantly a small shareholding changes attitudes. Owners of a two hundred pounds British Telecom stake spoke as if they were close relatives of the Duke of Westminster' (*Sunday Times* 16 April 1989).

Arguments like these have become widely accepted, but in some respects the belief that privatization has boosted electoral support for the Conservatives seems implausible. We know, for example, that the spread of home ownership has had little effect on political alignments (see Saunders 1990), yet the purchase of a house is surely more likely to influence people's voting patterns than the purchase of a few shares in a privatization issue. It seems unlikely that small-scale share purchasing could be significant enough to overturn a lifetime of political socialization. We also know that privatization was never very popular with the electorate, and was by the late 1980s distinctly unpopular, in which case it is difficult to understand how this policy could have won the Conservative Party votes.

In this chapter we shall see that privatization has had some impact on voting patterns but that most of the commentators writing on this issue have failed to understand how or why this has happened and have therefore failed to recognize why it is unlikely to persist in the future.

The unpopularity of privatization

Following its wave of nationalizations after the war, the Labour Party's support for further nationalization won little public support throughout the 1950s, 1960s and 1970s. Figures cited by McAllister and Studlar (1989) indicate that support for more nationalization peaked at 25% in 1966 but fell to half that level during the 1970s. Public support for what was then termed 'denationalization' grew correspondingly over the same period, from just 19% in 1966 to 37% on the eve of Margaret Thatcher's first general election victory in 1979.

As the 'denationalization' or privatization programme proceeded through the 1980s, however, so public support for it dwindled. Data from the *British Social Attitudes Survey* (Jowell and Witherspoon 1985), the 1983 election survey (Heath *et al.* 1985) and from MORI (see Figure 6.1) all indicate that privatization remained popular with 40% or more of electors for as long as the government did not actually sell anything of any consequence. But during the government's second term, when it sold BT and British Gas, the pattern began to change, and, by the 1987 election, support for further privatization was down to 30% according to the *British Social Attitudes Survey* (Jowell, Witherspoon and Brook 1988). Ever since then, the government has lacked any marked popular support for its privatization programme. By the government's third term, when basic utility industries like water and electricity were being sold, the programme was proceeding in the face of considerable public opposition, and by the end of the decade, the numbers favouring further privatization were overtaken by those favouring more nationalization (see Figure 6.1).

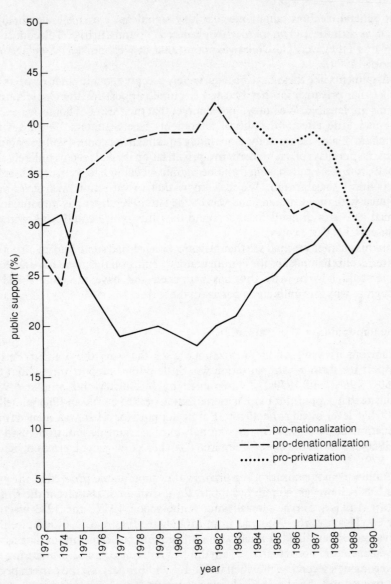

Figure 6.1   Support for nationalization, denationalization and privatization 1973–90

Source   MORI (personal communication). Questions on denationalization no longer asked after 1988; questions on privatization asked from 1984

This lack of public support for privatization by the end of the 1980s was reflected in our survey. In September 1989, less than a quarter of our respondents supported government privatization policies, while 57% opposed them; eighteen months later, opposition was still marked, with 52% of people still against privatization and just 30% in favour. Not surprisingly, people's attitudes to privatization varied according to their occupational class. While 37% of those in classes A and B (professional, administrative and managerial employees) supported it, this was true of only 26% of those in class C1 (routine white-collar workers) and 28% of those in class C2 (skilled manual workers), and in classes D and E support was down as low as 14% (differences significant at 0.003 confidence level). Support also varied markedly between people supporting different political parties. Fifty per cent of Conservative supporters in our sample supported privatization, but this was true of only 13% of Liberals and just 3% of Labour supporters.

At the June 1987 general election, the Conservative manifesto promised to privatize both the water and electricity industries. These, however, were the most unpopular privatizations of all. Even at the time of the election, most voters did not care for the idea – an opinion poll carried out by MORI (1988) reported that 56% of voters opposed electricity privatization with just 34% in favour, and that 59% opposed the privatization of water, with only 30% supporting it. The Conservatives won that election with a majority of over 100 seats and went on to claim a mandate for electricity and water privatization, but it is clear that there never was much public support for these particular sales, and as time went on, so opposition to them grew even greater. Water privatization, in particular, was intensely unpopular with the electorate.

Just three months before water was sold, 76% of the respondents in our (reweighted) survey opposed the policy (59% of them 'strongly'), while just 10% supported it. These sorts of figures were reproduced in opinion polls throughout the run-up to privatization. In December 1988, eighteen months after the election and a year before the water authorities were finally sold, a MORI poll found that 75% of voters were opposed to water privatization, with just 15% in favour. Support for the policy had halved since the general election, presumably because of the well-publicized problems which increasingly bedevilled the sale, and even among Conservative voters only 31% approved of the sale, with 57% against it (*Sunday Times*, 4 December 1988).

Nothing the government did could shift public opinion on this issue, and polls throughout 1989 continued to report similar levels of opposition. At the European Parliament elections, a strong Labour showing and an unprecedented level of support for the Green Party were widely interpreted as in part an expression of opposition to the water sale, and at Westminster a Conservative MP warned that the policy would prove an 'electoral disaster' at the next general election (*The Independent*, 5 July 1989). As time passed, opinion polls continued to report high levels of public resistance to the sale (in July a Harris poll in *The Observer* reported opposition at 79%) and some influential figures began to worry about what they saw as a 'public relations' problem. In March 1989, for example, the chairman of Thames Water, Roy Watts, criticized the government for its failure adequately to make the case for privatization, and his comments were echoed by the Prime Minister, who told a Conservative local government conference that 'Privatisation of water has not been handled well' (*The Independent*, 6 March 1989; see also *Financial Times*, 6

Table 6.1   Reasons for opposing privatization in general and water privatization in particular

	Privatization				Water privatization			
	1989		1991		1989		1991	
	No.	%	No.	%	No.	%	No.	%
Essential service	148	31	122	28	235	38	191	38
Prices will rise	109	23	112	26	141	23	85	17
Belongs to us all	111	23	88	20	143	23	77	15
Profits come first	59	12	68	16	88	14	58	12
Quality will fall	0	0	0	0	75	12	35	7
Monopoly	0	0	0	0	33	5	28	6
Environment suffers	0	0	0	0	26	4	4	1
Reduces efficiency	48	10	34	8	0	0	0	0
Total opposed	473	57	435	52	624	76	497	61

Source   Survey (reweighted data). Percentages are of respondents opposed. Responses unprompted (not all opponents gave reasons and some gave more than one).

March 1989). The evidence suggests, however, that the level of opposition to water privatization had little to do with poor public relations, but rather reflected some very basic and widely held sentiments which were particularly offended by this specific sale. As Table 6.1 indicates, a general public unease about privatization seems to have been concentrated and focused by the privatization of water.

Table 6.1 makes clear, first of all, why it is that opposition to privatization grew from the mid-1980s onwards. As the table shows, the main reason why people oppose privatization is their feeling that essential services should remain in the public sector, but from the mid-1980s on, it was precisely the essential core utility industries like electricity and water which were targeted for sale. Given that water is the most essential of all services, it is not surprising that it became the most unpopular of all privatizations and it is doubtful whether any public relations campaign could have done much about this deeply rooted and essentially ethical objection to the sale. As Gordon (1989, p. 141) suggests, there is a widespread 'public perception that water is a common need which no special interest should be allowed to exploit for private gain'.

Three other reasons were also commonly cited by our respondents to explain their general antipathy towards privatization. First, there was a widespread belief that privatization increases prices. Because privatized industries have to pay dividends to their shareholders, many people reason that they would have to charge higher prices than nationalized industries which have no share-holders. The *New Statesman and Society* (15 July 1988) estimated, for example, that the privatized water companies would have to raise prices to cover £400 million in dividend payments and another £350 million in corporation tax. This argument, however, ignored any efficiency gains which might accrue as a result of privatization, and it also ignored the fact that even in the public sector these industries were expected to show a rate of return on capital equivalent to that which they would have to earn were they in the private sector. Nevertheless, justified or not, the fear that privatization would create a price hike was certainly common, and nearly a quarter of those of our respondents who opposed the sale in 1989 cited increased prices as their reason.

Linked to this concern about prices was the further belief among many opponents of privatization that privatized companies would put profit considerations above all others to the detriment of their customers and other users (an argument considered in Chapter 3). Around one in eight of those of our respondents who were against privatization gave this distrust of the profit motive as their reason, and the same argument was applied by a similar percentage of people to explain their opposition to the sale of water.

The final major factor explaining public hostility to privatization was the view held by between a fifth and a quarter of opponents that they already owned these industries and that it was therefore wrong for the government to sell them. As the TUC (1985, p. 10) put it:

> One of the Government's more amazing claims for privatisation is that it extends public ownership by selling shares in concerns to 'the public'. In fact, of course, the public already owned all the enterprises con-cerned . . . Privatisation simply takes away most people's stake in an organisation like British Telecom and hands it to those willing and able to buy shares in something they already owned.

The same argument surfaced again during the water sell-off, when the Labour Party and trades unions, in particular, suggested, in the words of a Water Industry Unions Committee leaflet, that: 'You have already paid for and own the industry. It's nonsense for the government to talk of selling it back to the public.'

Theoretically, this argument can be and has been refuted. Property ownership consists of three crucial rights – the right to control, benefit and alienate – but members of the public enjoy none of these in the case of public sector industries. As Pirie (1988) argues, individual citizens can hardly be said to have enjoyed common ownership of enterprises like the British Gas Corporation or the Southern Water Authority when they had no control over company decision-making (the right of control), they received no dividend from company profits (the right of benefit), and there was no way in which they could dispose of their share by selling it or giving it away (the right of alienation). The argument nevertheless retained considerable ideological force, and in the specific case of water privatization it was reinforced by the view that water, as a 'natural' resource, belonged naturally to everybody.

There was something about selling water which people found morally disturbing, and it had to do with the idea that property rights cannot legitimately be claimed in respect of natural resources which are 'God-given'.

Of course what was being offered for sale in the privatization of the water authorities was not God-given water, but was rather the humanly constructed pumping stations, pipes, purification plants and sewage farms which made up the industry. Nevertheless, the concern lingered that this was in some way a morally illegitimate sale. As Angela Lambert wrote in *The Independent* (4 February 1989):

> Even more than gas and electricity, it [water] is seen as a primal natural resource, and indignation is aroused by the thought of anyone claiming to 'own' what naturally springs (or falls, or droppeth as the gentle rain from heaven) and thus belongs to everyone, or no one.

John Locke could not have put it better.

Essentially, water was an unpopular privatization because it exemplified the fundamental misgivings which many members of the public had about privatization as a whole. The public did not favour privatizing essential services, and water was the most essential service of all. The public feared that privatized companies would push up prices, and in the case of water even the government accepted that charges were going to have to increase. And at least some members of the public believed that public sector industries already belonged to them, none more so than the water industry which was in their view also unique in supplying a natural and God-given resource which it was morally wrong to sell. The government never succeeded in countering these arguments, and together with the ill-fated 'poll tax', water privatization was implemented in the teeth of huge public opposition.

How an unpopular policy may still win votes

Given that nobody ever suggested that the poll tax was going to win the Conservatives the next election, why did politicians and pundits cling fast to the belief that privatizing water or electricity would help the Conservatives do just that? How could anybody believe that a policy attracting the heartfelt opposition of 60%, 70% or even 80% of electors could still be a vote winner?

In fact, the logic of the argument is not as perverse as it might at first sight appear. To understand why not, we need to make a short excursion into a body of political science literature known as 'public choice theory' (for a review, see McLean 1987).

The theory of public choice seeks to explain political behaviour, whether by voters, politicians or administrators, using the terminology and assumptions of micro-economics. Thus, just as producers and consumers in a marketplace are assumed rationally to pursue their self-interest and to attempt to maximize utility, so, too, in the political 'marketplace', voters, politicians and state bureaucrats rationally pursue their self-interest, whether it be the interest of voters in improving their material well-being by voting for parties offering the most beneficial policies, or the interest of politicians in getting elected, or the interest of bureaucrats in expanding their office empires.

This theory has generally been used to predict that state intervention and government spending will continually increase in a vicious spiral. This is obviously in the interests of public sector administrators who expand their offices, their status, and their salaries when government pumps more money into a new or existing programme, but it is also in the short-term interests of politicians and voters. Thus, politicians compete for votes by offering ever greater 'bribes' to specific sections of the electorate, while rational voters respond by electing the party which offers to spend most money on things from which they expect to benefit. Politicians find it easy to add new programmes, for the additional cost can be spread thinly across all taxpayers such that nobody really notices and nobody bothers to complain. They find it extremely difficult to cut programmes, however, for cuts always reduce the benefits of some specific group within the population which will then make a lot of noise and cause a lot of problems until the funding is restored.

How, then, might self-interested rational politicians and voters be expected to respond to a policy like water privatization? On the face of it, rational politicians seeking re-election will not support such a policy because it is enormously unpopular with the voters. Indeed, in the specific case of water, it might have seemed that there were votes to be gained by promising to renationalize it once it had been privatized, for in our survey in 1991, 54% of respondents favoured returning water to the public sector while only 22% opposed the idea.

However, even though, by the late 1980s, a great majority of voters disapproved of privatization, and the apparent underpricing of many of the share issues can be said to have cost the general public millions of pounds, these sentiments were unlikely to have been enough to make them switch their votes. As rational utility maximizers, they knew that any loss they may have sustained was tiny. Like the millions of taxpayers who fund a new programme from which few will benefit, the millions of voters who disapproved of privatization and who saw industries sold at below their full value may not have liked what the government did, but its impact upon them personally was so minuscule as to be unnoticeable.

Compare this with the impact of the policy on those who gained. Some 2½ million people bought water shares. On the first day of trading, they saw the value of their holdings appreciate by between 36% and 57%. Those who held on to their shares later received dividends above the prospectus forecast and above the Stock Market average. As we shall see in Chapter 7, virtually all those who bought were pleased with the returns they had received on their investment. Privatization was for these people a significant policy with tangible personal financial benefits.

It is for this reason that privatization might be thought to have won votes for the Conservatives. Millions of people, including many Conservative voters, opposed the policy, but the theory suggests that this will not have affected the way they cast their votes. A significant minority, including some Labour voters, gained from it personally, however, and the theory suggests that this just might have been enough to influence the way some of them voted, for they would have been grateful for the gains they had made from previous privatizations and would have wanted to ensure that the opportunity to make such gains was repeated in the future. As Vickers and Wright (1988, p. 26) succinctly observe: 'The underpricing of privatisation issues is appreciated more by those who gain than deprecated by the general public which loses'.

Applied specifically to the impact of privatization on voting, the predictions of public choice theory are further strengthened by the position adopted by the Labour opposition through the 1980s. The Labour Party, together with the trade union movement, not only promised to end the privatization programme, thereby abruptly turning off the tap of windfall gains to small buyers, but also continually threatened to take back some or all of the shares which had already been sold. As we have seen, in the case of water at least, the Party's policy seems to have had public opinion behind it, yet it is still possible that this stand cost Labour dearly in terms of votes won and lost.

The threats began in 1980 when the TUC and Labour Party conferences passed resolutions calling on a future Labour government to renationalize without compensation all industries sold by the Conservatives. The no-compensation clause was abandoned in 1982, but at the 1983 general election, the Labour manifesto still promised to renationalize all privatized companies and to pay shareowners no more than the original offer price of the shares. At that election, the Party won fewer votes per candidate than at any election since its foundation.

By the 1987 election, the policy had changed. This time the Labour manifesto said that British Gas and BT shares would not be compulsorily repurchased, but owners would instead have the choice of selling their shares back to the government at the original purchase price, or exchanging them for 'special new securities' rather like non-voting bonds with a guaranteed rate of interest. The chairman of the Conservative Party, Norman Tebbit, took the opportunity to write to all BT shareowners in Labour constituencies informing them of the Labour Party's plans. The Conservatives were subsequently returned to power with a majority of over 100 seats.

In its 1989 policy review, designed to make the party more electable, Labour envisaged taking BT back into public ownership by extending the government's holding from 49% (as it then was) to 51%, and returning to 'some form' of public ownership the gas, water and electricity industries by stripping shareholders of their voting rights. This was followed by a press article (*Financial Times*, 14 August 1989) in which the Party's trade and industry spokesman, Brian Gould, warned those thinking of buying water shares that a future Labour government would fix water prices so as to exclude dividend payments to shareholders and would therefore seek to depress the share price below the original offer price before buying back the shares. By the time of the 1992 election, the Party had abandoned its plans to renationalize BT and British Gas, but it still targeted water and the National Grid to be 'restored to public control' although it gave no details as to how this was to be done. The Conservatives unexpectedly won that election as well, giving them a record sequence of four consecutive victories.

If public choice theory has any validity to it, then this long history of Labour threats to renationalize privatized companies looks to have been politically suicidal. The millions who disapprove of privatization will presumably have applauded Labour's intention to stop the programme (although some may have been uneasy about the plan to claw back shares), but few of them will have been motivated to switch their vote since they would not personally be affected either way. Those who held shares in privatized stock will, however, have been shocked to learn of Labour's intentions, for a Labour victory not only would deny them the chance to buy into future sales, but also threatened the stakes they had built up in previous ones. Even in opposition, Labour's pronouncements were depressing the value of their shares (when the Conservatives surprisingly won the 1992 election, for example, water shares rose by as much as 20%, while the market as a whole rose only 5%). How much worse, then, would it be for them were Labour to form a government and actually carry out its threats?

It would not, therefore, be surprising if shareowners with Labour leanings decided to vote Conservative in the elections between 1983 and 1992 in order to protect their investments. According to public choice theory, this would have been the rational thing for them to do, and according to many commentators this is exactly what they did.

How opposition to privatization lost Labour votes

Water privatization was slightly less unpopular with our panel of interviewees in 1991 than it had been in 1989. While 76% of them opposed the sale three months before it happened, only 61% were still opposed eighteen months after it happened.

This shift in attitudes is largely explained by a dramatic change in the views of those who bought water shares. Fifty-nine people in our original (weighted) sample bought water shares (the sample was weighted to overrepresent middle-class people in order to increase the number of share-buyers contacted – see Appendix). When we first interviewed these future buyers, before water was privatized, their views on the sale were little different from those of others in the sample – only 13% of them approved of the sale while 70% disapproved (reweighted figures are 12% of buyers approving and 70% disapproving, as compared with 10% and 77%, respectively, for non-buyers). At that time, of course, many of them did not know that they would later buy shares in the water flotation – three months before the sale only 5% of those who eventually bought believed they were certain to buy, while a further 14% thought they were very likely to, but over half (52%) believed they were either 'not very likely' or 'not at all likely' to buy. In other words, in the autumn of 1989, most of those who later went on to buy water shares did not expect to, and their views on the sale were little different from those of the people who did not subsequently buy shares.

By the spring of 1991, however, this pattern had changed completely. Six out of ten people in the sample remained consistent in their views over this period – 53% consistently opposed water privatization and 7% consistently supported it. Only 3% changed from approving in 1989 to disapproving in 1991, but 11% of initial opponents of the policy ended up supporting it. Most of these were people who bought shares.

While those who had not bought shares became, on average, a little less critical of the sale as time passed, those who had bought them became much less critical and more supportive. Thus, where just 13% of buyers had approved of the sale before they bought their shares, 59% of them approved of it afterwards. Buyers similarly became much more positive when asked to evaluate the effects which water privatization had had. They were, for example, less likely than non-buyers to believe that the privatization was to blame for increased prices (47% as against 68% of the sample as a whole), less likely to believe that the environment had suffered as a result of the sale (15% as compared with 28%), more likely to believe that privatization had improved accountability (44% as compared with 33%), and so on.

What is clear from all this is that the act and experience of buying shares does significantly alter the views which people have about privatization. This is not necessarily surprising, for people who originally opposed water privatization yet who nevertheless purchased shares are likely to experience a degree of 'cognitive dissonance' unless they subsequently rationalize their action by finding appropriate justifications for it.

This change, though not surprising, is nevertheless important, for it indicates that the spread of share ownership is producing an interest group within the electorate which not only objectively benefits from privatization, but also becomes subjectively much more in favour of it. Even in the case of water, which was the most unpopular privatization ever, a majority of those who bought shares had within eighteen months become supportive of the sale, and this group had become much less likely than other people to see negative consequences (such as increased prices or environmental neglect) arising from it. Any threat to renationalize, therefore, would not only represent an attack on their pockets, but would also appear to them to be unreasonable and therefore something to be resisted in principle. Although 22% of buyers said in 1991 that they would approve of taking the water industry back into some form of public ownership, this was much lower than the 56% of non-buyers who said they would support such a move, and it still left a majority of buyers (51%) opposing any proposal to renationalize.

The question, however, is whether this specific concern is enough to influence the way these share-buyers cast their votes at election time. Such evidence as we have suggests that, in some cases, it may indeed be enough, although considerable caution has to be exercised in evaluating the relevant data.

We know from various surveys that those who buy shares are more likely to vote Conservative than those who do not. Between 1983 and 1987, for example, there was a 2.5% swing to the Conservatives among first-time share-buyers, contrasting with a 3% swing to Labour among non-buyers (see Marsh 1990). The data from the 1987 general election itself show that the Conservatives won 17% more of the vote among new shareowners than among those who have never owned shares, while Labour won 18% less. While 54% of new shareowners voted Conservative, only 20% of them voted Labour (see McAllister and Studlar 1989).

The same pattern is repeated in our survey. In 1989, 34% of those who had never owned shares supported Labour, compared with 26% who favoured the Conservatives (by 1991 the figures were 31% and 27%, respectively). Among those with shares, by contrast, only 20% supported Labour, while 43% said they would vote Conservative (17% and 40%, respectively, in 1991).

We also know, however, that those who buy shares tend to be more affluent, more middle-class and more likely to live in the South of England (see Chapter 7), and all of these factors also correlate positively with Conservative voting. The question, therefore, is whether share-buyers are more likely to vote Conservative even when we take account of all these other variables.

Some evidence suggests that they are. In their analysis of the 1987 election data, McAllister and Studlar (1989) construct a regression model which includes socio-economic factors such as occupational status, age, trade union membership and family income as well as share ownership and housing tenure. They find that the Conservatives won 10% more of the vote among new shareowners than among non-owners, while Labour won 9% less, even after the effects of factors like occupation and income have been taken into account.

Using the results of their regression equation, McAllister and Studlar were able to estimate the likely impact of share ownership on the 1987 election result. Given that 16.5% of the sample were new share-buyers, and that share ownership correlated independently with Conservative voting with a co-efficient of $+0.095$, they conclude that the overall impact on the election result was to raise the Conservative vote by 1.6% (the proportion of new shareowners in the electorate divided by the strength of the statistical association). As the authors conclude, the effect of share ownership on voting is not large, but 'it could represent the difference between winning or losing in a closely fought election' (1989, p. 174), and 1992 was one such election which the Conservatives won by only twenty seats.

This still leaves us with a familiar 'chicken and egg' problem, however. That there is a statistical correlation between share ownership and Conservative voting seems clear, but it is far from clear that this represents a causal relation in the way that McAllister and Studlar believe. It could be, as they argue, that the act of buying shares itself causes people to change their vote, but it could also be that people who are most likely to change their vote to the Conservatives are also those who are most likely to buy privatization shares (see Heath *et al.* 1989). Particularly in contentious and unpopular sales like water and electricity, those who decide to buy are presumably less committed to an anti-Conservative ethos than others who refuse to buy on principle.

In a later paper, Studlar *et al.* (1990) claim to refute this second interpretation by determining the direction of causation through a path analysis. This seems to indicate that share-buying increases support for the Conservatives due to its association with more positive assessments of the state of the economy. However, Heath and McMahon (1991) show that the analysis was incorrectly conducted; reanalysing the same data set, they find that there is no significant independent association between share-buying and Conservative voting, and that the posited explanation of the link between share ownership and voting – a more positive evaluation of the economy by those who buy shares – does not hold. Interestingly, however, Heath and McMahon do accept that there does still appear to be a significant direct causal link between first-time share-buying and a decline in support for Labour (a partial correlation coefficient of -0.08, significant at a confidence level in excess of 99%). In other words, having taken all other factors into account, new share-buyers are still 8% less likely to vote Labour than those who did not buy shares. The direction of causation remains, however, unclear.

One way of making this link a little clearer is through an analysis of how the same sample of people change their votes over time, and this is precisely what our survey allows us to do. In our (original weighted) sample at the time of the second interviews in 1991, 50% of respondents had never owned shares (this proportion rises to 64% when the sample is reweighted to reflect the class composition in the population from which it was drawn). A further 30% (20% adjusted) of 'inactive owners' had owned shares at some point before the first interview in 1989 but had not bought since. Sixteen per cent (11% adjusted) of 'active owners' had owned prior to 1989 and had also bought shares in between the two interviews, while just 4% (5% adjusted) were new owners since 1989.

If it is the case that share purchase influences people to change the way they vote, then we should expect the 4% of new owners in our sample to show the most marked shift towards the Conservatives and/or away from Labour between 1989 and 1991. We might also expect a shift to the Conservatives or away from Labour among the 16% of people who already had experience of owning shares in 1989 and who bought again afterwards. These two groups should behave noticeably differently from the rest of the sample for whom the share ownership profile did not change between the two sets of interviews. Table 6.2 indicates how each of these four categories of voters changed their voting intentions between 1989 and 1991.

The results of Table 6.2 do show some evidence that new or recent buyers were more likely to move towards the Conservatives than were non-owners or inactive owners. If we focus on the 69 voters who switched to the Conservatives between 1989 and 1991, we find that 17 of them previously supported Labour while the others changed from the Liberals (12), the Greens (16) and those who were undecided or who said they would not vote (24). Let us first consider those who changed from Labour to Conservative.

There were twenty-seven people who supported Labour in 1989 and who bought shares between 1989 and 1991. When these people were reinterviewed in 1991, seven of them (26%) had switched to the Conservatives. There were, in comparison, 142 Labour voters in 1989 who have never bought shares, just eight (6%) of whom later switched to the Conservatives, and 51 Labour voters in 1989 who had owned shares at some point but have not bought again since 1989 ('inactive owners'), just two (4%) of whom went Conservative. Put simply, Labour supporters who bought shares between 1989 and 1991 were

Table 6.2 Changes in voting intentions comparing new share-buyers, non-owners and those having previous experience of share ownership, 1989–91

	Never owned shares		Owned in 1989 but not bought since		Owned pre-1989 and bought since		New buyer since 1989	
	No.	%	No.	%	No.	%	No.	%
Stayed Con.	100	27	87	37	67	52	7	25
Stayed Lab.	103	27	39	16	11	9	4	14
Stayed other	31	8	27	11	11	9	1	4
Stayed DK/NV	8	2	2	1	0	0	0	0
Changed Lab. to Con.	8	2	2	1	6	5	1	4
Changed Lab. to other/ DK/NV	29	8	9	4	3	2	1	4
Changed Oth./DK/NV to Con.	26	7	17	7	5	4	4	14
Changed Con. to Lab.	7	2	5	2	2	2	1	4
Changed Con. to Oth./ DK/NV	20	5	14	6	11	9	3	11
Changed Oth./DK/NV to Lab.	16	4	10	4	2	2	0	0
Other patterns and refused	30	8	26	11	10	8	6	21
Total	378	(417)	238	(250)	128	(130)	28	(31)

$N = 772$ (missing cases = 56; marginal totals in parentheses)
Source Survey (original weighted sample; percentages rounded)
DK = don't know; NV = non-voter

around five times more likely to desert to the Conservatives than those who did not.

What Table 6.2 also indicates, however, is that it was only Labour share buyers who were influenced to change their allegiance. This becomes clear when we look at the pattern of voting changes among share buyers and non-buyers who supported the Liberals and the Greens in 1989 or who were simply undecided at that time, for in this group, share ownership histories appear to be unimportant in influencing voting intentions.

Overall there was, as one would predict, much more switching among this group of 1989 voters than among the 1989 Labour supporters. Liberal support is notoriously fickle, the national surge in support for the Greens in 1989 swiftly petered out, and those who are undecided are by definition politically 'unstable'. What is interesting, however, is that, unlike Labour supporters who went Conservative, this group shows no significant variation as between people with different share-purchasing histories. Among new and recent share buyers in this group, nine out of 31 (29%) changed to the Conservatives. But among those in this group who have never owned shares, 26 out of 101 (26%) went Conservative, and among the 'inactive owners' who had not bought since 1989, 17 out of 67 (25%) changed to the Conservatives. In other words, new and recent buyers were no more or less likely to have changed to the Conservatives than those who had not bought since 1989 or than those who had never bought.

When we analyse the pattern of Conservative gains, therefore, it seems that recent share purchases were only significant as a factor in the change of voting intention for those who had previously supported Labour. Although our total number of cases is small, the pattern is a very sharp one, and it is a pattern which arguably has considerable theoretical (as well as political) significance, for it suggests that it is only among Labour supporters that new and recent purchases of shares play a part in influencing the way people vote. For some reason, a substantial proportion of Labour supporters who bought shares after 1989 were dissuaded from continuing their support for that party and pealed off to the Conservatives.

This pattern emerges even more clearly when we look specifically at the data from Table 6.2 on Labour desertions. We now see that only 15 out of the 27 Labour supporters who bought shares between 1989 and 1991 remained loyal to the party, while 11 deserted – seven to the Conservatives and four to the Liberals (one respondent refused to answer in 1991). This 'loyalty rate' of just 58% compares with one of 74% (103 out of 140 valid cases) among Labour supporters who have never owned shares, and with one of 78% (39 out of 50) among those who have but who have not bought any since 1989. The difference in the loyalty rate between new and recent buyers, on the one hand, and non-owners and inactive owners, on the other, is statistically significant at a confidence level of over 99%.

This same pattern of Conservative gains and Labour desertions is repeated when we consider the way voting intentions changed among the 59 people who bought water shares, although in this case the number of Labour voters is too small to allow us to test for statistical significance. We see from Table 6.3 that most (32 out of 59) of those who bought water shares in 1989 were already Conservative voters, and that most of these (25) remained Conservative in 1991. This level of loyalty (78%) is slightly better than that of 1989 Conservatives who did not buy water shares (74%) but the difference is not significant. It seems from this that the purchase of water shares had little effect as regards existing Conservative voters. The loyalty of 1989 Labour voters who did not buy water shares is also fairly high, for 70% of them continued to support Labour in 1991. Only 4% of Labour non-buyers switched to the Conservatives during this period, and this is matched by the 3% of Conservative non-buyers who switched to Labour.

The one group in this sample whose voting intentions seem to have changed quite dramatically between 1989 and 1991 is the small number of 1989 Labour supporters who bought water shares. Unfortunately, the numbers involved are too small for any serious statistical analysis, for in the whole sample there were only eleven Labour supporters who bought water shares. Nevertheless, their voting intentions eighteen months later are interesting. Only three of them still

Table 6.3 Changes in voting intentions between 1989 and 1991 comparing those
who bought water shares with those who did not

	Voting intention, 1991							
	Conservative		*Labour*		*Other*		*Don't know/ did not vote*	
Voting intention, 1989	*Buyer*	*Non-buyer*	*Buyer*	*Non-buyer*	*Buyer*	*Non-buyer*	*Buyer*	*Non-buyer*
Con.								
No.	25	188	1	8	2	28	4	30
%	78	74	3	3	6	11	13	12
Lab.								
No.	5	8	3	141	2	18	1	34
%	45	4	27	70	18	9	9	17
Other								
No.	0	16	1	10	4	41	3	17
%	0	17	13	13	50	48	38	22
Don't know/did not vote								
No.	2	36	0	16	2	45	1	82
%	40	20	0	9	40	25	20	46

$N = 774$ (missing = 54 including refusals)
Source Survey (original weighted sample)

favoured Labour – a loyalty rate of just 27% as compared with 70% among
Labour non-buyers. No fewer than five of them had switched from Labour to
Conservative, while two more had gone over to the Liberal Democrats.

Looking at these same data in a different way, we see that, just as Labour
attracted nine former Conservatives during this eighteen months, so the
Conservatives recruited only thirteen new supporters from the Labour camp.
The proportions switching between the two main parties were therefore very
small – only 3% of Conservatives changed to Labour, and only 6% of Labour
supporters changed to the Conservatives. But when we look at the characteristics of the former Labour supporters who switched to the Conservatives, we
find that five of these thirteen people (38%) had bought water shares. Although
these numbers are too small to permit a significance test, the pattern is
consistent with that found in Table 6.2 regarding the statistically significant
association between voting intention and new or recent share ownership, for
again we find that Labour support looks particularly vulnerable among those
of its erstwhile supporters who have recently bought privatization shares.

The most plausible explanation for this pattern is simply that these Labour
supporters changed their vote because Labour made it clear in the period
under investigation that it intended to take the most recently privatized
industries back into public ownership. In the case of water, in particular, this
intention was well publicized and widely understood.

This explanation for the high rate of Labour desertions among water and electricity share buyers seems to be the only one which is entirely consistent with the findings we have discussed. In Table 6.2, for example, we saw that there is no significant difference in the Labour loyalty rate between those who have never bought shares and the 'inactive' shareowners who have not bought since 1989. It cannot, therefore, be share ownership as such which is costing Labour support, for those of its supporters who bought in earlier privatiz-ations, or who have purchased non-privatization stock, are no more likely to switch their vote than those who never bought at all. The point here is that, by 1991, Labour was not threatening to take back into public ownership those industries like BT or British Gas which had been privatized years earlier. Its threat was to the most recently privatized industries – water and electricity – and it is only those of its supporters who had bought shares in these companies who showed a clear tendency to switch their vote to some other party.

Conclusion

The evidence from the survey, especially when put in the context of previous studies, seems quite compelling. The privatization programme has helped the Conservative Party to win a small but possibly crucial electoral advantage over Labour. This is not (as so many commentators have assumed) because buying a few shares somehow turns lifelong socialists into Conservative supporters. It would indeed be strange if purchase of a few hundred pounds of water shares could effect such a change when we know with a fair degree of confidence that council tenants who spend vastly greater sums on buying their houses from the council do not change their vote as a result. Rather, it is because the Labour Party has frightened off a substantial proportion of the relatively small number of its potential supporters who have bought shares in privatized companies targeted for some form of renationalization.

Privatization has in recent years become highly unpopular with the electorate as a whole. Perhaps the Labour Party leadership believed in 1992 that its promise to take water and the National Grid back into an unspecified form of public ownership would therefore prove a vote winner. It is our view that this proved a serious miscalculation, for the widespread public opposition to water and electricity privatization was not felt deeply and personally enough by voters to become a reason for supporting Labour or switching from the Conservatives. The threat to renationalize, by contrast, was certainly felt deeply and personally by the minority of voters who had bought shares in these industries and who saw their investments threatened by Labour's proposals. Labour, therefore, antagonized a small but important number of its own potential supporters while failing to win over anything like the same number of its potential opponents, even though they agreed with its policy on this particular issue.

The one shred of comfort for Labour in all this is that the programme of huge public flotations is virtually at an end. Those industries, like coal and the railways, which are scheduled for privatization during the Conservatives' fourth term in office will not be sold through share offers designed to attract millions of small investors. By the time the next election comes, it is therefore doubtful whether Labour will still be threatening to claw back from millions of ordinary people shares in industries privatized five or more years earlier. As this threat recedes, so we may predict that the owners of these shares are likely to allow other issues to sway them in the way they decide to cast their votes.

7 The new shareowners

We saw in Chapter 1 that a major factor behind the government's promotion of wider share ownership during the 1980s was the desire to foster a new 'enterprise culture'. There was a belief that Britain's long-standing economic weakness was at root a cultural problem and that any long-term solution would therefore necessitate a fundamental challenge to a set of attitudes, values and norms of behaviour which had become entrenched in the British way of life and which were now stifling the traditional inventiveness and self-reliance of the British people.

The 'cultural revolution' which came to be known as 'Thatcherism' entailed many different policies and initiatives which were intended to make the British people more 'enterprising', but none was more central to the government's strategy than the privatization programme. Privatization was the flagship of the Thatcher armada, for it not only dramatically reduced the size and significance of the public sector, but also created millions of new shareholders. For the first time, ordinary men and women were invited to invest their savings directly in British capitalism. The hope and the intention was that people would become more 'enterprising' through direct experience and participation in the free enterprise system.

The attempt to create mass share ownership was a national project aimed at the working class and the middle class alike. As we shall see, there was disturbing evidence that the middle class, traditionally the pillar of bourgeois culture, was becoming culturally detached from the core values which underpin a capitalist system of free enterprise. The privatization programme was, therefore, intended to reincorporate the middle class as well as the working class into a mainstream capitalist culture.

The collapse of bourgeois culture

In the government's view, both the working class and the middle class had been afflicted by the extension of state responsibility and power into every nook and cranny of everyday life. The rise in real incomes through the twentieth century should have reduced people's sense of dependency upon the state and should have encouraged increasing numbers of people to assert responsibility for their own lives. Yet in reality, the reverse seemed to have occurred. The belief that it was the government's duty to take responsibility for major areas of people's lives had become increasingly widespread and the solid 'Victorian values' of independence, personal initiative and self-reliance were being lost in what Digby Anderson (1992, p. xix) has referred to as an 'endless demand for rights and . . . neglect of obligations'. Bourgeois culture seemed to be collapsing, and the values arising in its place were in many respects antithetical to the system of private property and free enterprise.

Although these fears came to be associated in the 1980s with the so-called 'New Right' in British politics, they were not 'new', nor were they inherently or necessarily 'right-wing'. The problem of the erosion of bourgeois culture had originally been identified nearly half a century earlier by the American political economist, Joseph Schumpeter, but in the long years of the postwar boom Schumpeter's warnings had been largely forgotten, and it was not until the turbulent decade of the 1970s that Western academics of Left and Right rediscovered it and that British Conservative politicians began to take notice.

In 1943, Joseph Schumpeter argued that bourgeois culture was in terminal decline in the West and he identified two principal causes. First, the extension of education and the commitment to a spirit of critical rationality had produced a new intellectual class (those often referred to today as 'the chattering classes') with no direct responsibility for practical affairs and no direct material stake in the survival of capitalism. This new class had developed a 'vested interest' in criticism and 'social unrest', with the result that society's opinion leaders and opinion formers no longer believed in or endorsed the values of capitalism (Schumpeter 1943, p. 146).

The second cause identified by Schumpeter was the decline of the independent entrepreneur and the erosion of the bourgeois family as an independent economic unit. The virtual disappearance of the owner-manager had, he said, depersonalized and therefore delegitimated the private property system, for it had removed from society the one class of people who recognize a strong personal identification with private capital as a social institution:

> The very foundation of private property and free contracting wears away in a nation in which its most vital, most concrete, most meaningful types disappear from the moral horizon of the people . . . [T]he figure of the proprietor and with it the specifically proprietary interest have vanished from the picture.
>
> (1943, pp. 140–1)

Schumpeter referred to this phenomenon as 'the evaporation of the substance of property'. He recognized, of course, that there is in modern capitalism a class of rich and powerful company executives who have taken the place of the old independent proprietors, but he denied that they have the same personal allegiance or commitment to the property that they control. Significantly for our concerns in this chapter, he also dismissed the idea that ownership of shares in a company could stimulate the sentiments of symbolic attachment and personal identification with capital which characterized the earlier independent entrepreneurs: 'Dematerialized, defunctionalized and absentee ownership does not impress and call forth moral allegiance as the vital form of property did. Eventually there will be nobody left who really cares to stand for it' (1943, p. 142). For Schumpeter, the erosion of bourgeois culture was irreversible.

The basic issue addressed by Schumpeter in the 1940s was rediscovered by Western academics in the 1970s, and thirty years on they were no less gloomy in their prognoses. In the mid-1970s, for example, the conservative sociologist, Daniel Bell, identified a growing tension between economic efficiency, on the one hand, and a culture of self-gratification, on the other. For Bell, there was a clash between the spirit of functional rationality which drives the economy, and the anti-rational, unrestrained spirit of individuality which pervades contemporary culture, and he believed that this contradiction has brought us to 'a watershed in Western society: we are witnessing the end of the bourgeois idea' (Bell 1976, p. 7).

Contemporary ('postmodern') culture is characterized, for Bell, by an emphasis on personal experience and unrestrained self-fulfilment: 'Impulse and pleasure alone are real and life-affirming; all else is neurosis and death' (1976, p. 51). This narcissism runs directly counter to the continuing dull and irksome economic requirement that individuals commit themselves to a narrowly defined occupational role. The puritan emphasis on work as a vocation has disappeared, and the traditional rationalism and sobriety of the middle class now finds little support in the intellectual culture of contemporary capitalist societies. There is no longer any widely held set of moral values which legitimate the capitalist order, and the spirit of individualism which in earlier times underpinned economic activity now undermines it.

The irony in all this is that it is the expansion of the capitalist economy itself which has led to the erosion of the traditional bourgeois culture on which it finally depends. The era of mass consumption, fuelled by instant credit, has rendered the puritan values of saving and abstinence obsolete. What Bell terms the old 'goodness morality', linking work and moral virtue to reward and happiness, has been displaced by what he calls a 'fun morality' in which any failure to achieve instant gratification becomes an occasion for critical self-examination. Yet having undermined the old puritan morality, capitalism has failed to find anything to replace it. Called upon to justify itself, capitalism has either tried to reassert the old values which now appear incongruent with current practice, or has remained silent: 'The social order lacks either a culture that is a symbolic expression of any vitality or a moral impulse that is a motivational or binding force' (Bell 1976, p. 84).

Like Schumpeter, Bell is pessimistic about the possibility of reconstructing the old bourgeois values which have been lost and he is clear that a new morality cannot be constructed or imposed from above. No government can, in his view, hope to engineer 'a cultural revolution' (Bell 1976, p. 30).

This inability to find new moralities or to recycle old ones has also been explored in the Marxist literature. Like Daniel Bell, Marxists such as Jürgen Habermas have explored the 'cultural crisis' of contemporary capitalism and have concluded that the legitimations and motivations which once underpinned capitalist economic activity may now be collapsing.

For Habermas, crisis tendencies within the economy have necessitated an increased role for the state in managing and directing economic activity. Like Bell, he argues that this has encouraged people to look to government to solve problems and to meet demands which in an earlier period would never have been seen as the responsibility of the political system. Vicissitudes of life which were once accepted as inevitable and even natural now provoke demands for government to use public funds to ameliorate the costs of change and to compensate the losers. The failure of governments to meet these escalating demands and expectations has in turn generated a crisis of legitimacy: 'If governmental crisis management fails, it lags behind programmatic demands that it has placed on itself. The penalty for this failure is withdrawal of legitimation' (Habermas 1976, p. 69).

Habermas argues that the 'socio-cultural system' is also in crisis, for the motivations which are necessary if capitalism is to function have been eroded. Traditional morality has been undermined by a pluralism of competing beliefs and has become detached from the holistic religions and philosophies which once invested it with meaning. Modern bourgeois moralities are no substitute, for they fail to motivate people. The ideology of personal achievement fails to provide adequate motivation because people see no clear link between hard work, educational achievement and eventual occupational success. The ideology of possessive individualism has likewise failed as individuals no longer believe that acquisition of commodities is the means through which to achieve happiness and personal fulfilment. And the ideology of materialism has been undermined as growing state involvement in people's lives has weakened the link between labour and material sustenance.

The analyses offered by Schumpeter, Bell and Habermas indicate that the 'cultural problem' dimly perceived by Thatcherite Conservatives in the 1970s and 1980s was both deeper and more widespread than they seem to have appreciated. The growth of an intellectual class antagonistic to or ambivalent about capitalism, the decline of independent entrepreneurship and of the corresponding ethic of personal risk and reward, the erosion of the sober puritan morality stressing work as a vocation and saving as a virtue, the failure of traditional values to provide effective motivation, and the apparent inability of capitalist societies to generate new ideologies which can claim widespread moral commitment – all of these are problems which reflect structural changes consequent upon the development of capitalism and about which governments can probably do very little.

Anti-enterprise values in Britain

Added to these generic tendencies within contemporary capitalism are some specific features of British culture which may also threaten the vitality of capitalist enterprise. Wiener (1981) has argued that Britain never fully came to terms with the Industrial Revolution and the emergence of the capitalist system. In his view, Britain has its own unique cultural legacy of anti-industrialism, aristocratic class snobbery, rural romanticism, antipathy to explicit commercialism, ambivalence towards science and technology, anti-materialistic austerity, concern for stability, fear of innovation, and a deep-rooted distrust of the profit motive. This cultural legacy reflects the way in which the new industrial bourgeoisie adapted itself to the culture of the British aristocracy in the nineteenth century through, for example, the purchase of country houses and the pursuit of an elite education by means of the public schools. Rather than reforging the national culture in its own image, the Victorian middle class simply adapted itself to the pre-industrial and anti-capitalist culture of its social 'superiors'.

Wiener believes that Britain's failure to establish a self-confident capitalist culture explains its long-term economic decline, and at the start of the Thatcher era he warned: 'The least tractable obstacle to British economic "redevelopment" may well be the continuing resistance of cultural values and attitudes' (Wiener 1981, p. 163). In support of his view that these values and attitudes were now entrenched, he cited a survey in *New Society* (28 April 1977) suggesting that most British people are 'remarkably unambitious', do not want to be rich, and do not want to work any harder in order to raise their standard of living. Comparable evidence charting British cultural shifts through the 1980s indicates that very little seems to have changed and that Wiener's pessimism may have been well founded.

One source is the series of *British Social Attitudes Surveys*. These have consistently shown, first, that social attitudes change very slowly, and second, that a culture of 'collectivism', which is in many ways antithetical to the capitalist ethos which government was trying to cultivate, remained strong throughout the 1980s and may even have strengthened the more government tried to attack it.

In their 1986 report, for example, Jowell, Witherspoon and Brook found that 'Collectivism seems to be an integral feature of public attitudes in [Britain], shared by those of quite differing ideological viewpoints on other issues' (1986, p. 133). Distrust of free enterprise was also widespread – only 58% of the public agreed that we would all be better off if British firms made bigger profits, and their 1988 report found that legislation limiting free enterprise (price controls, subsidies and import restrictions) was widely favoured. This series of social attitude surveys also reveals that, if there was a shift in public attitudes through the 1980s, it was *away* from the Thatcherite project, for the increasing support during the late 1970s for tax cuts and reduced government spending apparently reversed itself once such policies were actually implemented. As the 1987 report commented: 'Public attitudes run counter to the policies of the 1979 and 1983 Conservative governments' (1987, p. 4).

Other public opinion surveys paint a similar picture. In 1988, MORI conducted a survey designed to discover how large a proportion of the British population subscribed to 'Thatcherist' values as compared with those committed to 'socialist' values. The results, less than a year after the electorate had returned the Conservatives to power for the third time with a Parliamentary majority of over 100 seats, were surprising: 'We found that 54% of the British public hold essentially socialist values while 39% are essentially Thatcherists in the values they hold' (Worcester 1988, p. 41).

This conclusion was based on responses to a range of questions in which people were asked to choose between different sets of ideals. Perhaps most remarkable was the finding that 49% of the population favoured a 'mainly socialist society' involving a controlled economy, while only 43% favoured a 'mainly capitalist society' based on free enterprise. Furthermore, only 40% valued an individualistic self-help ethic, as compared with 55% who found collective provision more attractive, and a paltry 16% wanted to see 'wealth creators' rewarded more highly than 'carers'.

Perhaps the most eloquent testimony to the failure of Margaret Thatcher's attempt at bringing about a 'cultural revolution' in Britain was revealed, however, in another MORI survey conducted in 1989 to mark the tenth anniversary of her administration. This found that, while just 30% of the population opted as an ideal for 'a country in which private interests and a free market economy are more important', 62% preferred the ideal of 'a country in which public interests and a more managed economy are more important' (*The Independent*, 4 May 1989). After more than 200 years, it seems that the British still feel ambivalent about the values underpinning the capitalist system in which they live, and that the brief Thatcher era did little to change this.

Evidence like this does much to put empirical flesh on the analytical bones of the arguments of writers like Bell, Habermas and Wiener. If more people feel comfortable with a socialist ethic than a capitalist one, and if more people want to live under a managed economy than in a free one, then there does indeed seem to be a problem, if not a crisis, in what Habermas calls the 'socio-cultural system'. And if, after nine years of a radical programme of cultural reconstruction, only one in six of the population wished to reward wealth creators more highly than the 'caring professions', then Wiener's fears that the British antipathy towards profit-making may be too entrenched to be reversed would seem to have been well grounded.

A nation of shareowners?

The government's attempt to make capitalism popular seems to have failed. Yet the attempt to build a 'popular capitalism' by extending the basis of ownership of capital to a larger proportion of the population has equally clearly succeeded. Whatever the opinion polls and attitude surveys might tell us about how people in Britain feel about capitalism, the fact remains that many of us took the opportunity during the Thatcher years to buy ourselves a small slice of it. As we saw in Chapter 1, around 2½ million people owned shares in 1979, yet this figure had grown to an estimated 11 million, or around a quarter of the adult population, thirteen years later.

The *General Household Survey* for 1988 (Central Statistical Office 1990) contained the results of an in-depth analysis of share ownership based upon a survey of over 18,000 people in 9,000 households in Great Britain. It reported that 21% of adults at that time owned shares. Thirteen per cent owned shares in privatized companies, and nearly half of these (46%) also owned shares in other companies. Four per cent of the population (but 8% of those who were employees) owned shares in the company for which they worked, and 1% had taken out Personal Equity Plans (PEPs).

As we saw in Chapter 1, shareholders were found to be drawn disproportionately from among males, the middle-aged, and the middle classes. Fifty-five per cent of all shareholders in the *General Household Survey* were men and 40% were aged 45–64 (as compared with just 28% of the sample as a whole). Forty-six per cent were in professional or managerial occupations (as compared with 26% in the sample as a whole) while just 10% were in semi- or unskilled manual jobs (22% in the sample overall). Thirty per cent of shareholders (but only 14% of the sample) had a weekly income in excess of £250, and the average gross income of those owning shares was almost twice that of those who did not.

Looking at those who owned only privatization stock, there was still a skewed distribution by social class and income, but it was less marked. For example, while 32% of all shareowners were in manual occupations, this was true of 39% of those owning only shares in privatized companies. Similarly, while 33% of all shareowners had a weekly income of less than £100, this was true of 37% of those owning only privatized company stock. Thus, the privatization programme had not only massively expanded the number of shareholders in Britain, but also extended ownership further into lower-income and lower socio-economic groups.

Share ownership was therefore broadened during the 1980s, but it was not deepened. A 1990 survey for the CBI estimated that, of 10.6 million individual shareholders, only 1.5 million, or 14%, owned shares in four or more companies, while no fewer than 61% owned shares in only one (CBI 1990, p. 15). As Grout (1987a, p. 61) observes: 'The recent growth in share ownership . . . is almost as thin as it possibly could be'.

In our survey, 70% of shareholders owned shares in only one company. Half of the shareholders in classes A and B had only one holding, and this proportion rose to 68% in class C1 and to over three-quarters in classes C2, D and E. There was also a slight tendency for multiple share ownership to be associated with higher-income groups. Taking those in our sample for whom we have information on gross household income, and dividing them into 'low' ($N = 166$), 'medium' ($N = 217$) and 'high' ($N = 153$) income groups, we find that just 7% of households in the 'low' income band owned two or more shares as compared with 13% of those in both the 'medium' and 'high' bands. Conversely, 76% of the lowest-income households owned no shares, compared with 66% of those in the middle band and 54% of those in the highest band. The relationship between multiple ownership and income is not, however, a strong one, with a correlation coefficient of just 0.1.

It would seem from the data on depth of ownership that most of the 8 million or so new owners have either bought shares in one privatization issue and then never bought again, or have bought and sold in successive privatization issues, recycling the same small sum of money in order to achieve a capital gain each time. Either way, there is little evidence from these figures to support the view that millions of ordinary people have begun to invest in shares to any significant extent. Rather, it seems likely that in millions of living rooms up and down the country, there is in a bottom drawer somewhere a British Gas or BT share certificate lying alongside the Premium Bond numbers or the building society account book and gathering dust.

Chapman (1990, p. 8) concludes from these figures:

> If the Conservative's [*sic*] purpose of privatization was to introduce popular capitalism – to turn the British into a nation of shareholders – then this objective has not been achieved . . . The British have certainly not developed a real taste for share ownership or share trading.

This conclusion may, however, be too pessimistic. While it is true that, by the late 1980s, only around one-quarter of the adult population owned shares and that most of these people held holdings in only one company, it is also true that, first, a much larger proportion of the population has at some time had experience of buying and selling shares; second, most of those who have bought in the privatization sales have held on to their shares; and third, some of those who buy privatization stock have been encouraged later to go on and buy other shares. These three points indicate that the privatization programme may have had a more significant impact in encouraging a shareowning and share-trading culture than Chapman admits.

How widespread is experience of share ownership?

The first point concerns the extensiveness of the experience of share ownership. We can see from Table 7.1 that 31% of our (adjusted) sample owned shares of some kind in 1989. This is rather higher than the *General Household Survey* 1988 estimate of around one-quarter of all adults, and the difference is probably explained by the huge 1989 Abbey National flotation when 5½ million savers and borrowers became shareholders, some 4 million of whom had never owned shares before.

Not only does our survey suggest that share ownership may be rather more widespread than previous estimates have indicated, but we can also see from Table 7.1 that only 59% of our sample had never owned any shares of any kind. We therefore estimate that something like four out of ten adults in Britain have had some experience of share ownership, and among the professional and managerial classes this figure rises to 60%. Share ownership and/or share dealing is therefore now a common experience, particularly among the middle classes, and this should make us cautious about accepting Chapman's cavalier judgement that the Conservatives have failed in their quest to create a culture of share ownership.

Table 7.1   Share ownership careers

	Ever owned before 1989		Still owned in 1989		Purchases 1989–91	
	No.	%	*No.*	%	*No.*	%
Abbey National	121	15	87	11	na	
BA	16	2	11	1	na	
BAA	21	3	10	1	na	
BP	17	2	13	2	na	
Brit Aerospace	10	1	4	1	na	
Brit Gas	115	14	76	9	na	
Brit Steel	16	2	10	1	na	
BT	68	8	46	6	na	
Rolls Royce	21	3	12	2	na	
TSB	55	7	39	5	na	
Other privatizations	17	2	9	1	na	
Employee*	55	7	35	4	na	
Other shares	64	8	46	6	62	7
Unit trusts	59	7	41	5	19	2
PEP	14	2	8	1	19	2
Electric supply	na		na		62	8
Electric gen	na		na		34	4
Water	na		na		44	5
None	485	59	570	69	697	84

* Shares in a company which the respondent works for, or used to work for, or which a partner works or worked for.
$N = 825$ (missing = 3)
Source   Survey (reweighted)

Do people keep hold of their shares?

Table 7.1 also provides some evidence on the stability of ownership, the second issue on which Chapman's conclusion may need to be challenged. It has become a commonplace observation among the critics of the government's privatization programme that large numbers of people buy privatization shares simply to cash in quickly on the rise in share price once trading begins. Indeed, it is frequently argued that the government has deliberately undervalued these industries in order to guarantee healthy first day profits, thereby encouraging investors to stag the issues rather than take a longer-term perspective.

The evidence, however, indicates that 'stagging' of privatization issues may not be as common as Chapman and others have suggested, and that large numbers of new shareowners are sticking with their investments over substantial periods of time.

Considerable research has been done on the attrition rate of ownership of privatization stock. Figures cited by Hyman (1989) show that rapid selling of BT and British Gas shares was quite limited: six months after these sales 80% and 70%, respectively, of buyers still held their shares, although there was a steady erosion over the years that followed. Figures given by Price Waterhouse (1989) reveal that when the first tranche of BT was sold in 1984, 2.3 million people bought shares, but this had declined by March 1989 to just 1.2 million. Similarly, the number of British Gas shareholders fell from 4.4 million in 1986 to 2.3 million by March 1991 (Hansard, 10 February 1992, vol. 203, col. 336w). In both cases, therefore, the number of shareholders halved in a period of five years.

In some of the other privatization issues, early selling was more marked. Nearly 35% of BA buyers deserted within six months, for example, and the number of shareholders in British Aerospace fell from 157,829 to just 27,175 in the first year of trading (Veljanowski 1987, p. 105). As for the water PLCs, taking Southern Water as an example, the number of shareholders fell from 183,000 at flotation to 128,000 six months later (a 30% decline) and by another 18% to 105,000 a year after that (Southern Water annual reports, 1990 and 1991). Taking the water industry as a whole, the number of shareholders fell from 2.7 million in December 1989 to 1.1 million in June 1991 (Hansard, 10 February 1992, vol. 203, col. 336w).

Although the pattern has varied between different sales, the figures suggest that, on average, most of the privatized companies have lost around half their shareholders over the first few years of their existence in the private sector, with perhaps a quarter going in the first few months after the sale.

While it is therefore true that a substantial minority of people 'stag' privatization issues, it does seem that most remain loyal, at least for a few years. The 1990 CBI survey looked at people's reasons for buying shares and found that only 20% of respondents were initially motivated by the prospect of making a quick profit (cited in Oldham 1990). Furthermore, our own survey of water share buyers suggests that people may buy shares with the intention of selling quickly, only to hold on to them after they have purchased. Of those people in our sample who said in 1989 that they were likely to buy water shares and who did then go on to buy, more than half (58%) said they were intending to stag the issue, but in the event, most of them actually chose to hold on to their investments.

In our (weighted) sample there were fifty-nine people who bought water shares. Nearly half of these bought no more than £250 worth and less than a quarter bought more than £500 worth. All of them bought shares in the water company serving their own region, and only seven also bought shares in other water PLCs.

When we reinterviewed these people fifteen months after the flotation, thirty-nine of them (two-thirds) still owned all their shares and one had sold some and kept some. Of the nineteen who had sold, ten had done so in the first month and another six had sold in the first six months. This indicates that only around 16% had bought and followed through their intention of selling quickly

– a figure which is broadly consistent with the 20% in the CBI survey for whom quick profits provided the motivation to purchase.

The fact that so many buyers had originally intended to stag the issue, yet so few had actually done so, cannot be explained by inadequate potential profits. Like most previous privatizations, that of water offered a considerable incentive to sell early and cash in on capital gains. Looking at the two companies in which the people in our sample invested, both of which were offered for sale at 100p (part-paid), we see that the share price for North West Water opened at 135p and moved to 137p after one week and to 153p after one month, while that of Southern Water opened at 141p, moved to 142p at the end of the first week, and stood at 159p after one month. Anyone looking to take a quick profit would surely have been happy to accept a gain of over 50 per cent, yet most investors chose not to sell.

One factor which has sometimes been suggested as a cause of people holding on to their shares is the relatively high cost of commission charged on sales. According to the CBI (1990), transaction costs on small deals in Britain are among the highest in Europe, and as Grout (1987a, p. 73) argues, 'With large exit transaction costs small traders may simply choose to hold the particular share as a passive investor'. It is unlikely, however, that high relative transaction costs would deter many potential stags. Those in our sample who bought only 250 water shares, for example, stood to lose as much as one-fifth of their initial capital gain in commission payments, but this would still have left a net return in excess of £100 – a substantial inducement to cash in quickly.

There are two more likely reasons why most water investors held on to their shares. One is inertia – they simply never got around to selling. The other is that at least some of them came to realize early on that they stood to gain more by holding the shares than by selling them. When we asked those in our sample who still owned water shares how satisfied they were with their performance as compared with other possible investments, 40% thought their shares had performed 'well above average', 17% saw the performance as 'slightly above average', and 40% described it as 'about average'. Only one person was dissatisfied.

In fact, water share prices far outstripped the FT index of a hundred leading shares after 1989, and dividend growth, too, was strong at a time of deep recession. As we saw in Chapter 3, water company profits since privatization have exceeded forecasts, and higher than expected profits have enabled the companies to pay dividends to shareholders far above those paid by most other companies quoted on the London Stock Exchange. In the financial year 1991–2, when average dividends on the Stock Market rose by just 3%, dividends paid by the water PLCs rose by an average of 16% (*Sunday Times*, 31 May 1992). These healthy dividend payments have in turn boosted water share prices. Over the first three years following privatization (a period when much of British industry was in a deep recession), the FT index of one hundred leading shares rose just 10% while the water sector rose by over 60%. In 1992, water was the best performing sector on the London Stock Exchange (*Financial Times*, 20 January 1993).

Other privatization shares have also performed well in recent years, both as regards dividend levels and share price. Bishop and Kay (1988) calculated the returns on a privatization portfolio of eleven companies assuming an investor put an equal amount of money into each at the time when they were sold. The calculations showed that the value of the portfolio would have risen by 166% by October 1988. Had the same investor put the same amount of money into non-privatization stock at the same dates, he or she could have expected an average return of just 77%. Part of this difference is explained by the substantial first day gains registered by most privatization shares, but even discounting these high initial gains, Bishop and Kay calculated that the privatization portfolio would still have risen by 128%.

Drawing all this evidence together, it is plausible to suggest that many small investors, having bought privatization stock, decide to hold it as a high-yielding medium- to long-term investment. This would in turn indicate that the government's aim of creating a sustainable shareowning culture has been rather more successful than some of the critics have suggested.

Is a momentum building up?

We noted in Chapter 1 that the scope for new privatization issues is now severely limited, for very little now remains to be sold and it is unlikely that much if any of this will be achieved through large public flotations. Given that there is a small but continuing rate of disinvestment by small shareholders in all the privatized companies, it is clear that there is now little scope for further extending the popular share ownership programme through privatization, and this has led some commentators to suggest that the number of shareholders in Britain has probably peaked and is now set to decline gradually in the future.

There are two possible developments which could prevent such a decline. One is that ever increasing numbers of people are set to inherit substantial sums of money in the future as a result of the growth in the rate of home ownership over the last fifty years. Saunders (1990) discussed this trend elsewhere, showing that, by the late 1980s, around 150,000 houses, most of them fully paid-off and with a total value of some £6 billion, were being inherited in Britain each year. This figure was anticipated to rise to around 200,000 by the turn of the century. About 80% of these houses are sold by those who inherit them, and much of the revenue from these sales is likely to be invested in one way or another. This has led *The Economist* (28 November 1987) to suggest that inheritance of housing may do more in the long run to build 'popular capitalism' than the whole of the government's privatization programme, for thousands of beneficiaries each year will be looking to invest at least some of their inheritance.

There is, however, no guarantee that this money will find its way into stocks and shares. In their pioneering analysis of housing inheritors, Hamnett *et al.* (1991) found that 49% of inheritors put most or all of their money into financial assets. However, while 27% put most of the money in a building society and 8% put it in a bank account, only 4% used it to buy shares or unit trusts (the remaining 8% chose other types of investment). Judging by these figures, the growth of housing inheritance in the years to come will have only a modest impact on the number of shareholders in Britain, for most of us apparently remain very cautious about risking our windfall by putting it into shares. Assuming that 200,000 housing bequests occur each year in the future, and that just 4% of inheritors use the money to invest in shares, we might predict an annual rate of increase in share purchasers of, say, 8,000 people at most – a figure which is certainly not enough to counter the likely rate at which existing shareholders disinvest.

The second way in which the number of shareholders could continue to rise is if the experience of purchasing privatization stock encourages people to go on to buy other, non-privatized company shares. We saw earlier that no more than 14% of shareowners own shares in four or more companies, and, on this evidence, it seems unlikely that many purchasers of privatization stock have been going on to buy shares in other companies. However, the *General Household Survey* also found that, while 18% of British households contained individuals who owned privatization shares in 1988, only 7% contained individuals who owned *only* privatization shares. Furthermore, of those households where somebody owned privatization shares, 9% contained somebody who owned shares through an employee ownership scheme (other than that of a privatized company), 6% contained somebody with a PEP, and no fewer than 51% contained somebody who also owned shares in a non-privatized company. Thus, more than half of those owning privatization shares also own shares in companies which were always in the private sector.

We can estimate from this that of the (approximately) 10 million shareholders in Britain today, 5 or 6 million own both privatized and non-privatized stock. Given that in 1979 there were only about 2½ million shareholders altogether, it must be the case that some 3 million 'novices' have acquired and retained non-privatization stock since the privatization programme began.

These estimates are consistent with the data from our survey, summarized in Table 7.1, showing that, in the period 1989–91, the rate of new purchases of non-privatization shares was as great as that for the purchase of the new water and electricity privatization issues. Eight per cent of our sample bought shares in the electricity distribution companies, 5% bought shares in water, and 4% bought shares in the electricity generators, but we also found that 7% had bought shares in other companies over this same period and that 2% had bought unit trusts and 2% had opened a PEP. Of those who bought water shares in 1989, nearly two-thirds went on to buy in the electricity privatization, but over one-third (37%) bought shares in companies other than those offered by the government in its privatization issues. Only 12% bought no other shares at all in the period between the two interviews. Evidence like this casts some doubt on the assertions of those such as Hutton (1988) and Turner (1990) who have argued that the purchase of privatization shares does little to encourage people to buy more conventional shares. It should also lead us to question the view that share ownership has now peaked and is set to decline in the years to come as new privatization issues dry up and investors in earlier issues sell their shares.

In the 1980s, people became more attuned to the idea of share purchase, and experience of buying in privatization issues seems to have spilled over into a willingness to try non-privatized company stock purchases, especially when share offers were made by well-known High Street companies. The Tie Rack issue, for example, was 85 times oversubscribed, Sock Shop was 53 times oversubscribed and the Pickwick record group was 55 times oversubscribed (*Sunday Times*, 23 August 1987). The massive amount of equity required to finance the Channel Tunnel was attracted partly on the strength of a share-purchasing culture created by earlier privatizations (see Letwin 1988). Individuals who just a few years earlier would never have considered the possibility of share ownership have in recent years been encouraged to apply in flotations like these. Application forms appear in popular newspapers inviting people to clip a coupon and send off a cheque. Advertisements appear regularly for 'penny shares', or for 'ethical' unit trust investments. The tabloid press has regular financial advice columns highlighting the performance of the most popular shares and advising readers about PEPs. In the High Street, banks, building societies and even specialist share shops offer swift and simple transaction services. And as we saw in Chapter 4, millions of workers now acquire shares regularly through employee ownership schemes.

In his 1986 speech, the minister responsible for privatization, John Moore (1986a, p. 6), suggested that a 'general and widespread movement' towards wider share ownership had been kick-started by the privatization programme. Our evidence suggests he may have been right, for there are signs of a self-sustaining momentum in the growth of share ownership which may be enough to maintain current levels of ownership even after the privatization programme ends.

Of course, Britain is still a long way from being a 'nation of shareowners', and predictions of how the future may work out are extremely hazardous. Nevertheless, there may be a parallel between the history of the expansion of home ownership and the future development of share ownership. Mass home ownership in Britain began in the 1930s when the middle classes started to buy rather than rent their homes. It may be that the boost to share ownership provided by the privatization programme in the 1980s will prove comparable to this boost to home ownership provided by the building boom of the 1930s, for what the privatization programme has done is to establish a shareowning 'bridgehead' among the middle classes. Just as the 1930s finally banished the idea that ownership of a house was only for the rich, so the 1980s demolished the idea that ownership of shares was only for the privileged. In both cases, a form of property ownership previously thought of as 'alien' to ordinary people's culture became acceptable, desirable and unexceptional within the culture and lifestyle of middle England.

Share ownership and cultural values

The privatization programme has shifted the cultural 'norms' regarding investment in shares. The government's ambition has, however, been bolder than this. As we saw in the first section of this chapter, the government hoped not only to change cultural norms, but also to influence cultural values. It wanted to bring share ownership within the everyday experience of ordinary people *and* thereby to change the way they thought, felt and behaved.

Popular capitalism was intended to create a more 'enterprising' society. In particular, the hope was that, by introducing millions of people to share ownership, the culture of 'state dependency' could be broken, the virtue of individual responsibility and self-help could be promoted, and the resistance to the profit motive – what Lord Young (quoted in Turner 1990, p. 121) referred to as the notion that 'profit-making, making money, was somehow not quite nice' – could be overcome. As Aharoni (1988, p. 41) noted at the time:

> For Mrs. Thatcher, privatization is first and foremost a means of transforming attitudes by transferring ownership. She strongly believes that a new 'enterprise culture', based on wider private ownership and competition, is needed to revive Britain. According to official proclamations, privatization has been pursued to promote both.

The assumption seems to have been that share ownership would perform an educative function. Most people were thought to be ignorant about how a capitalist economy works, and this ignorance explained why so many were ambivalent or even hostile towards the ethic of private enterprise. The way to get people to empathize with capitalist entrepreneurship was therefore to involve them in some way in the system, to educate them through experience. As enlightenment dawned, a change of attitudes would follow. As the CBI (1990, p. 13) suggested:

> The vast majority of the adult population have only the haziest understanding of how value is added and wealth is created in a free market economy . . . Investment made directly in UK companies gives individuals more than just a financial interest. It brings them closer to the wealth creating process and the economic realities of life.

The question of whether wider share ownership actually has fostered a greater understanding of and sympathy for the capitalist mode of enterprise can be examined on three dimensions. At the simplest level, we can consider whether people who buy shares show any increased interest in the companies in which they have invested. If share ownership is to play an 'educative' function as regards people's knowledge and understanding of the wealth creation process under capitalism, then it must presumably encourage individuals to become involved at some minimal level in the affairs of the companies in which they have bought a stake. Next, we can investigate how people see their share holdings. If, as Hutton (1988) suggests, shares are no more significant to most people than other more traditional forms of saving, then the likelihood of any profound attitude shift when people buy shares is no greater than when they invest a few pounds in National Savings or in a life assurance policy. Finally, and most broadly, we can see whether people who buy shares become any more 'enterprising' in their attitudes regarding self-reliance, profitability and financial success.

An interest in the company?

Justifying his government's privatization programme, the then Chancellor of the Exchequer, Nigel Lawson, claimed: 'The new shareholders follow the prices of their shares in the newspapers, receive regular information about how the company is performing, can attend the annual general meetings . . . That is real ownership' (quoted in Bishop and Kay 1988, p. 32).

Our survey included fifty-nine people who bought water shares, forty of whom still owned them at the time of the second interview. We asked these forty whether or not they now 'felt more involved' with the company in which they had bought shares. The majority – twenty-six people or 65% – said that they did not, and only eleven, or 27%, said that they did (three people had no opinion). This finding is consistent with Schumpeter's argument that 'mere shares' are insufficient to form the basis for any strong sense of expressive identification with capitalist property. It does not, however, support Lawson's claims. Indeed, all of our evidence indicates that Lawson was guilty of hyperbole.

He claimed, for example, that small shareholders could attend their company AGM. This is true in principle, but none of the water shareowners in our sample had done so (although nearly one-quarter had returned a proxy voting slip). Attendance at an AGM is potentially the most active form of shareholder involvement, for it offers the opportunity to put questions to the chairman and to vote for members of the board, but small shareholders do not attend in any significant numbers. At the first AGM of Southern Water, for example, just 760 people attended. This figure included representatives from financial institutions with substantial holdings in the company, so the number of personal shareholders was probably nearer 500. This means that approximately one shareholder attended this very first AGM for every 240 who stayed away. Figures supplied by Southern Water do, however, indicate that as many as 40% of the company's shareholders send in a proxy vote.

Lawson also claimed that shareholders receive regular information about company performance and follow the share price in the newspapers. In our sample, about half claimed to have read the annual report which is issued to all shareholders, and 70% said that they regularly checked the current share price. We have no independent evidence to gauge whether or not those who claimed to have read the annual report had actually done so, nor to assess how much attention they might have paid to it. We do, however, have a way of evaluating the claim by 70% of shareholders that they regularly checked the price of their shares, for we asked them whether they knew the price at the time of the interview. Of the forty buyers who still held water shares, twenty-five could not offer an estimate of the current share price and only six were able to quote a price which was within the actual range of price movements over the previous month. Clearly there is little evidence here to support the view that holders of privatization shares know much about or show much interest in the companies in which they have invested.

Share ownership and the 'spirit of capitalism'

If share ownership is to foster more 'enterprising' attitudes, then it is important not only that shareholders should show some interest in their investments, but also that they should see their shares as 'capital' and act accordingly. According to Max Weber, the spirit of modern capitalism is acquisitive yet sober. The enterprising individual under capitalism is neither so cautious as to avoid all risks, nor is so reckless as to pursue short-term gains with little thought for longer-term strategies of accumulation. As Weber (1930, p. 17) puts it:

> Unlimited greed for gain is not in the least identical with capitalism, and is still less its spirit. Capitalism *may* even be identical with the restraint, or at least a rational tempering, of this irrational impulse. But capitalism is identical with the pursuit of profit, and forever *renewed* profit, by means of continuous, rational, capitalistic enterprise.

Applied to the case of shareholders, this means two things. On the one hand, shareholders should be aware of the risks they are taking with their money and should be ready to disinvest if circumstances change. They should understand that shares are not like those forms of saving which offer regular and guaranteed flows of revenue in the form of interest payments, and they should understand (as all advertisements for share issues are now obliged to state) that 'the value of shares can go down as well as up'.

On the other hand, shareholders should take a sober view of their investments. They should understand that shares are not like those forms of gambling which offer the prospects of sudden, short-term, dramatic gains, and they should be looking for a strong and steady rate of return through dividends rather than hoping to cash in as soon as the value of the shares rises. As Weber says, the true spirit of capitalism entails the search for ever renewed profits rather than for windfall gains.

If popular shareholding is to foster a spirit of enterprising capitalism, therefore, shareholders should be neither 'savers' nor 'gamblers' but rational risk-taking 'investors'.

In our survey we asked all those who had ever owned privatization shares why they had first purchased them. Their answers may not be very reliable for they depend upon people's ability to think back several years to recapture the motives which originally lay behind their actions. Nevertheless, their responses can provide a rough indication of what motivated ordinary people to respond to the government's invitation to become shareholders.

A wide scatter of responses to this question was recorded, but in two-thirds (68%) of cases it was possible to classify people's answers into one of three main categories. As a rough estimate, it seems that around one in five people were drawn into share ownership as 'gamblers' (21% said that they had first bought in order to make a quick profit). This figure corresponds with that in the CBI survey discussed earlier and is probably, therefore, quite reliable. About a quarter (27%) said that they had been drawn to share purchase as a long-term investment for themselves or their families. These are the 'savers' for whom the opportunity to buy shares was little more than an attractive alternative to leaving their cash on deposit with a bank or building society. Only 20% of the sample represent true capitalist 'investors'. These were the people who said that they had bought shares because they expected the value to rise or that they anticipated a good rate of return on their money.

Of the remaining 34% of the sample, 7% had been given their shares by their employer while the rest responded with a bewildering diversity of motives which often suggested that the original decision to purchase was not always carefully thought through. Many people seem to get caught up in the mounting frenzy surrounding these privatizations and, like shoppers worried about missing a bargain in the sales, simply buy on impulse, or because 'everybody else' is intending to buy. There is certainly evidence that some people simply do not understand what is going on when they apply for shares. A survey by the Wider Share Ownership Council in 1988 found that some people had bought BT shares under the misapprehension that they would lose their telephones if they did not. The same survey also found that some people continued to buy shares in the aftermath of the Stock Market crash of 1987, apparently oblivious of what had happened (*The Independent*, 18 February 1988).

Our findings lend considerable support to those who have suggested that the privatization programme has little in common with an 'enterprise culture', for it has attracted 'gamblers' and 'savers' as much as 'investors'. Moreover, neither the 'gamblers' nor the 'savers' seem to become any more 'enterprising' once they have bought their shares. If anything, the reverse seems to be the case.

As regards the 'gamblers', the initial 'casino mentality' (Vickers and Yarrow 1988, p. 25) has probably been reinforced by the experience of purchasing shares in privatization issues. Many critics have pointed out that the 'underpricing' of many of these issues, whether deliberate or not, has created an expectation in the public mind that there will be an immediate and substantial increase in the value of shares once trading begins, and this has encouraged an orientation to share purchasing which is antithetical to a true 'spirit of capitalism'. The chairman of the CBI is worried that this has led new investors 'to see share ownership rather as a sophisticated gamble than a long-term investment in the wealth-creating process' (CBI 1990, p. 7). Rather than educating the public about how capitalism creates wealth, the huge first day profits on many privatization issues are likely to have reproduced existing prejudices and folk myths about how the wealthy make their money.

The clearest illustration of this was the sale of the electricity distribution companies in December 1990. Press forecasts of a high demand for shares fuelled predictions of large early profits which in turn further stoked up the rate of applications. Six million individuals – one in ten of the entire population of Britain – eventually applied for the 100p shares which opened at between

142p and 166p – an enormous windfall gain which bore no relation to the idea of profit as a return to enterprise and risk. As *The Times* (6 December 1990) editorial observed:

> A substantial number of those who subscribed for shares in the electricity sell-off knew little of what they were buying. They did not know, nor care . . . all that was at stake was how much they were going to make.

Nor has the privatization programme made the 'savers' any more enterprising, for many share buyers remain remarkably ignorant of the risks entailed in this form of investment. A survey of BT purchasers, conducted by MORI in 1986, found that around 80% believed they were buying a low-risk investment and that about half of them thought that purchase of BT shares was no more risky than putting their money in the building society (Veljanowski 1987, p. 105). A later survey for the CBI came up with similar findings and showed that most investors remain averse to risk and are more concerned to safeguard their capital than to earn high rates of return. Only 10% of them even recognized that investing in shares could bring them a better rate of return than saving in a bank or building society (CBI 1990, p. 17).

The CBI survey also found that many shareholders still have little experience of how to trade in shares. Asked where they would seek guidance on where to buy shares, 54% could not answer (see Oldham 1990). There is little sign here of people having been 'educated' through the experience of share ownership, for not only do most shareowners still fail to adopt an appropriate 'investor' orientation, but many do not even seem to know how they might buy more shares if they so desired.

Enterprising individuals?

Keat (1991) has identified four basic elements in the ideal type of the capitalist 'enterprising individual' which government policy has aimed to encourage. The first is self-reliance. The enterprising individual does not depend upon others and is willing to take responsibility for his or her own actions. The second is motivation. Enterprising individuals know the goals at which they are aiming and are motivated to pursue them effectively. The third is initiative. These individuals seize opportunities and are optimistic about making things happen. And the fourth is success. Enterprising individuals are happy to compete for monetary rewards, are not embarrassed about winning, and do not envy or resent the success of other people.

We attempted to assess whether share ownership had encouraged these sorts of values by means of a series of attitude questions. One set of questions was designed to tap people's attitudes towards reward structures by asking them to evaluate three normative statements regarding the determination of incomes (Table 7.2). One of these (the 'egalitarian' position, which would increase tax on higher earners and redistribute income according to need) was explicitly antithetical to the values of capitalist enterprise, and one (the 'free market' position, which recognizes that rewards should follow the demand for one's

Table 7.2 Share ownership careers and changes in attitudes regarding determination of incomes

	1989		1991		Change in % yes
	Yes %	*No* %	*Yes* %	*No* %	
1 Free marketeers People's incomes should depend on market demand for their services					
Non-owners	51	32	57	25	+ 6
Inactive owners	53	31	58	25	+ 5
Active owners	67	23	70	18	+ 3
New owners	57	28	62	28	+ 5
2 Meritocrats People's incomes should depend on hard work and ability					
Non-owners	86	8	84	7	− 2
Inactive owners	94	3	89	5	− 5
Active owners	88	9	93	4	+ 5
New owners	94	6	87	4	− 7
3 Egalitarians People's incomes should be made more equal by taxing higher earners					
Non-owners	64	24	62	23	− 2
Inactive owners	59	35	60	28	+ 1
Active owners	46	42	57	31	+13
New owners	56	35	58	28	+ 2

$N = 828$
Source Survey, original weighted sample

services) is clearly consistent with such values. The third statement (the 'meritocratic' position, which seeks to link rewards to effort and ability) is only partially consistent with the values of capitalist enterprise, for although the emphasis on hard work is certainly a key element in the rhetoric of enterprise, there is in capitalism no necessary relation between merit and reward. As Hayek (1960, p. 94) points out: 'The value which a person's capacities or services have for us and for which he is recompensed has little relation to anything that we can call moral merit or deserts'.

Several points emerge from Table 7.2. One is that all three statements attracted majority support although they are logically incompatible and inconsistent. It seems – as Parkin (1971) and others have long argued – that many people subscribe to contradictory sets of beliefs and attitudes. This being the case, we should be cautious about research, such as the MORI surveys discussed earlier in this chapter, which seeks to differentiate the population into mutually exclusive categories such as 'socialist' and 'Thatcherist', for many people evidently fall into both categories. Public attitudes are complex and often contradictory.

A second point about the data in Table 7.2 is that there is precious little difference between the responses of people with different share ownership careers. The only group which stands out at all is the 'active owners', for they score noticeably higher on the free market item and (in 1989 at any rate) lower on the egalitarian item, but this difference is probably a function of the social class differences between the groups (while classes A and B accounted for only 15% of the sample, they made up one-third of the 'active owners', and these classes tend to be less egalitarian than others).

The third, and most important, point about these findings is that share purchasing activity between 1989 and 1991 seems to show little or no association with attitude change over this period. If share ownership did contribute to more 'enterprising' values, we should expect this to show up most clearly in attitude changes among new owners and active owners. We saw in Chapter 6 that it was in these two groups that voting shifts appear to have occurred, but we argued there that this had little to do with any fundamental change of values, and the data in Table 7.2 confirm this. If anything, the results are counter-intuitive, for the one substantial attitude shift which is apparent from Table 7.2 is the thirteen point *increase* in the proportion of active owners endorsing the egalitarian statement. As for the new owners, there is no significant change on any of the three items as compared with the other groups, yet it is in this group that we would expect the greatest shifts to have occurred if shareowning had any association with a move to more 'enterprising' attitudes.

The suspicion that share ownership does nothing to encourage the sort of values identified in Keat's ideal type of the 'enterprising individual' is further reinforced by the responses given by the sample to four further statements designed to differentiate 'individualistic' and 'autonomous' sets of values from those which are more 'collectivistic' and 'state-dependent'. Enterprising individuals do not look to the government or to trade unions to provide for them, they have faith in the efficiency of private enterprise, and they believe in the importance of monetary incentives. Table 7.3 summarizes how those with differing share ownership histories judged these issues.

Much the same pattern emerges as in the previous questions. Again we see that a large majority of respondents in all categories endorse all the statements and that share ownership careers have no association with variations in the pattern of answers. Comparing the changes in answers between the two interviews, we also find that those who were active in buying shares in this period show no significant shifts in attitudes when compared with those who were not. Indeed, just as in Table 7.2, the most striking shift occurs against the direction which would have been predicted, for those who bought shares for

Table 7.3 Share ownership careers and changes in attitudes regarding the state, trade unions and private enterprise

	1989		1991		Change in % yes
	Yes %	*No* %	*Yes* %	*No* %	
1 Government duty to ensure everyone has decent living standard					
Non-owners	85	10	88	8	+ 3
Inactive owners	86	10	81	13	− 5
Active owners	77	19	80	15	+ 3
New owners	79	13	89	9	+10
2 Trade unions are an essential safeguard					
Non-owners	70	19	71	16	+ 1
Inactive owners	64	26	60	23	− 4
Active owners	70	25	67	19	− 3
New owners	66	21	70	19	+ 4
3 High tax destroys incentive and discourages risk					
Non-owners	70	18	71	16	+ 1
Inactive owners	74	17	69	23	− 5
Active owners	74	14	75	13	+ 1
New owners	74	17	79	9	+ 5
4 Private sector is more efficient than public sector					
Non-owners	54	26	54	23	0
Inactive owners	66	16	59	19	− 7
Active owners	67	16	76	12	+ 9
New owners	66	15	66	19	0

N = 828
Source Survey, original weighted sample

the first time after 1989 became more rather than less positive about the role of government in determining people's living standards.

The irrelevance of share ownership careers as an influence on people's attitudes can further be demonstrated by constructing a simple index of attitude scores based upon the four items in Table 7.3. Scoring each of our respondents on a range from 4 (strong agreement with items one and two and strong disagreement with items three and four) to 20 (strong disagreement with the first two items and strong agreement with the second two), we can

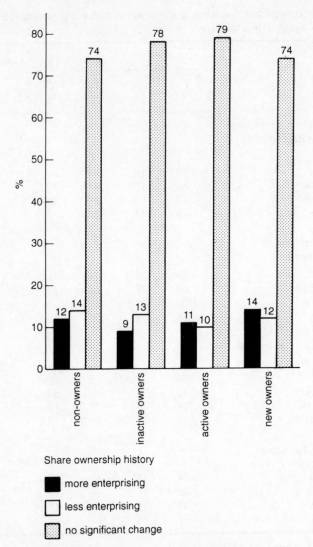

Figure 7.1 Share ownership careers and patterns of change in overall attitude scores
Source   Survey, original weighted sample

derive an overall attitude score in which pro-capitalist sentiments rank high
and pro-collectivist sentiments rank low.

We find, first, that scores overall remained remarkably consistent and in
both years were tightly clustered around the mode and median of 12. In 1989,
the mean score of the sample as a whole was 11.4 with a standard deviation of
2.8, and this compares with a 1991 mean score of 11.3 and standard deviation
of 2.5. Between 1989 and 1991, 277 people increased their scores (i.e. became

more 'enterprising'), 276 reduced them (i.e. became less 'enterprising') and 142 did not change at all (data are missing on the remaining 133). Furthermore, the degree of shift among those who changed was generally tiny. Only 12% of the sample shifted by as much as plus or minus four points and the mean total change in attitude scores over this period was just -0.061.

To investigate the crucial question of whether there was any significant difference in the way attitude scores changed between the four different categories of share ownership careers, we divided the sample into three – those who shifted by more than two points towards 'anti-enterprise' values (14% of the total); those who shifted by more than two points towards 'enterprise' values (11% of the total); and those whose scores varied by two points or less over the eighteen months between the two interviews. The results are set out in Figure 7.1.

The conclusion is obvious. There is virtually no difference between those with different share ownership histories. No matter which way we analyse the attitudinal data, it is impossible to detect any significant variations on the basis of share ownership careers.

All the indications from our survey are that the spread of share ownership has been irrelevant and inconsequential in the government's desire to foster an enterprise culture in Britain. Share ownership does not change people's attitudes about 'enterprise', capitalism, the market economy or the role of government. If Britain does become a 'nation of shareowners' over the next decades, this is unlikely to have any impact on the national culture.

Conclusion

The work of writers like Schumpeter, Bell and Habermas has suggested that there is a growing tension in Western capitalist societies between the requirements of the economy and the development of the culture. In addition, Britain is thought by analysts such as Wiener to face specific problems of its own as a result of the failure of the dominant culture ever fully to come to terms with the transition to industrial capitalism.

The evidence reviewed in this chapter does not suggest that British culture is antithetical to capitalism as such, but it does indicate cultural ambivalence and contradiction. Many people accept, for example, that individuals should be free to make as much money as they can, but they also feel, as Lord Young put it, that there is something 'not quite nice' about the profit motive, and they tend to trust the state rather than private enterprise to ensure a reasonable standard of living for all. The claim (in the 1988 and 1989 MORI surveys) that more Britons are 'socialistic' rather than 'capitalistic' is probably too crude, for most of us endorse different elements of each of these different belief systems, but it is true that British culture does not seem to place a high value on individual effort, self-reliance and entrepreneurship.

From 1979 onwards, Conservative governments have sought to change this, and central to their attempted 'cultural revolution' has been the drive to increase individual share ownership through the privatization programme. At face value, the programme has been a success, for a quarter or more of the adult population owned shares by the beginning of the 1990s and experience of share ownership had become commonplace among the middle classes. There is also some evidence that a momentum may have been established, for although something like one-third of investors in privatization issues tend to sell quite early to realize their profits, many have retained their holdings and have gone on to buy other shares, including those in non-privatized companies. Nevertheless, share ownership in Britain remains wide yet shallow, for most of the 10 million or so owners have holdings in only one or two companies.

Where the privatization programme has been conspicuously unsuccessful is in 'educating' the British public about capitalism and thereby changing the way it feels about private enterprise and the profit motive. Few new shareholders show much interest in or understanding of the companies in which they have invested, and most do not even know what their shares are currently worth. Few can be said to have developed any clear sense of what is entailed in share ownership, for most of them see shares either as a way of making a quick profit or as a safe long-term home for their savings. And there is absolutely no evidence to support the government's view that share ownership would transform the way people think about capitalism and free enterprise.

Outside of eastern Europe, Britain's privatization programme has been the most radical in the capitalist world. Such a dramatic and far-reaching change in the pattern of ownership of a country's basic industries might have been expected to have some social and political as well as purely economic effects. Yet outside of the companies themselves, where managers have become more autonomous and employees have become rather less secure, the sociological effects of this programme have been muted. The privatized companies have perhaps become rather more efficient, although even this is disputed, but individual customers have noticed little change in terms of the quality or accountability of the services they receive. There has probably been a marginal impact on voting behaviour, but this is unlikely to persist once the Labur Party ceases its threats to renationalize. Share ownership has for many people become 'normal', but this has done little to change the way they think about the capitalist system in which they live.

Privatization was the ideological flagship of the Thatcher years, yet its sociological significance has been minimal. Many more people today own shares than was the case in 1979, but, unlike the spread of home ownership, this has had precious little impact on their lives or on their values and beliefs. The inspirational dream of creating a nation of shareowners has in part been realized, but nobody has noticed any difference. Sociologically, the great privatization crusade has turned out to be much ado about nothing.

Methodological appendix

The research reported in this book took the form of a two-stage panel study. In each of two case-study areas, we drew samples from three different populations: a quota sample of householders who were water consumers; a stratified random sample of employees in the water industry; and a positional sample of individuals representing organizations with an interest in the industry. These people were interviewed in the autumn of 1989, approximately three months before the Regional Water Authorities were privatized, and then reinterviewed in the spring of 1991, approximately fifteen months after privatization. The panel design enabled us to trace changes in interviewees' views and experiences arising out of the transfer of the industry from public to private ownership.

Originally we had hoped to focus the study on three, or possibly four, of the ten regions into which the industry was divided. Different RWAs served different types of customer, faced different types of problem, and adopted different strategies to prepare for the impending privatization. None was in this sense 'representative' of the industry as a whole. In the end it proved possible to secure the full cooperation of only two of the four authorities with whom we entered discussions: Southern Water, which serves a region covering most of Kent, Surrey, Sussex and Hampshire, and is seventh largest of the ten WSPLCs; and North West Water which serves Merseyside, Manchester and the surrounding areas, and is third largest behind Thames and Severn Trent. These were two starkly contrasting authorities, not only in terms of their size and their social and industrial geography, but also in terms of factors such as debt levels (although all debt was eventually written off by the government before the sale) and future investment requirements. North West, for example, faced some of the severest problems of crumbling infrastructure of any authority, while Southern had a specific problem regarding pollution of beaches and the disposal of sewage at sea.

Having selected our two case-study authorities, we commissioned MORI to conduct the household interviews with domestic consumers of water in each of the two regions. These householders were interviewed not only in their capacity as water consumers who could evaluate any changes that occurred in the service they received before and after privatization, but also as voters and as potential share buyers. Questions were mainly pre-coded and most interviews lasted for around fifteen minutes.

Because it was essential that our sample should include a significant number of people who would end up buying water shares, and because previous research has shown that working-class people are less likely than middle-class people to buy shares in privatization issues, the sample was weighted to include a disproportionate number of respondents in occupational classes A, B and C1. This weighted sample has been used in this book for the analysis of share buyers, but for analysis of the public as a whole (for instance, the discussion of consumers in Chapter 3), data have been reweighted to achieve a sample which is adjusted to represent the occupational class of the population of the two regions. Tables in the text carry notes stating whether data are based on the original (weighted) sample or on the adjusted (reweighted) sample. Table A.1 shows how weighting affected the social characteristics of the final sample.

In the first phase of the research, 1,444 householders were interviewed, 726 in the North West region and 718 in the Southern region. Eighteen months later, however, many of these either could not be contacted or refused to be interviewed again, and they have been dropped from the data set. We were finally left with 828 successful repeat interviews, and it is on these that our analysis has been based.

The loss of 516 cases from phase one was disappointingly high – a 'wastage' rate of 36% in just a year and a half. It did also introduce some biases into the final sample, as Table A.1 shows. Most noticeable is the skew which occurred in the balance of interviews between the two regions, for in the final sample we lost 100 more respondents in the North West than in the Southern region. The effects of this do not appear to be too serious, however, for there are few significant differences in the answers given by informants in the two regions. The final sample is also slightly biased towards women, homeowners and older people.

At the same time as the household interviews were being conducted, Colin Harris interviewed a sample of employees from the two case-study water PLCs. In the first phase, 179 interviews were conducted, but this figure was reduced to 107 repeat interviews eighteen months later and only 103 of these were fully completed. The 72 respondents who were lost included a disproportionate number of manual workers and the final sample was therefore skewed towards higher grades. At Southern Water both phases of interviewing were conducted during working hours at various company sites and offices throughout the region. At North West the first phase of interviewing took place at evenings and weekends at the homes of our respondents while the second phase was conducted with our respondents at their place of work.

In each case the company drew our sample for us following criteria designed to produce a representative random sample stratified by employment grade. Employees destined in 1989 to transfer to the NRA were excluded from the sampling frame. Interviews lasted on average fifteen to twenty minutes.

Table A.1 Characteristics of sample of water consumers comparing first and second phases and weighted and reweighted samples

	Autumn 1989 weighted (N = 1,444)		Spring 1991 weighted (N = 828)		Spring 1991 reweighted (N =828)	
	No.	%	*No.*	%	*No.*	%
Region						
North West	726	50	368	44	368	44
Southern	718	50	460	56	460	56
Gender						
Female	758	52	445	54	450	54
Male	686	48	383	46	378	46
Class*						
AB	425	28	242	29	143	17
C1	422	29	259	31	191	23
C2	314	22	184	22	240	29
DE	283	20	143	16	253	30
Age						
18–24	131	9	51	6	58	7
25–34	296	21	161	19	166	20
35–44	275	19	168	20	161	19
45–54	198	14	111	13	102	12
55–64	216	15	136	17	138	17
65+	328	23	201	24	204	25
Union member						
Yes	297	21	178	22	180	22
No	1113	77	634	77	633	76
Not known	34	2	16	2	15	2
Housing tenure						
Owner	441	31	267	32	249	30
Buying	732	51	430	52	401	48
Local authority tenant	155	11	79	10	115	14
Private tenant	75	5	34	4	43	5
None of above	41	3	18	2	20	2

* Based on 'head of household' to achieve comparability with 1981 Census data. Data were also collected on the class of respondents who did not claim to be head of household, and data on class in the text and in tables are based on the occupational class of respondent whether or not head of household.

Because we recognized that changes in employee attitudes or behaviour over the eighteen months could occur in response to factors other than those associated with the transfer of the industry into the private sector, the employee interviews were supplemented by a small 'control group' of 65 matched employees working in the water industry in Scotland, where water has remained in the public sector. This control group, based at Strathclyde Regional Council, completed short questionnaires in both phases of the project. Forty successful repeat cases were finally included in the control group.

The data from both the general public panel study and the employees panel study were coded and analysed using SPSS-X on the Solbourne mainframe computer at the University of Sussex. An SPSS-X system file containing data from the survey of the public, together with specimen questionnaires, a codebook and other documentation have been deposited with the ESRC Data Archive at the University of Essex where they are available to other researchers on open access.

The final part of the project, which was again conducted in two phases, involved unstructured interviews with representatives of organizations with an interest in the water industry. In phase one we interviewed local and national officers of various trade unions including NALGO, NUPE and GMB, plus fifteen other individuals including local and national officers of the National Farmers' Union, the Country Landowners' Association and the Confederation of British Industry; officers from the national and regional offices of the Nature Conservancy Council (later English Nature) and the National Federation of Anglers; and managers of large industrial users such as the Ford Motor Company at Halewood. We also had meetings with various officers of public sector agencies such as the former Water Authorities' Association, as well with senior management at the two RWAs themselves. In phase two, all the trade union interviews and ten of the fifteen 'interest-group' interviews were repeated (the other five were dropped as inappropriate). Notes were taken by hand during interviews and were later transcribed.

Various problems and weaknesses can be identified in the research. Some arise out of the delegation of interviewing on the household survey to a third party, in this case MORI. As I have suggested elsewhere (Saunders 1990, p. 383), there is much to be said for social scientists conducting their own interviews wherever possible, for it can be difficult to get a 'feel' for the data when one has not been involved in interviewing. It can also be difficult to keep detailed control over the research when this key stage of the work is contracted out. For example, MORI changed the wording on one attitude question between the first and second phases of interviewing, and this obviously rendered the item itself worthless (it has been ignored in subsequent analysis). Similarly, answers to open-ended questions are rarely fully recorded by interviewers who are paid on piece rates and who have no personal or academic interest in the research. Such experiences indicate that the quality of data is probably best safeguarded by keeping the interviewing task in-house.

Other, more serious, problems arose out of the research design itself. The 'wastage rates' between the first and second phases of interviewing (36% on the household interviews and 40% on the employee interviews) were higher than expected and left us with fewer final cases on both surveys than intended. This has had frustrating implications at certain points in the analysis. The very small number of relevant cases has meant that the shift in voting intentions among Labour supporters who bought water shares (discussed in Chapter 6) could not be evaluated in terms of statistical significance, and the small size of the employee sample, coupled with the eventual underrepresentation of manual workers, meant that contingency tables prepared for Chapter 4 rarely contained sufficient cases for significance tests to be applied. This is one of the two major weaknesses of the study, for it has meant that only tentative conclusions could be drawn on some of the crucially important questions. Larger initial samples would have helped overcome such difficulties.

The other major weakness in the research design was the relatively short period of time that elapsed before the second phase of interviewing. The managements at our two case-study companies have pointed out to us that many of the changes brought about by privatization may not become apparent to customers or to employees for some years, yet the study allowed only fifteen months to elapse after privatization before the follow-up interviews were conducted. Colin Harris hopes at some point in the future to conduct further interviews on the employee panel to track longer-term changes, but further panel wastage will probably make this impossible. It is in the nature of academic research like this that time and money are both limited, and, within these constraints, the maximum time possible was allowed between interviews. Clearly, however, a project like this cannot stand as the last word on the sociological impact of privatization, for changes which only become apparent in the longer term may well prove significant.

For all the problems in the panel design, however, the research can still be defended in terms of its overall reliability. Although wastage rates were high and the duration was limited, the panel design proved a powerful tool for tracking social change, for it generated some unique insights into the effect that privatization has had upon customers, employees, interest groups, voters and those who have bought shares.

References

Aharoni, Y. (1988) 'The United Kingdom: Transforming Attitudes' in R. Vernon (ed.), *The Promise of Privatization*. New York, Council on Foreign Relations.

Anderson, D. (1992) 'Introduction' in D. Anderson (ed.), *The Loss of Virtue*. London, Social Affairs Unit.

Atkinson, R. (1989) *The Failure of the State*. Swalwell, Compuprint Publishing.

Barclay, C. (1986) 'Privatisation'. London, House of Commons Library Research Division, *Background Paper*.

BBC (1989) *'Analysis': Profits for the People*. Transcript of a recorded documentary, tape number TLN928/89VT1028, broadcast on 14 July. London, BBC News and Current Affairs Department, Radio 4.

Beesley, M. and Littlechild, S. (1986) 'Privatisation: Principles, Problems and Priorities' in J. Kay, C. Mayer and D. Thompson (eds), *Privatisation and Regulation*. Oxford, Clarendon Press.

Bell, D. (1976) *The Cultural Contradictions of Capitalism*. London, Heinemann.

Bird, P. and Jackson, C. (1967) 'Economic Charges for Water' in A. Seldon (ed.), *Essays in the Theory and Practice of Market Pricing*. London, Institute of Economic Affairs.

Bishop, M. and Kay, J. (1988) *Does Privatization Work?* London, London Business School.

Bowers, J., O'Donnell, K. and Ogden, S. (1988) 'Privatisation of the Water Industry: Some Outstanding Issues'. Unpublished paper, School of Economic Studies, University of Leeds.

Brennan, L. (1988) *Sharing the Family Silver with the Staff*. London, New Bridge Consultants.

Brittan, S. (1984) 'The politics and economics of privatisation', *Political Quarterley*, 55, 109–28.

Byatt, I. (1991) 'New pricing in the pipeline', *Economic Affairs*, 11, 14–15.

Carney, M. (1992) 'The cost of compliance with ever higher quality standards' in T. Gilland (ed.), *The Changing Water Business*. London, Centre for the Study of Regulated Industries.

Carsberg, B. (1989) 'Injecting competition into telecommunications' in C. Veljanovski (ed.), *Privatisation and Competition*. London, Institute of Economic Affairs.

CBI (1990) *A Nation of Shareholders*. London, Confederation of British Industry.

Central Statistical Office (1990) *General Household Survey 1988*. London, CSO.

Challen, D. (1987) 'Water: The City View'. Paper given at the conference on 'The Privatisation of the Water Industry', organised by *The Economist*, London, September.

Chapman, C. (1990) *Selling the Family Silver*. London, Hutchinson.

Clarke, P. (1987) 'The argument for privatisation' in J. Neuberger (ed.), *Privatisation: Fair Shares for All or Selling the Family Silver?* London, Papermac.

CRI (1992) *The UK Water Industry: Water Services and Costs 1990/91*. London, Public Finance Foundation Centre for the Study of Regulated Industries.

Department of the Environment and the Welsh Office (1986a) *Privatisation of the Water Authorities in England and Wales*, Cmnd. 9734. London, HMSO.

Department of the Environment and the Welsh Office (1986b) *The Water Environment: The Next Steps*. London, HMSO.

Dick, B. (1987) *Privatisation in the UK: The Free Market versus State Control*. York, Longman.

Dockray, M. (1987) 'A natural monopoly facing complex privatisation', *Municipal Journal*, 95, 398–403.

Dunn, M. and Smith, S. (1990) 'Economic policy and privatisation' in S. Savage and L. Robins (eds), *Public Policy under Thatcher*. Basingstoke, Macmillan.

Dunn, S., Richardson, R. and Dewe, P. (1991) *The Impact of Employee Share Ownership on Worker Attitudes*. London, Centre for Economic Performance, London School of Economics.

Edmonds, J. (1987) 'Privatisation of Water: A View from the GMB'. Paper presented at the conference on 'The Privatisation of the Water Industry' organised by *The Economist*, London, September.

Estrin, S. and Wilson, N. (1986) 'The micro-economic effects of profit-sharing'. Centre for Labour Economics *Discussion Paper*, no. 7, London School of Economics.

Ferner, A. (1991) 'Privatisation of the British Utilites'. Paper presented at the conference on 'International Privatisation: Strategies and Practices', St Andrews University, September.

Fogarty, M. and White, M. (1988) *Share Schemes – As Workers See Them*. London, Policy Studies Institute.

Fraser, R. and Wilson, M. (1988) *Privatization: The UK Experience and International Trends*. Harlow, Longman.

Gordon, S. (1989) *Down the Drain: Water, Pollution and Privatisation*. London, Macdonald & Co.

Grimstone, G. (1988) 'The financial processes of privatisation' in V. Ramanadham (ed.), *Privatisation in the UK*. London, Routledge.

Grout, P. (1987a) 'The wider share ownership programme', *Fiscal Studies*, 8, 59–74.

Grout, P. (1987b) 'Wider share ownership and economic performance', *Oxford Review of Economic Policy*, 3, 13–29.

Habermas, J. (1976) *Legitimation Crisis*. London, Heinemann.

Hamnett, C. Harmer, M. and Williams, P. (1991) *Safe as Houses*. London, Paul Chapman Publishing.

Hanke, S. and Walters, S. (1987) 'Privatizing waterworks' in S. Hanke (ed.), *Prospects for Privatization*. New York, Academy of Political Science.

Harper, W. (1988) 'Privatisation in the water sector' in V. Ramanadham (ed.), *Privatisation in the UK*. London, Routledge.

Harper, W. (1992) 'Business excellence everyone wins' in T. Gilland (ed.), *The Changing Water Business*. London, Centre for the Study of Regulated Industries.

Hayek, F. A. von (1960) *The Constitution of Liberty.* London, Routledge and Kegan Paul.

Heald, D. and Steel, D. (1986) 'Privatising public enterprises: An analysis of the government's case' in J. Kay, C. Mayer, and D. Thompson (eds), *Privatisation and Regulation: The UK Experience.* Oxford, Clarendon Press.

Heald, D. and Thomas, D. (1986) 'Privatization as theology', *Public Policy and Administration*, 1, 49–66.

Heath, A. and McMahon, D. (1991) 'Privatisation and the British electorate: A comment' Joint Unit for the Study of Social Trends *Working Paper*, no. 8 (Nuffield College, Oxford).

Heath, A., Jowell, R. and Curtice, J. (1985) *How Britain Votes.* Oxford, Pergamon Press.

Heath, A., Jowell, R., Curtice, J. and Evans, G. (1989) 'The extension of popular capitalism', *Papers on Government and Politics*, no. 60, University of Strathclyde.

Henig, J., Hamnett, C. and Feigenbaum, H. (1988) 'The politics of privatization', *Governance*, 1, 442–68.

Henney, A. (1986) *Regulating Public and Privatised Monopolies.* London, The Public Finance Foundation.

Hill, S. (1989) *Taking Stock: Privatisation of Water Services.* London, Arthur Collins & Co.

Hutton, P. (1988) 'How sophisticated is the private investor now?' Paper presented at the forum on 'Retailing Personal Financial Services: 1992 and beyond', London, MORI.

Hyman, H. (1989) 'Privatisation: The facts' in C. Veljanovski, (ed.), *Privatisation and Competition.* London, Institute of Economic Affairs.

Jones, G. (1985) 'A management view of the privatisation possibilities' in F. Terry (ed.), *Privatisation in the Water Industry:* London, Public Finance Foundation.

Jones, G. (1987) 'Setting the scene: The government's objective'. Paper presented at the conference on 'The Privatisation of the Water Industry', organised by *The Economist*, London, September.

Jordan, A., Richardson, J. and Kimber, R. (1977) 'The origins of the Water Act of 1973' *Public Administration*, 55, 317–34.

Jowell, R. and Witherspoon, S. (1985) *British Social Attitudes: The 1985 Report.* Aldershot, Gower.

Jowell, R., Witherspoon, S. and Brook, L. (1986) *British Social Attitudes: The 1986 Report.* Aldershot, Gower.

Jowell, R., Witherspoon, S. and Brook, L. (1987) *British Social Attitudes: The 1987 Report.* Aldershot, Gower.

Jowell, R., Witherspoon, S. and Brook, L. (1988) *British Social Attitudes: The 5th Report.* Aldershot, Gower.

Kay, J. (1987) *The State and the Market: The UK Experience of Privatisation.* New York and London, Group of Thirty Occasional Paper, no. 23.

Keat, R. (1991) 'Introduction: Starship Britain or international enterprise?' in R. Keat and N. Abercrombie (eds), *Enterprise Culture.* London, Routledge.

Kirby, C. (1979) *Water in Great Britain.* Harmondsworth, Penguin.

Labour Research Department (1983) *Privatisation: Who Loses, Who Profits.* London, Labour Research Dept Publications.

Leadbeater, C. (1987) 'The Sid in us all', *Marxism Today*, 31, 18–23.

Letwin, O. (1988) *Privatising the World.* London, Cassell.

Littlechild, S. (1986) *Economic Regulation of Privatised Water Authorities*. London, HMSO.

Margisson, P. and Sisson, K. (1990) 'Single table talk', *Personnel Management*, May, 46.

Marsh, D. 1990: 'Privatisation in Britain: An idea in search of a policy', *Essex Papers in Politics and Government*, no. 72, University of Essex.

Massey, D. and Catalano, A. (1978) *Capital and Land*. London, Edward Arnold.

McAllister, I. and Studlar, D. (1989) 'Popular versus elite views of privatization', *Journal of Public Policy*, 9, 157–78.

McLean, I. (1987) *Public Choice: An Introduction*. Oxford, Basil Blackwell.

Meade, J. (1986) *Different Forms of Share Economy*. London, Public Policy Centre.

Morris, P. (1991) 'Freeing the spirit of enterprise' in R. Keat and N. Abercrombie, (eds), *Enterprise Culture*. London, Routledge.

Moore, J. (1983) *Why Privatise?* London, Conservative Political Centre.

Moore, J. (1986a) *The Value of Ownership*. London, Conservative Political Centre.

Moore, J. (1986b) 'The success of privatisation, in J. Kay, C. Mayer and D. Thompson (eds), *Privatisation and Regulation: The UK Experience*. Oxford, Clarendon Press.

MORI (1988) 'Prospects for the new year', *British Public Opinion*, 10, 4.

NALGO and NUPE (1991) *The Water Companies: Information and Data for NALGO and NUPE Local Negotiators*. London, NALGO and NUPE.

Nelson, A. and Cooper, C. (1993) 'The impact of privatisation on employee job satisfaction and well being'. Working Paper, UMIST (University of Manchester).

NFC (1989) *Introduction to the Rights Issue*. London, NFC.

Nichols, T. and O'Connel Davidson, J. (1992) 'Employee shareholders in two privatised utilities', *Industrial Relations Journal*, 23.

O'Connel Davidson, J., Nichols, T. and Sun, W. (1991) 'Privatisation and change: Employee attitudes to privatised utilities' Working Paper. University of Leicester.

Ofwat (1992) *1991 Report of the Director General of Water Services*. London, HMSO.

Okun, D. (1977) *Regionalisation of Water Management*. London, Applied Science Publishers.

Oldham, G. (1990) 'TAURUS and the private shareholder', *Economic Affairs*, 11, 14–20.

Parker, D. and Penning-Rowsell, E. (1980) *Water Planning in Britain*. London, Allen & Unwin.

Parkin, F. (1971) *Class Inequality and Political Order*. London, MacGibbon & Kee.

Pearce, F. (1982) *Watershed: The Water Crisis in Britain*. London, Junction Books.

Pirie, M. (1988) *Privatization*. Aldershot: Wildwood House.

Porter, E. (1978) *Water Management in England and Wales*. London, Cambridge University Press.

Poulantzas, N. (1973) *Political Power and Social Classes*. London, New Left Books.

Price Waterhouse (1989) *Privatisation: The Facts*. London, Price Waterhouse.

Price Waterhouse (1990) *Privatisation: The Facts*. London, Price Waterhouse.

Pryke, R. (1986) 'The comparative performance of public and private ownership' in J. Kay, C. Mayer and D. Thompson (eds), *Privatisation and Regulation: The UK Experience*. Oxford, Clarendon Press.

Redwood, J. (1990) 'Spreading popular capitalism' in E. Butler (ed.), *Privatization Now!* London, Adam Smith Institute.

Rees, J. and Synnott, M. (1988) 'Privatisation and social objectives: the water industry' in C. Whitehead (ed.), *Reshaping the Nationalised Industries*. Oxford, Transaction Books.

Rentoul, J. (1987) 'Privatisation: The case against' in J. Neuberger (ed.), *Privatisation: Fair Shares for All or Selling the Family silver?* London, Papermac.

Richardson, J. and Jordan, A. (1979) *Governing under Pressure. The Policy Process in a Post-Parliamentary Democracy.* Oxford, Martin Robertson.

Richardson, J., Maloney, W. and Ruedig, W. (1992) 'The dynamics of policy change', *Public Administration*, 70, 157–75.

Rouse, L. (1990) 'Why privatize utilities?' in E. Butler (ed.), *Privatization Now!* London, Adam Smith Institute.

Sapper, S. (1991) 'Do members services packages influence trade union recruitment?', *Industrial Relations Journal*, 22, 309–16.

Saunders, P. (1984) '"We can't afford democracy too much": Findings from a study of regional state institutions in South-East England', *Urban & Regional Studies Working Papers*, no. 43, University of Sussex.

Saunders, P. (1985) 'Corporatism and urban service provision' in W. Grant (ed.), *The Political Economy of Corporatism.* Basingstoke, Macmillan.

Saunders, P. (1990) *A Nation of Home Owners.* London, Unwin Hyman.

Savas, E. (1982) *Privatizing the Public Sector.* Chatham, NJ, Chatham House Publishers.

Schumpeter, J. (1943) *Capitalism, Socialism and Democracy.* London, George Allen & Unwin.

Shackleton, J. (1984) 'Privatisation: the case examined', *National Westminster Bank Quarterly Review*, May, 59–73.

Southern Customer Service Committee (1991) *Annual Report 1990/91* London, Ofwat.

Southern Water (1992) *Customer Charter.* Worthing, Southern Water PLC.

Speight, H. (1985) 'Understanding privatisation', *Water Services*, 89, 465.

Stafford, B. (1980) 'Water services', *Town Planning Review*, 51, 257–60.

Steel, D. and Heald, D. (1984) *Privatizing Public Enterprises: Options and Dilemmas.* London, Royal Institute of Public Administration.

Studlar, D., McAllister, I. and Ascui, A. (1990) 'Privatization and the British electorate', *American Journal of Political Science*, 34, 1077–1101.

Swann, D. (1988) *The Retreat of the State.* Hemel Hempstead, Harvester Wheatsheaf.

Synnott, M. (1986) 'Change and conflict in the local planning/water authority relationship since 1979', *Planning Practice and Research*, 1, 14–18.

Thomas, D. (1986) 'The union response to denationalisation' in J. Kay, C. Mayer and D. Thompson (eds), *Privatisation and Regulation: the UK Experience.* Oxford, Oxford University Press.

Thompson, D. (1988) 'Privatisation: Introducing competition, opportunities and constraints' in V. Ramanadham (ed.), *Privatisation in the UK.* London, Routledge.

TUC (1985) *Stripping Our Assets.* London, Trades Union Congress.

Turner, R. (1990) 'Mrs. Thatcher's "Enterprise Culture"', *Social Studies Review*, 5, 120–2.

Veljanovski, C. (1987) *Selling the State.* London, Weidenfeld & Nicolson.

Veljanovski, C. (1989) 'Privatisation: Monopoly money or competition?' in C. Veljanovski (ed.), *Privatisation and Competition.* London, Institute of Economic Affairs.

Veljanovski, C. (1993) *The Future of Industry Regulation in the UK.* London, European Economic Forum.

Vickers, J. and Wright, V. (1988) 'The politics of industrial privatisation in western Europe', *West European Politics*, 11, 1–30.

Vickers, J. and Yarrow, G. (1985) *Privatization and the Natural Monopolies*. London, Public Policy Centre.

Vickers, J. and Yarrow, G. (1988) *Privatization: An Economic Analysis*. Cambridge, Mass., MIT Press.

Vickers, J. and Yarrow, G. (1989) 'Privatization in Britain' in P. MacAvoy, W. Stanbury, G. Yarrow and R. Zeckhauser (eds), *Privatization and State-Owned Enterprises*. Boston, Kluwer Academic Publishers.

Walters, A. (1989) 'Comment on Vickers and Yarrow' in P. MacAvoy, W. Stanbury, G. Yarrow and R. Zeckhauser (eds), *Privatisation and State-Owned Enterprises*. Boston, Kluwer Academic Publishers.

Water Industry Unions Committee (1985) *Public Ownership: A Watertight Case*. London, GMBATU, MATSA, NALGO, NUPE, TGWU, TWSA and UCATT.

Watts, R. (1987) 'Prospects for water services PLCs'. Paper given at the conference on 'The Privatisation of the Water Industry', organised by *The Economist*, London, September.

Weber, M. (1930) *The Protestant Ethic and the Spirit of Capitalism*. London, Unwin University Books.

White, A. (1992) 'The profitability of regulated industries' in T. Gilland (ed.), *The Changing Water Business*. London, Centre for the Study of Regulated Industries.

Whitfield, D. (1983) *Making it Public: Evidence and Action Against Privatisation*. London, Pluto Press.

Wiener, M. (1981) *English Culture and the Decline of the Industrial Spirit 1850–1980*. New York, Cambridge University Press.

Wiltshire, K. (1987) *Privatisation: The British Experience*. Melbourne, Longman Cheshire.

Wiseman, J. (1991) 'Nationalisation and privatisation', *Economic Affairs*, 11, 27–31.

Wolfe, J. (1989) 'Reorganising interest representation: A political analysis of privatization in Britain' in R. Foglesong and J. Wolfe (eds), *The Politics of Economic Adjustment*. New York, Greenwood Press.

Woodward, N. (1988) 'Managing cultural change on privatisation' in V. Ramanadham (ed.), *Privatisation in the UK*. London, Routledge.

Worcester, R. (1988) 'Polls apart', *New Socialist*, Summer, 39–41.

Wright, J. (1992) 'Economic regulation in the water industry' in T. Gilland (ed.), *The Changing Water Business*. London, Centre for the Study of Regulated Industries.

Wright, N., Thompson, S. and Robbie, K. (1990) 'Management buy-outs: Achievements, limitations and prospects', *National Westminster Bank Quarterly Review*, August.

Yarrow, G. (1989) 'Does ownership matter?' in C. Veljanovski (ed.), *Privatisation and Competition*. London, Institute of Economic Affairs.

Zeckhauser, R. and Horn, M. (1989) 'The control and performance of state-owned enterprises' in P. MacAvoy, W. Stanbury, G. Yarrow and R. Zeckhauser (eds), *Privatization and State-Owned Enterprises*. Boston, Kluwer Academic Publishers.

Index

IMPLEMENTING HOUSING POLICY

Peter Malpass and Robin Means (eds)

Following its radical housing policy reforms of the early 1980s the British government carried out a fundamental policy review in 1986–87 and launched into a further bout of major legislative change in the Housing Act 1988, and the Local Government and Housing Act 1989. These Acts introduced a range of new policy instruments which are being applied with differing degrees of success. *Implementing Housing Policy* provides the first full and detailed account of the new housing policy in action, each chapter written by a well-known specialist in the field.

But the book is much more than a policy review, its distinctive focus on implementation makes it a particularly valuable addition to the literature. Implementation too often remains a taken-for-granted aspect of the policy process, but the contributors to this book explicitly address the importance and complexity of the policy–action relationship. As a result the book will appeal to a wide range of readers interested in public policy and policy processes in general.

Contents
Introduction: focus and outline – Perspectives on implementation – Housing policy and the housing system since 1979 – The re-privatization of housing associations – Rebuilding the private rented sector? – Remodelling a HAT: the implementation of the Housing Action Trust legislation 1987–92 – The new financial regime for local authority housing – Housing renewal in an era of mass home ownership – The enabling role for local housing authorities: a preliminary evaluation – The decentralization of housing services – Large-scale voluntary transfers – The politics of implementation – Index.

Contributors
Glen Bramley, Ian Cole, Valerie Karn, Peter Kemp, Philip Leather, Sheila Mackintosh, Peter Malpass, Robin Means, David Mullins, Pat Niner, Bill Randolph, Moyra Riseborough, Matthew Warburton.

208pp   0 335 15750 5 (Paperback)   0 335 15751 2 (Hardback)

RESOURCE POLITICS
FRESHWATER AND REGIONAL RELATIONS

Caroline Thomas and Darryl Howlett (eds)

A systematic study of the international politics of freshwater resources is long overdue. This is a serious omission, for life, agriculture and industry depend on an assured supply of a certain quality of freshwater. Demand for this resource is constantly growing but its quantity and quality is threatened by various human activities. Moreover, with over two hundred river and lake basins shared by two or more states – and the number is increasing with the disintegration of the Soviet Union – the potential for inter-state hostilities over water is increasing.

This book furthers our understanding of the international political dimensions of the freshwater issue. It takes a regional approach since it is at the regional level that conflict between states over the resource is most likely to occur and where cooperation must be expedited. It explores the implications of freshwater availability in the interlinking contexts of environmental, developmental and security needs. *Resource Politics* argues that a holistic analysis is integral to the formulation of politically viable, environmentally sensitive and developmentally sustainable water management strategies.

Contents
The freshwater issue in international relations – The Great Lakes: exploring the ecosystem – Water politics in Latin America – The issue of water in the Middle East and North Africa – South-east Asia: the Mekong river – South Asia: the Ganges and the Brahmaputra – Sub-Saharan Africa – Eurasia – The European Community and freshwater – Anthropogenic causes of freshwater pollution – Geomorphological alteration by water – Index.

Contributors
Chris Brady, Peter Calvert, Frank Gregory, Anne Guest, Darryl Howlett, Adrian Hyde-Price, C. Ian Jackson, George Joffé, Paikiasothy Saravanamuttu, Caroline Thomas, Peter Wilkin, Sandra Wilkins.

224pp   0 335 15775 0 (Hardback)

GOVERNMENT, INDUSTRY AND POLITICAL ECONOMY

Peter Barberis and Timothy May

The state of the economy has been the most important political issue in Britain for the last thirty- years. Industrial performance plays a crucial part in determining the UK's economic fortunes. This book presents a detailed analysis of contemporary industrial policy in Britain. After an introduction on the nature of industrial policy, a number of different views about the role of the state in relation to industry and the economy are examined. A discussion of the major characteristics of the UK's industrial structure follows, concentrating on the most significant debates over the last fifteen years. The parts played by political parties and the major organized interests in developing various industrial policies are dissected. There is a detailed examination of major areas of contemporary industrial policy, including privatization, monopolies and mergers, regional policy, small business and local initiatives. The book concludes by posing the question 'could policy-makers have done better?'

The book draws together a wide range of material from official sources and academic analysis. It is written in a clear and accessible style and will be a key text for a variety of politics and economics courses.

Contents
Part I: The elements – The political economy of industrial policy – The anatomy of British industry – Britain's industrial decline: some explanations – The international dimension – Part II: The participants – Political parties – Employers and unions – The intelligentsia and informed opinion – Part III: Institutions and policies – Direction from the centre – Regional policy – Local industry: the regeneration of inner cities – Public ownership and privatizaton – Small business – Monopolies, mergers and competition policy – Conclusions – Appendix – Recommended reading – Bibliography – Index.

272pp   0 335 15680 0 (Paperback)   0 335 15681 9 (Hardback)